Modern System Administration
Managing Reliable and Sustainable Systems

Jennifer Davis

Beijing · Boston · Farnham · Sebastopol · Tokyo   

Modern System Administration

by Jennifer Davis

Copyright © 2023 Jennifer Davis. All rights reserved.

Published by O'Reilly Media, Inc., 1005 Gravenstein Highway North, Sebastopol, CA 95472.

O'Reilly books may be purchased for educational, business, or sales promotional use. Online editions are also available for most titles (*http://oreilly.com*). For more information, contact our corporate/institutional sales department: 800-998-9938 or *corporate@oreilly.com*.

Acquisitions Editor: John Devins
Development Editor: Virginia Wilson
Production Editor: Katherine Tozer
Copyeditor: Kim Wimpsett
Proofreader: Piper Editorial Consulting, LLC

Indexer: Ellen Troutman-Zaig
Interior Designer: David Futato
Cover Designer: Karen Montgomery
Illustrator: Kate Dullea, Tomomi Imura

November 2022:   First Edition

Revision History for the First Edition

2022-11-16:   First Release

See *http://oreilly.com/catalog/errata.csp?isbn=9781492055211* for release details.

The O'Reilly logo is a registered trademark of O'Reilly Media, Inc. *Modern System Administration*, the cover image, and related trade dress are trademarks of O'Reilly Media, Inc.

While the publisher and the author have used good faith efforts to ensure that the information and instructions contained in this work are accurate, the publisher and the author disclaim all responsibility for errors or omissions, including without limitation responsibility for damages resulting from the use of or reliance on this work. Use of the information and instructions contained in this work is at your own risk. If any code samples or other technology this work contains or describes is subject to open source licenses or the intellectual property rights of others, it is your responsibility to ensure that your use thereof complies with such licenses and/or rights.

978-1-492-05521-1

[LSI]

Table of Contents

Part III.   Assembling the System

Part IV. Monitoring the System

Foreword

After a few years of job hopping, I finally landed a full-time job as a system administrator at a sizable financial institution. The people managing servers and executing shell scripts sat on the second floor, and the developers who wrote the applications sat on the third. I never questioned why an elevator separated us or why more communication happened over support tickets than in person, but that was the hierarchy.

I joined the company during the winter holidays, and guess who didn't have any vacation time. I found myself sitting alone on the second floor processing support tickets. Developers opened deployment request tickets, and I ran scripts on each server to fulfill the requests and close the tickets. I eventually got tired of that process and wrote a script that basically did my job for me. Instead of spending 30 minutes running scripts across a set of machines, I was able to do it in less than one. I was closing tickets almost as fast as they were being opened. One day someone from upstairs came to visit and asked me how I was moving so fast. I showed them how I automated myself out of a job, and somehow I ended up with a better one. I was continuously being presented with new challenges, at which point I decided to cut out the go-between, and moved my desk to the third floor, blurring the lines between dev and ops.

No good deed goes unpunished. My management chain informed me that I was compromising existing processes designed around industry regulations and setting the wrong expectations for the rest of the team, because nowhere in the job description did it require system administrators to learn how to code, help Q/A automate tests, or define new ways of doing things. The more I colored outside the lines, the more problems I had with those who drew them.

After about a year of successful projects, I grew to understand why my unconventional working style was useful and important. I came to realize that operating as a lone wolf wasn't sustainable, and better tools were no substitute for a better team. Around this same time, my director (the one I once betrayed by pushing the bar without permission) had just returned from a conference and pulled me to the side. He said, "I finally understand what you are doing, and there is a word for it: DevOps."

For the last decade, DevOps has been mistakenly used to describe modern system administration, but the reality is that DevOps is just one of the new practices we must adopt to thrive in our ever-changing environments. Modern system administration is about more than a single practice. And it can't be fully defined by a single tool, or set of individual contributions, either. Although it may have felt to some that the advancement of our profession finally had a North Star in DevOps, far too many have set out on a DevOps-only journey and gotten lost. This book represents a map that highlights the many starting points and paths toward modern system administration, written by someone who has traveled many of them. Jennifer doesn't simply give you the directions; she gives you the context to help you understand why the trail exists—not only so you can follow in the footsteps of others but to help you blaze your own.

— *Kelsey Hightower*

Preface

When I started my first system administrator job, my mentors told me I needed to read the Red Book (aka the second edition of *UNIX System Administration Handbook* by Evi Nemeth et al. [Addison-Wesley]) and attend USENIX LISA (the first conference dedicated to system administration and targeting large-scale sites—which back then meant serving more than one hundred users). Those mentors were right; I learned so much from both experiences. Reading the Red Book gave me a solid grounding on specific hardware and Unix services. It was much more valuable than any available manuals because of its authors' collective, practical wisdom. At my first USENIX LISA, I learned from tutorials about the importance of continuous learning (Evi Nemeth's "Hot Topics in System Administration" tutorials) and documentation techniques (Mike Ciavarella's Documentation Techniques for SysAdmins). I met countless other sysadmins at informal gatherings and information-sharing sessions, like the Birds of a Feather (BOF) and hallway tracks.

Beyond all of the specific skills or technologies, I learned the following:

- System administration work is often interdisciplinary, requiring collaboration across different types of teams.
- Random knowledge can turn out to be unexpectedly useful.
- Stories are crucial to how we learn and teach (which is how those random pieces of knowledge are sticky enough for use).

I still felt like there was a gap, a distance for me between system administration as described and my experience of system administration in practice. Since then, I've realized there is never going to be *the book* that tells me exactly what I need to do for every given situation. Of course, we learn from sharing stories, but each of us forges our paths for the specific systems we need to maintain in the particular environments we find them.

Today, system administrators have an ever-growing list of technologies and third-party services to learn about and use when building, deploying, and running systems that have thousands, sometimes even millions, of users.

With that in mind, in this book, I want to share some of my stories and focus on a distilled set of fundamentals and practices that will support your journey to assemble, run, scale, and eventually hand off your systems.

Who Should Read This Book?

I wrote this book for all the experienced system administrators, IT professionals, support engineers, and other operation engineers looking for a map to understand the landscape of contemporary operation technologies and practices.

This book may also be helpful to developers, testers, and anyone who wants to level up their operations skills. I recognize that sometimes a team is made up of folks who only sometimes do "ops stuff" but have a need to understand the systems more clearly to be effective in their roles.

I've tried to focus on the principles and practices that support all modern operations work. Still, I recognize that my experiences (lots of Unix-flavored administration, primarily with distributed systems) have shaped my perspectives. All of this book is relevant to most sysadmins, but every organization has different needs that will drive the activities of those sysadmin teams. For example, suppose your activities are primarily managing site-based infrastructure (i.e., WiFi hotspots, printers, and phones). In that case, the material in Part III will not be as relevant.

What This Book Is Not

This book is not a "how-to" reference for tools, software applications, or specific operating systems, as there are many quality reference materials to dig into those particular topics. (However, where relevant, I will point out some recommended materials to level up your skills.)

If you are looking for the instruction manual for a specific tool that gives you a step-by-step guide to administering a system, this isn't that book. There are plenty of operating system and application-specific books and resources out there. These are a few options I recommend:

- For general Unix administration, the latest version of the Red Book, *UNIX and Linux System Administration Handbook*, 5th edition, by Trent R. Hein et al. (Addison-Wesley)
- For general system and network administration and decades of experience, two books from Thomas A. Limoncelli et al.

- *The Practice of System and Network Administration: Volume 1: DevOps and Other Best Practices for Enterprise IT*, 3rd edition (Addison-Wesley)

- *The Practice of Cloud System Administration: DevOps and SRE Practices for Web Services*, Volume 2 (Addison-Wesley)

- For a deep dive on data application system concerns: *Designing Data-Intensive Applications* by Martin Kleppmann (O'Reilly)

- If you're focused on managing microservices, check out *Building Microservices* 2nd edition, by Sam Newman (O'Reilly)

Scope of This Book

As system administrators, our time focuses on the system level and how the whole works holistically (for whatever slice of systems we are responsible for). No one can tell you how to do everything, but I can guide you to practices and tools that will help you engage with the craft, boost your confidence, and connect with others who are on the same journey.

If I Could Tell You Only One Thing

Systems are fundamentally messy. We want to imagine that somewhere out there someone has figured out how to manage systems perfectly and that their processes and tools lead to pristine systems. Of course, there are people with experience who can share recommendations, and while this can be helpful, it's important to keep the following ideas in mind:

- Their experience might not apply to your environment or challenges.

- They don't know what they don't know. They might not be aware of additional factors that influenced their successful outcomes.

- Their best practices may exist because their systems reflect their design and how they run them.

You're not working alone anymore. Sometimes, your instinctual approach might not be the right one. Technology evolves, change is constant, and there is more than any one person can know. You can have shallow, broad, generalist knowledge or in-depth, specific knowledge and still have insufficient knowledge. Adopting collaborative practices allows you to plan with insight from multiple perspectives and administer your systems effectively. Working with others may mean taking a different approach than usual. Collaboration also requires communicating intent so that others can better understand the problem you are solving, why it matters to solve, and your process.

If I Could Tell You Only One More Thing

When something goes wrong—and it will go wrong—it's not your burden to bear alone. Mistakes are going to happen. Ask for help. You carry a great weight of responsibility in maintaining systems, and that responsibility can lead to issues with your physical and mental health. There are multiple ways to keep your systems running (and thriving) without sacrificing yourself for that perfectly running system. Support yourself so that you can have a lifelong career.

Conventions Used in This Book

The following typographical conventions are used in this book:

Italic
> Indicates new terms, URLs, email addresses, filenames, and file extensions

`Constant width`
> Used for program listings, as well as within paragraphs to refer to program elements such as variable or function names, databases, data types, environment variables, statements, and keywords

`Constant width bold`
> Shows commands or other text that should be typed literally by the user

 This element signifies a tip or suggestion.

 This element signifies a general note.

 This element indicates a warning or caution.

O'Reilly Online Learning

 For almost 40 years, *O'Reilly Media* has provided technology and business training, knowledge, and insight to help companies succeed.

Our unique network of experts and innovators share their knowledge and expertise through books, articles, conferences, and our online learning platform. O'Reilly's online learning platform gives you on-demand access to live training courses, in-depth learning paths, interactive coding environments, and a vast collection of text and video from O'Reilly and 200+ other publishers. For more information, please visit *http://oreilly.com*.

How to Contact Us

Please address comments and questions concerning this book to the publisher:

O'Reilly Media, Inc.
1005 Gravenstein Highway North
Sebastopol, CA 95472
800-998-9938 (in the United States or Canada)
707-829-0515 (international or local)
707-829-0104 (fax)

We have a web page for this book, where we list errata, examples, and any additional information. You can access this page at *https://oreil.ly/modern-sysadmin*.

Email *bookquestions@oreilly.com* to comment or ask technical questions about this book.

For news and information about our books and courses, visit *https://oreilly.com*.

Find us on LinkedIn: *https://linkedin.com/company/oreilly-media*.

Follow us on Twitter: *https://twitter.com/oreillymedia*.

Watch us on YouTube: *https://youtube.com/oreillymedia*.

Acknowledgments

Writing a book is immensely hard. Writing a book through a pandemic where millions of people perished and worldwide systems were strained to capacity, creating inhumane conditions, is indescribable (especially when writing a book about managing systems).

I am immensely grateful to many people for helping this book become a reality.

I appreciate Evi Nemeth (*https://oreil.ly/vmPXm*), who established the culture of sharing and continuous learning in system and network administration with her "bibles" of system administration and conference tutorials.

Thank you to the people who have reviewed drafts and provided feedback: Chris Devers, Yvonne Lam, Tabitha Sable, Brenna Flood, Amy Tobey, Tom Limoncelli, David Blank-Edelman, Bryan Smith, Luciano Siqueira, Steven Ragnarök, Æleen Frisch, Jess Males, Matt Beran, and Donald Ellis. I take all responsibility for any mistakes in the final draft.

Thank you, Chris Devers—you've been there since that early first draft of chapters contributing your ideas, words, and perspectives from your personal experience.

Special thanks to Tomomi Imura for her incredibly gifted illustrations throughout this book.

Thank you to the entire team at O'Reilly, who made this book a reality. Special thanks to Virginia Wilson, the ever-patient development editor who was crucial in helping me find the right words. This book and my writing have immensely improved with her support.

I'm incredibly grateful for the love and patience that my family showed me throughout this writing process. Without the support of Brian, keeping the household running and Frankie entertained and being my first reader, this book would not have been possible. Thank you, Frankie, for keeping me mindful of the joy and imagination possible. I love you very much, Frankie, Brian, and George.

Many thanks to everyone who has been active in the USENIX LISA, SREcon, CoffeeOps, and DevOps communities who have shared their stories and contributed to the evolution of industry technology and practices. Much love to you all.

Introducing Modern System Administration

Systems are made up of a group of components and their relationships to one another to form a complex whole. You are fundamentally trying to navigate the chaos to manage your systems sustainably. There is no one right way of system management, but there are paths you can take on your journey to understanding your systems to reduce their physical and mental toil and build a lifelong career tackling interesting challenges.

I've organized this book to provide the resources you need to prepare for your journey to adopt modern system administration technologies, tools, and practices. In this introduction, I will give you some high-level goals that will help you forge your own path to take care of your systems reliably and sustainably.

Map Your Journey

In many ways, system administrators are like hikers embarking into the wilderness. Like Figure I-1 shows, we like to think that somewhere out there is a map that will tell us exactly what to do and when to do it, and if we follow that map, we will achieve a perfectly maintained system. We imagine that the path we're about to walk is well lit and that the map we find will have clearly defined milestones and goals.

But modern system administration is more like Figure I-2. You can prepare yourself for the journey with some universal tools: the fundamental and critical practices of assembling, monitoring, and scaling any system. You can't predict which specific tools you'll need on your journey or how you're going to need to use them, but you'll be ready to make those decisions and enact them when the time comes. And you don't have to do it alone!

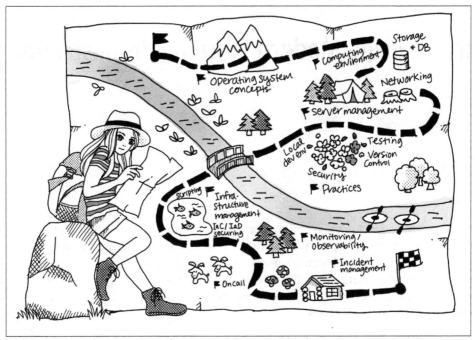

Figure I-1. This image shows what most of us imagine is possible—a clear map with clear goals and a solitary journey—if only we find the right resources and learn the right things. This is not the reality (image by Tomomi Imura).

You must tailor your journey to achieving effective system administration at every organization and on every team you join. Ultimately, the milestones and goals will vary.

When hiking, you don't know each and every turn along the way. Even if you've walked the same path, you may encounter new challenges: a path washed out or wild animals you don't want to disturb. In system administration, you're going to run into unexpected problems (twists and turns) that impact the outcomes of your efforts. So you learn from your mistakes, try different routes, ask for help, and keep trying until you reach your goal.

Figure I-2. There is no such thing as the one resource that will tell us exactly what to do to manage our systems. The path before us is unclear, and the terrain never matches the map, but with the right tools and collaborators we can move forward with confidence that we'll be able to handle whatever lies ahead (image by Tomomi Imura).

This book supports you in establishing the patterns and behaviors to focus your time and energy where you need to so that you can build quality, reliable, and sustainable systems. The size and scope of your responsibilities will vary. You may be responsible for everything and must balance supporting the whole organization and specific engineering initiatives. You may manage the "IT infrastructure" and how the company conducts business. You may support the specific infrastructure for one product.

When something goes wrong, you need to maintain your systems without harming your own physical and mental health. You are not done when you reach your goal. For a lifelong career, you'll be constantly adjusting to new trails and terrain as technology and practices evolve.

Embrace a Mindset Shift

Being prepared starts with a growth mindset, in which you believe you can grow your capacities and talents over time. You can continue to update your skills and knowledge and persist in facing challenges and failures.

Throughout the book, I share different models to enable you to think about the systems you manage. Models enable understanding and communication and help to explain concepts, represent ideas, and provide common ways of talking to one another. No model is flawless. They aren't meant to be. As you think about the systems that the models represent, remember what Vincent van Gogh wrote, "[Y]our model is *not* your final aim,"[1] and be cautious when the model isn't giving you a good frame to maintain your systems.

Take models like infrastructure as code and the five-layer Internet model to process, visualize, and explain your systems. And build from your experiences to develop new models to advance the practices and technologies in system administration.

At the heart of modern system administration is the fact that your systems are continuously growing in complexity and size as "software eats the world." To be effective, you must recognize change and develop your understanding of what it means to do the job in practice, whether adopting new practices or technologies.

What Is the Job?

You are responsible for building, configuring, and maintaining reliable and sustainable systems, where systems can be specific tools, applications, or services. While everyone within the organization should care about uptime, performance, and security, your perspective focuses on these measurements within the constraints of the organization or team's budget and the specific needs of the tool, application, or service consumer.

Whether you manage hundreds or thousands of systems, you are a sysadmin if you have elevated privileges on the system. Unfortunately, many people strive to define system administration in terms of the tasks involved or what work the individual does. That's often because the role is not well defined and usually takes on an outsized responsibility of everything that no one else wants to do.

---

1 Vincent van Gogh quoting Dickens: "[Y]our model is not your final aim, but the means of giving form and strength to your thought and inspiration" in a letter to his brother (*https://oreil.ly/5nkDi*).

Many describe system administration as the digital janitor role,[2] responsible for cleaning up the systems, especially when they aren't working as needed. While the janitor's role in an organization is critical, equating the two is a disservice to both positions.

Closer metaphors for system administrators include plumber, electrician, or HVAC specialist. People take it for granted that modern homes and businesses have running water, electricity, and climate control systems, but these systems require trained specialists to build, install, maintain, and repair them so they run correctly and safely.

A Role by Any Other Name

I have experienced dissonance over the past 10 years over the role of "sysadmin." There is so much confusion about what a sysadmin is. Is a sysadmin an operator? Is a sysadmin the person with root? There has been an explosion in terms and titles as people try to divorce themselves from the past. So when someone said to me, "I'm not a sysadmin; I'm an infrastructure engineer," I realized that it's not just me feeling this.

Recognize that organizations have retitled their system administration postings to keep current with the tides of change within the industry. Don't limit your opportunities by the name of the role.

Flavors of System Administration

The name for the people who manage systems widely varies (e.g., sysadmin, SRE,[3] DevOps engineer, platform engineer, and cloud engineer are just a few). The name of the role may indicate that slightly different skill sets are required. For example, with "SRE," there is often an expectation that engineers are also software engineers with operability skills. With DevOps engineers, there is often an assumption that engineers are strong in at least one modern language and have expertise in continuous integration and deployment. More often, it's just a name and not always a consistent one. Sometimes a team defines the role completely differently and requires specific skills based on the needs of the organization. To avoid a mismatch in expectations, check with the team directly when assessing whether a role is a good fit for you. For example, the acronym SRE can mean site, system, service reliability, or resilience engineering at different organizations.

---

2 Check out the many roles of system administrators in Appendix B (*https://oreil.ly/JYWCK*) of Thomas Limoncelli et al.'s book *The Practice of System and Network Administration* (Addison-Wesley Professional).

3 Learn more about being an SRE from Alice Goldfuss's blog post "How to Get into SRE" (*https://oreil.ly/wALwU*) and Molly Struve's blog post "What It Means to Be a Site Reliability Engineer" (*https://oreil.ly/35Es6*).

As an engineering discipline, system administration is one part art and one part science. It's an approach to your work (designing, building, and monitoring your systems) that considers the implications to safety, human factors, government regulations, practicality, and cost. There can be hundreds of different ways to accomplish something. Your knowledge, skills, and experiences will inform which of those many ways you will take while leveraging your analytical skills to monitor for impact and success, identifying when to spend (or save) money or time, and factoring in the cost to humans to support the system.

Embrace Evolving Practices

As technology evolves, the practices to manage the technologies have also adapted. Be prepared to adopt new techniques to stay abreast of changing platforms to reduce a system's impact and maintainability.

The fundamental sysadmin and dev dynamic changes when you measure your system's reliability and the organization shifts who is responsible for reliability improvements. Today, it's more common for everyone to improve a product's reliability than for a single team to carry the brunt of the support work to keep a system or service running. SRE teams are empowered to help reduce the overall toil of the systems.[4]

Embrace Collaboration

The pace of change, complexities of our environments, and risks inherent to their failure require the following actions:

- Bringing together expertise from different areas (e.g., development, operations, security, and testing)
- Integrating proposals rather than compromising so that the final solution addresses multiple perspectives

It takes real effort to build the trust and psychological safety that encourages people to voice their opinions and perspectives. When team members have achieved psychological safety with one another, they feel safe to take risks and be vulnerable. For example, an individual on a team who feels high amounts of psychological safety will proactively share when they need help. This can help prevent failures in the system because of an established mutual support system.

Encourage a culture that enables and supports people asking probing questions to help everyone come to a shared understanding (we're working toward the same goal)

---

4 Learn about the reduction of toil and its impact on teams from Stephen Thorne's Medium article on the tenets of SRE (*https://oreil.ly/SpiwZ*).

and promotes intellectual courage (experts are fallible). Some questions include the following:

- Why? Why are we doing this? Why does it work this way?
- Could you help me understand your perspective?
- What other ways did you think about solving this?

 Learn more about psychological safety, the number-one key dynamic of high-performing teams that Google's People Operations identified from its research with the re:Work program (*https://oreil.ly/uTpZU*).

Embracing collaboration leads to working well with others so that when you most need them, your collaborators will be available (and willing) to provide support because you have already built up and prepared for that eventuality.

Embrace Sustainability

Sustainability is the measurement of a system that enables the humans in the system to thrive, leading healthy lives while working. Regardless of the size and scope of your work, eight measurements inform the sustainability of your work:

Performance
Measures the system's capability of doing useful work for a period of time. System performance is defined differently depending on the service or product you build.

Scalability
Measures the system's adaptability to add and remove individual components.

Availability
Measures the length of the time the system functions as expected.

Reliability
Measures how well a system consistently performs its specific purpose for a period of time.

Maintainability
Measures the ease of deploying, updating, and deprecating a system.

Simplicity
Measures the ease of a new engineer understanding the system.

Usability
> Measures user satisfaction with the system.

Observability
> Measures how well you can figure out what is going wrong with a system under observation, recognizing not all systems need a high level of observability.

In the following chapters, I will share the different technologies and practices that improve the goals you set for these measures and, ultimately, the sustainability of your systems.

Wrapping Up

Your journey will be specific to your systems and the people who support those systems. No one can provide that perfectly defined checklist to tell you exactly what you need to learn or do and when. Still, you can better prepare yourself with the appropriate toolkit (understanding the fundamentals and key practices and assembling, monitoring, and scaling the systems).

What it means to be a system administrator is constantly evolving. Therefore, it would be helpful to adopt a growth mindset and foster the talents and skills necessary to sustain a lifelong career with new technology and practices.

Ask for help and build on collaborative practices that enable you to work effectively with your team by building psychological safety. Use models to inform your understanding, and build upon them to advance system administration practices.

Embrace sustainability. You deserve to thrive and have a whole career supporting the systems you manage.

PART I

Reasoning About Systems

The first four chapters share the fundamentals of systems and how to choose between options. It isn't helpful to talk about solutions in terms of the "best." Instead, you need to understand what is available and what it's "best for," and its context in your system. That context is an evolving set of conflicting goals, people, and the different parts that provide the functioning system. "Systems thinking" encourages you to think about the different parts of the system and how they interact in alignment with your current problems, which leads to a better understanding of the system's evolution over time.

CHAPTER 1

Patterns and Interconnections

Imagine you are making a cake with a friend. You followed the recipe, mixing all the ingredients (oil, flour, eggs, and sugar), and it looks OK, but when you taste it, something isn't quite right. To be an accomplished baker, you must understand all the elements of a cake (ratios of flour to fat, etc.) and how they work together to impact the finished product's quality (e.g., taste and texture). For example, in Figure 1-1, our bakers didn't understand that sesame oil wasn't an appropriate oil to include in the cake.

Now replace *baker* with *sysadmin*, and replace the golden ratios of a baker's ingredients with the interconnected components in your system (e.g., smartphones, embedded devices, large servers, and storage arrays). To be an accomplished sysadmin, you need to understand how the components connect in common patterns and impact your system's quality (e.g., reliability, scalability, and maintainability).

In this chapter, I will help you reason about your systems to see the patterns and interconnections in them so that you understand what informed the choices behind your system's design.

Figure 1-1. Modeling understanding a system (image by Tomomi Imura)

How to Connect Things

Engineers choose *architecture patterns*, the reusable solutions to address typical work-loads (e.g., batch processing, web servers, and caching). These patterns are models that convey "a shared understanding of the system's design."[1]

From on-prem to cloud computing environments, the reusable solutions are evolving to support decomposed sets of smaller sets of services.[2] These patterns shape systems' reliability, scalability, and maintainability by determining the components of the system and the connection between the components.

Let's examine three common architecture patterns used in system design so you can see how their use informs (and limits) their evolution and system qualities (reliability, scalability, and maintainability):

---

[1] Martin Fowler, "Software Architecture Guide," martinfowler.com, last modified August 1, 2019, *www.martin-fowler.com/architecture*.

[2] Learn more about decomposing services from Chapter 3 of Sam Newman's *Building Microservices* (*https://oreil.ly/SSx0B*) (O'Reilly).

Layered architecture

The most common and familiar pattern is a general-purpose layered or tiered architecture pattern. Engineers commonly use this pattern for client-server applications like web servers, email, and other business applications.

Engineers organize components into horizontal layers, with each layer performing a specific role, separating the concerns of each layer from the other layers. Layers are generally tightly coupled depending on a request and response to and from the adjacent layers. As a result, you can update and deploy components within each layer independently from other layers.

A two-tier system is composed of a client and a server. A three-tier system comprises a client and two other layers of servers; the presentation, application, and data tiers are abstracted into different components. Each tier may be split into separate logical layers in an N-tier or multitier system. There may be more than three tiers depending on the system's needs (e.g., resilience, security, and scalability). With each tier, scalability and reliability increase as the tiers create additional separation between concerns that can be deployed and updated independently.

Microservices architecture

A microservice system is a distributed architecture that, instead of tiers, consists of a collection of small units of business code decoupled from one another. Microservices are small and autonomous. Because each service is separate, code can be developed and deployed independently. In addition, each service can leverage the best language or framework for its use case.

Microservices increase the system's scalability and reliability because they can be independently deployed as needed and isolated from the points of failure in the system.

Decomposing a service into microservices decreases maintainability due to the increased cognitive load on the sysadmins. To understand your system, you need to know all the details about each separate service (i.e., languages, frameworks, build and deploy pipelines, and any relevant environments).

Event-driven architecture

An event-driven architecture is a distributed asynchronous pattern that enables loose coupling between applications. Different applications don't know details about one another. Instead, they communicate indirectly by publishing and consuming events.

Events are something that happens, a fact that can be tracked.[3] Systems generate events. In event-driven systems, event producers create events, brokers ingest events, and consumers listen and process events.

There are two main models for event-driven systems: messaging (or pub/sub) and streaming.

The event producer or publishers publish events to a broker in an event messaging system. The broker sends all posted events to event consumers or subscribers. The message broker receives published events from publishers, maintains the order of received messages, makes them available to subscribers, and deletes events after they are consumed.

In an event streaming system, events are published to a distributed log, a durable append-only data store. As a result, consumers consume events from the stream that they want and can replay events. In addition, the distributed log retains events after they have been consumed, meaning that new subscribers can subscribe to events that occurred before their subscription.

Because components are loosely coupled, individual parts of the system don't have to worry about the health of other components. Loosely coupled elements increase the resiliency of the overall system as they can be independently deployed and updated. Event persistence enables the replaying of events that occurred in the case of a failure.

Table 1-1 summarizes the relative comparisons of reliability, scalability, and maintainability of the three common architecture patterns you will see in systems.

Table 1-1. Comparison of reliability, scalability, and maintainability of architectures

	Layered	Microservices	Event driven
Reliability	Medium (tightly coupled systems)	High	High
Scalability	Medium (limited within layers)	High	High
Maintainability	High	Low (decreased simplicity)	Medium (decreased testability)

Of course, these are not the only patterns you'll see in system design. Check out Martin Fowler's comprehensive website, the Software Architecture Guide (*https://oreil.ly/Sf5IC*).

---

3 CloudEvents (*https://cloudevents.io*) is a community-driven effort to define a specification for describing event data in a standard way that can be implemented across different services and platforms.

How Things Communicate

A component of a system doesn't exist in isolation—each component will communicate with other components in the system, and that communication may be informed by the architecture pattern (REST (*https://oreil.ly/CmRCT*) for N-tier architecture, gRPC (*https://oreil.ly/MzO9n*) for event-driven architecture).

There a few different models used to represent how components communicate, e.g., the Internet model, five-layer Internet model, TCP/IP five-layer reference model, and TCP/IP model. While these models are very similar, they have slight differences that may inform how people think about the applications and services they build to communicate.

When an individual or group of engineers identify an area for improvement, they author a Request for Comment (RFC) and submit it for peer review. As an open international community that works to maintain and improve the internet's design, usability, maintainability, and interoperability, the Internet Engineering Task Force (IETF) (*https://oreil.ly/ydfJn*) adopts some of the proposed RFCs as technical standards that define the official specifications and protocols. The protocol specifications define how devices communicate with one another while loosely following the Internet model. And these protocols continue to evolve as the Internet grows and the needs of people change (for an example of this, check out Appendix B).

As depicted in Table 1-2, the five-layer Internet model shows five discrete layers. Each layer communicates via the interfaces above and below via a message object specific to the layer. Layering a system separates the responsibilities at each layer and enables different system parts to be built (and changed). It also allows differentiation at each of the layers.

Table 1-2. Five-layer Internet model and example protocols

Layers	Example protocols
Application	HTTP, DNS, BGP
Transport	TCP, UDP
Network	IP, ICMP
Data Link	ARP
Physical	Copper, optical fiber, WiFi

Like the cake in Figure 1-1, there aren't any crisp layers that inform you precisely where a problem emerged. Protocol implementations are not required to follow the specifications strictly and overlap layers. For example, the protocol that determines the fastest and most efficient route to transmit data is the Border Gateway Protocol (BGP). Because of the implementation of the protocol, people may classify BGP at either the application layer or the transport layer.

The layers in the Internet model give you a way to frame the context and narrow your focus to the ingredients of your application—the source code and dependencies— or at a lower physical level, simplifying the complex communication model into understandable chunks. However, sometimes you will run into situations where the reduction in context doesn't help you understand what is happening. To level up your comprehension, you have to know how everything works together to impact your system's quality.

Learning More About Protocols

If your role entails managing networks or implementations of protocols, check out Andrew Tanenbaum's *Computer Networks* (Pearson), Kevin R. Fall and W. Richard Stevens's *TCP/IP Illustrated, Volume 1: The Protocols*, 2nd edition (Addison-Wesley), and the website the RFC Series (*https://oreil.ly/1DYQT*).

Let's look in more detail at the application, transport, network, data link, and physical layers.

Application Layer

Let's start at the top of the Internet model with the application layer. The application layer describes all the high-level protocols that applications commonly interact with directly. Protocols at this layer handle how applications interface with the underlying transport layer to send and receive data.

To understand this layer, focus on the libraries or applications that implement the protocols underlying your application. For example, when a customer visits your website using a popular browser, the following steps happen:

1. The browser initiates library calls to obtain the IP address of the web server using the Domain Name System (DNS).

2. The browser initiates an HTTP request.

The DNS and HTTP protocols operate within the Internet model's application layer.

Transport Layer

The next layer in the Internet model, the transport layer, handles the flow between hosts. Again, there are two primary protocols: the Transmission Control Protocol (TCP) and the User Datagram Protocol (UDP).

Historically, UDP has been the foundation of more rudimentary protocols, such as ping/ICMP, DHCP, ARP, and DNS, while TCP has been the foundation for more "interesting" protocols like HTTP, SSH, FTP, and SMB. However, this has been changing, as the qualities that make TCP more reliable on a per-session basis have performance bottlenecks in specific contexts.

UDP is a stateless protocol that makes a best-effort attempt to transfer messages but does not attempt to verify that network peers received messages; TCP, on the other hand, is a connection-oriented protocol that uses a three-way handshake to establish a reliable session with a network peer.

The essential characteristics of UDP are as follows:

Connectionless
UDP is not a session-oriented protocol. Network peers can exchange packets without first establishing a session.

Lossy
There is no support for error detection or correction. Applications must implement their fault-tolerance mechanisms.

Nonblocking
TCP is vulnerable to the "head of line blocking" problem, in which missing packets or nonsequential receipt of data can cause a session to get stuck and require retransmission from the point of the error. With UDP, nonsequential delivery is not a problem, and applications may selectively request retransmission of missing data without resending packets that have been successfully delivered.

By comparison, the essential characteristics of TCP are as follows:

Acknowledgment
The receiver notifies the sender of the data receipt for each packet. This receiver acknowledgment does not mean that the application has received or processed the data, only that it arrived at the intended destination.

Connection-oriented
The sender establishes a session before transmitting data.

Reliability
TCP keeps track of data that is sent and received. Receiver acknowledgments can be lost so that a receiver won't acknowledge segments out of order; instead, it sends a duplicate of the last observed ordered packet or duplicate cumulative acknowledgment. This reliability can lengthen latency.

Flow control
The receiver notifies the sender of how much data can be received.

Notice that security wasn't part of TCP or UDP's design or fundamental characteristics. Instead, lack of security in the initial designs of these protocols drove additional complexity in application and system implementation and further changes in the protocols.

Network Layer

In the middle, the network layer translates between the transport and data link layers, enabling the delivery of packets based on a unique hierarchical address, the IP address.

The *Internet Protocol* (IP) is responsible for the rules for addressing and fragmentation of data between two systems. It handles the unique identification of network interfaces to deliver data packets using IP addresses. The IP breaks and reassembles packets as necessary when passing data through links with a smaller maximum transmission unit (MTU). IPv4 is the most widely deployed version of the IP with a 32-bit address space represented in a string of four binary octets or four decimal numbers separated by dots or quad-dotted decimal notation. The IPv6 standard brings advantages such as a 128-bit address space, more sophisticated routing capabilities, and better support for multicast addressing. However, IPv6 adoption has been slow partly because IPv4 and IPv6 are not interoperable, and making do with the shortcomings of IPv4 has generally been easier than porting everything to the new standard.

The underlying binary definition informs the range in decimal notation for IPv4 addresses of 0 to 255. In addition, RFCs define reserved ranges for private networks (*https://oreil.ly/QkHVN*) that aren't routable via the public internet.

The network layer's IP protocol is focused on providing a unique address for network peers to interact with, but it is not responsible for data link layer transmission, nor does it handle session management, which is dealt with at the transport layer.

Data Link Layer

Next, the data link layer uses the physical layer to send and receive packets.

The *Address Resolution Protocol* (ARP) handles hardware address discovery from a known IP address. Hardware addresses are also known as *media access control* (MAC) addresses. Each *network interface controller* (NIC) assigns it a unique MAC address.

The industry intended for MAC addresses to be globally unique, so network management devices and software assume this is true for device authentication and security. Duplicate MAC addresses appearing on the same network can cause problems. But duplicate MAC addresses do appear due to production errors in the manufacturing of hardware (or intentional software design with MAC randomization).[4] Still, it can

---

4 Learn more about the issues with MAC randomization from "MAC Address Randomization: Privacy at the Cost of Security and Convenience" (*https://oreil.ly/31Hsf*).

also happen with virtualized systems, such as VMs cloned from a reference image. However it happens, if multiple network hosts report having the same MAC address, network functionality errors and increased latency can occur.

 People can mask the MAC address presented to the network through software. This is known as *MAC spoofing*. Some attackers use MAC spoofing as a layer 2 attack to attempt hijacking communication between two systems to hack into one of the systems.

The *Reverse Address Resolution Protocol* (RARP) examines IP address to hardware address mapping, which can help identify if multiple IP addresses are responding for a single MAC address. If you think you have a problem with two devices on the network sharing an IP address, perhaps because someone has assigned a static IP when a DHCP server has already allocated the same address to another host, RARP helps identify the culprit.

Physical Layer

The physical layer translates the binary data stream from upper layers into electrical, light, or radio signals that are transmitted across the underlying physical hardware. Each type of physical media has a different maximum length and speed.

Even when using cloud services, you still have to care about the physical layer, even though you don't have to manage the racking and stacking of physical servers. Increased latency can be due to the physical routing between two points. For example, if something happens to a data center (lightning strikes or squirrels damage cables (*https://oreil.ly/miV4u*)), resources might get redirected to alternate services farther away. Additionally, the networking gear within a data center may need to be rebooted or have a degraded cable or faulty network card. As a result, requests sent through those physical components may experience increased latency.

Wrapping Up

You'll find a mix of these patterns (layered, microservices, and event-driven) and protocols in your environment. Understanding the system's architecture informs how the components relate and communicate with one another, and your requirements impact the system's reliability, maintainability, and scalability.

In the next chapter, I'll share how to think about these patterns and interconnections and how they impact your choices for your computing environments within your organization.

CHAPTER 2

Computing Environments

Let's dig deeper into the fundamentals of reasoning about your system, starting with your computing environment.

This chapter examines the fundamental building block of the system: compute. *Compute* is the generic term used to encompass an instance that has a set of resources (i.e., processing power, memory, storage, and networking) associated with it. Contemporary computing is not just about the technical implementation of a system; it's also about enabling methods of collaboration when building, configuring, and deploying the compute that your organization needs. In this chapter, we'll explore the ways to distinguish the types and environments of compute infrastructure so you can customize your choices to your organization's or team's needs and technology.

Common Workloads

Workloads are characterized by the amount and type of pressure on resources that an application puts on a system.

The systems you manage will have a number of applications or services to install, maintain, and run in production environments. Each of the applications or services you manage will have a minimal and recommended set of compute requirements (CPU, memory, and storage) that inform the categorization of your application: CPU-bound, memory-bound, and storage-bound.

 I will share more about storage and networks in Chapters 3 and 4, respectively.

CPU-bound applications benefit from high-performance processors. Example workloads include the following:

- Batch processing
- Gaming servers
- High-performance computing (HPC)
- Media transcoding
- Machine learning
- Scientific modeling
- Web servers

Memory-bound applications benefit from more memory, and most of the execution time is spent reading and writing data. Example workloads include the following:

- Caching
- Data analytics
- Databases

Storage-bound applications benefit from low-latency and random I/O operations. Example workloads include the following:

- Data warehouses
- Data lakes
- Databases
- Distributed filesystems
- Hadoop
- Log or data processing applications

Knowing what type of workloads are part of your system informs how you evaluate what you need for building out your system. For cloud architectures, your options will often be framed in terms of systems that are optimized for these workloads, i.e., CPU-, memory-, and storage-optimized.

 You don't have to make the exact right choice of compute when you build out your systems in the cloud.

As long as you have guardrails that limit your spending, you can choose options that, while not perfect, may be good enough. See Chapter 11 to learn about provisioning your infrastructure with infracode.

Choosing the Location of Your Workloads

Your computing environments may be hosted in private data centers that are self-maintained and controlled, otherwise known as *on-prem*. Or, you may leverage service providers, otherwise known as *cloud computing*.

On-Prem

In an on-prem computing environment, you either rent or purchase hardware to host the services that you need to power your organization's requirements.

You may decide to deploy different resources for your applications, depending on each application's workload. Standardized hardware simplifies your deployments and configuration but can starve some applications while not fully utilizing others. Deploying different hardware specific to your application's needs better matches the expenditure and utility for those resources but increases the complexity required to manage your infrastructure.

With the dedicated hardware, you may deploy different-sized hardware for your different applications depending on whether they are CPU-, memory-, or storage-bound. Having different hardware increases the complexity of the server deployment and software configuration of the system.

Maintaining your own data centers may be advantageous if your organization specializes in data center management or you have custom needs not available from typical cloud service providers (e.g., compliance requirements).

Consider New Ways Of Doing Things

Managing a data center, from sourcing equipment to deploying and managing hardware, was an interesting chapter in my career. I managed the purchase of millions of dollars' worth of gear to support a development environment that required hardware testing and evaluation across a wide variety of storage and networking devices. From this experience, I learned that I'm really good at figuring out the complex project and vendor management and navigating schedules of deliveries and installs. But I really don't like all the paperwork involved or the brain-numbing experience of cabling and tracking system components. I'm grateful for the advent of cloud computing and readily accessible compute.

In Chapter 17, I'll talk about monitoring your work and finding the work you enjoy. It's really easy to fall into the trap of doing what you're good at without considering that you might not enjoy it.

When deploying standardized hardware, you may find it useful to deploy complementary applications on the same system. For example, hosting a web server and a database server (two-tier system architecture) on the same system can work well because it minimizes the network latency between these services. On the other hand, running these services together can create resource contention for the CPU, memory, or storage, and this, in turn, can make it more difficult to make decisions about scaling vertically or horizontally. Pay attention to your hot spots of resource-constrained services and your cold spots of idle services and consider how best to balance and grow your system's ability to meet demand expectations.

Cloud Computing

Service providers use different terms to describe their offerings. Sometimes this can cause confusion, especially when the same term means something different.[1]

Take a look at Figure 2-1. This matrix of terms shows how these different concepts overlap. At the top of the stack, with functions as a service (FaaS), you have the least amount of control over the running compute infrastructure. At the bottom of the stack, with virtual machines, you have the most control and flexibility in the use of the hardware but also the most maintenance.

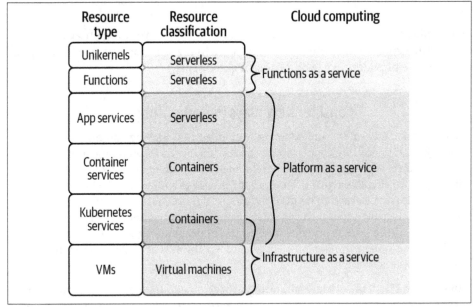

Figure 2-1. Cloud computing environments

---

1 As an example of this, check out Julia Evans's fantastic blog post (*https://oreil.ly/bCBhT*) explaining the difference between IAM offerings from Google Cloud and Amazon Web Services.

Compute Options

Let's look at the different types of compute (serverless, containers, and virtual machines) available within these computing environments so you have a standard frame of reference.

Serverless

Serverless architectures cover unikernels, functions, and app services (and depending on the provider, occasionally also containers).

Unikernels

Unikernels are lightweight, immutable operating system (OS) images compiled to run a single process. I've included them here based on their specialized nature and size.

 MirageOS is one of the longest-running library OSs for constructing unikernels. For a hands-on approach to learning more about unikernels, try the MirageOS tutorial (*https://oreil.ly/fwZex*).

Functions

Functions are small (and ideally single-purpose) blocks of code. You pay a hosted service to maintain the physical infrastructure that you need based on demand, otherwise known as FaaS. The platform may provide you with a specific runtime or allow custom-built runtimes. Runtime limitations may include specific languages (e.g., Java or Go), specific versions of the language, or specific embedded libraries. Popular hosted FaaS include the following:

- AWS Lambda
- Azure Functions
- Google Cloud Functions

You can also deploy function frameworks to provide a functions service to your organization with the following:

Fn (https://oreil.ly/nZxd5)
    A lightweight Docker-based functions platform

OpenFaaS (https://oreil.ly/UTsko)
    A framework for deploying functions to Docker or Kubernetes

OpenWhisk (https://oreil.ly/KHVsw)

A framework to execute functions in response to events, a large variety of supported language runtimes, and customized runtimes supported through Docker

Each platform has strengths and weaknesses depending on your use case. In some cases, your implementation choices may lock your application to a specific FaaS platform. This doesn't mean you can't migrate your application, but the extra work to maintain the application's capabilities may be more than you want to spend.

Examples of additional FaaS capabilities include high availability, endpoint load-balancing, request processing time, concurrency of requests, and traffic management. You may be able to configure the number of CPUs and the amount of memory you want. A key feature of using a FaaS platform is that instances are ephemeral and up only when needed. For initial prototyping of a new application and for test environments, spinning up an environment can be inexpensive depending on the storage and networking configurations.

Rather than designated instances of compute, service providers charge for function invocation, network utilization, and length of time that a function runs. Triggers define how a function is invoked. Common supported triggers include the following:

- Scheduled
- HTTP requests
- Event-based triggers

App services

App services are generally larger than functions. Platforms cover the physical infrastructure, including scaling the application to additional physical infrastructure as needed, application runtimes, and the dependencies needed for the offered languages.

Hosted app services include the following:

- DigitalOcean App Platform (*https://oreil.ly/uqDV3*)
- Google App Engine (*https://oreil.ly/tMR6F*)

While you get more configuration choices than FaaS, many of the same capabilities of FaaS are handled for you. You can then focus on building and deploying the application and monitoring the necessary system environments.

Containers

Conceptually, a *container* is an isolated process with a portable runtime environment. When talking about containers, it's often more helpful to talk about the container image and the container runtime as separate concepts.

A *container image* is the immutable packaged application along with any of its required dependencies, including system libraries, utilities, and configuration settings. Images are composed of layers added on top of a base image or parent image.

A *container runtime* is the setup and running of the container. Low-level runtimes have a limited set of capabilities (e.g., resource allocation and process setup) and generally perform the key setup steps. High-level runtimes have a rich set of capabilities (e.g., image management and networking) and are where you will normally interact with the container runtime.

Here are some examples of commonly used runtimes:

containerd
　　An open source low-level container runtime supported by Linux and Windows

Docker
　　A high-level container system

runC
　　A standard low-level container runtime written in Go Windows Containers

A container orchestrator manages clusters of containers taking care of scaling, networking, and security.

Examples of orchestrators include the following:

- Kubernetes
- Google Cloud Run
- Amazon App Runner
- Amazon Elastic Container Service (ECS)
- Amazon Elastic Kubernetes Service (EKS)
- Azure Container Instances (ACI)
- Azure Kubernetes Service (AKS)
- Google Kubernetes Engine (GKE)
- Red Hat OpenShift

> Read Julia Evans's "What Even Is a Container: namespaces and cgroups" (*https://oreil.ly/1XDJQ*) for a visual guide to containers.

Virtual Machines

Whether virtual machines (VMs) are hosted or managed by your team, server virtualization is the process of creating an environment where multiple OS instances can run on a single physical server. With VM technology, individuals can install and simultaneously run completely different OSs on a single computer.

In practical terms, virtualization gives you the ability to use more of the hardware resources that were idling on dedicated servers.

Packer (*https://oreil.ly/IPzf8*) is an open source software tool from HashiCorp for creating identical machine images from a single configuration file for a variety of platforms, including Amazon EC2, Microsoft Azure Virtual Machine, Docker, and VirtualBox. This can help you build similar images in a repeatable fashion across providers as well as for local use.

The key to server virtualization is the hypervisor that coordinates the low-level interactions between the VMs and host hardware.

Hypervisors can be specialized hardware, firmware, or software. There are a variety of specialized and comprehensive resources depending on your area of focus.

For example, check out Brendan Gregg's blog post "AWS EC2 Virtualization 2017: Introducing Nitro" (*https://oreil.ly/8Lisl*) for a deep dive into Nitro, the virtualization technology in use on Amazon Elastic Compute Cloud (Amazon EC2).

The configuration file specifies the virtualized hardware resources, including memory, CPU, and storage, that are allocated to the VM. Popular desktop VM software includes the following:

- Microsoft Hyper-V (Windows) (*https://oreil.ly/BIFBK*)
- Oracle VM VirtualBox (Windows, Mac, and Linux) (*https://oreil.ly/0LAc3*)
- Parallels Desktop (Mac) (*https://oreil.ly/TlcYV*)
- VMware Fusion and Workstation (Windows, Mac, and Linux) (*https://oreil.ly/WfLYx*)

With virtualization, you don't have to buy specialized hardware for each service you run. You still have to manage the software on the VMs. Hosted VM options include the following:

- Amazon Elastic Compute Cloud (EC2)

- Azure Virtual Machines
- DigitalOcean Droplets (*https://oreil.ly/r8mgZ*)
- Google Compute Engine

Guidelines for Choosing Compute

Consider the following questions to identify impacts and choose appropriate compute for your needs:

Do you have existing physical hardware that you want to use?
> You can customize this dedicated hardware based on your internal and external users' needs. You could do the following:
>
> - Dedicate a server explicitly to the system you need to manage
> - Manage VMs (and the physical hardware)
> - Manage containers (and the physical hardware)

Do you need a specific language or framework to run your application (that you don't want to manage)?
> Can you implement them with small units of business code? Use a functions service. Otherwise, use an app service if your language is supported, or a container service if not and customize your build image.

Do you need a specific OS?
> You can use platform as a service (PaaS) or infrastructure as a service (IaaS).

Do you need to respond to increased demand quickly?
> Choose FaaS or PaaS.

How geographically distributed does your application need to be?
> Check specific cloud providers to identify the best match of region distribution.

Ethical Considerations in Service Choices

You should also consider whether a potential provider is socially and ethically responsible (i.e., with regard to climate change, economic inequality, or ethical sourcing as potential concerns). Negative externalities in your supply chain are no longer opaque in the modern world of social media. Numerous companies have had to halt production and shift their suppliers due to public awareness of labor or ethical issues.

Your organization should vet suppliers, and the people who are responsible for supplier decisions should be able to make a business ethics judgment call. Ethical concerns are now necessarily part of an organization's financial concerns.

Server virtualization, containerization, and serverless compute options all enable running software in an isolated environment with consistent dependencies, libraries, binaries, and configurations that you can repeat reliably and consistently. There are differences in isolation, startup time, and portability:

Isolation

With serverless compute, isolation is opaque. Your function or hosted app may run in containers or a VM. With containers, a single Linux kernel hosts multiple containerized applications. With virtualization, a single hypervisor hosts multiple virtualized OSs, each with its own independent kernel.

Your function will ideally be small, single-purpose, and use a platform's managed runtime. Your container encapsulates an application that may be a few megabytes (MB). Finally, a virtual machine is going to be larger because it must include a complete, runnable OS image. This can run from hundreds of MB to a few gigabytes (GB) in size.

This means that isolation isn't complete on containers, and if there is a vulnerability with the container runtime or the host kernel, an attacker could escape from the container and have access to the host machine.

Startup time

VMs need to be booted like any other computer, which can take several minutes. Containers aren't initializing hardware at startup, which means they can be launched in seconds, and they can be spun down just as quickly when they are no longer needed.

Portability

Containers are more suited for running many application instances on the same host OS, while VMs are better suited for running a heterogeneous mix of OSs on shared host server hardware.

Ultimately, when you are architecting your systems and considering a serverless solution, there are three main areas to consider:

Greenfield development

Serverless compute can facilitate developing and scaling fast to deliver business value. You can experiment and try out different ways of doing something without investing large amounts on compute before you know the actual demand of the system you are developing.

Replacing admin tasks

Instead of a dedicated server for administrative tasks, you can define functions that have only the level of privilege and time needed. You save money and improve security by eliminating the one administrative server with root level privileges to ephemeral instances that spin up with only the permissions necessary to run their tasks (e.g., mail merge, infrastructure compliance runs).

Shifting operational and security concerns
If your team is comfortable with shifting the burden of operational and security concerns early in the decision process, a devops approach (with cooperation and collaboration between the different groups responsible for the system) will support the complex decisions around serverless patterns and implementation to avoid making costly mistakes (i.e., spending your entire budget or exposing your customer's data on poorly configured instances).[2]

It may be that, to begin with, the best choice is what gets you up and running fastest so that you can focus on what brings core business value to your organization. Over time, you'll figure out whether you need to refine and improve resource utilization.

By incorporating these considerations into your choice on compute, you will be able to choose compute infrastructure customized to your organization or team's needs and technology.

Wrapping Up

Compute comprises all the components associated with a computer: processing power, memory, storage, and networking and a runtime environment to make use of these resources. Each application you manage needs to be deployed with consideration of that application's requirements and constraints. For example, applications may be bound by CPU power, by memory capacity, or by storage. Similarly, applications may have specific needs, such as an ability to scale to support demand fluctuations, a need to interact with particular hardware, or a requirement to use particular languages, libraries, or operating systems.

Your computing environment will consist of a mix of compute systems connected in different architecture patterns. Choose based on your requirements, and factor in your needs for isolation, startup time, and portability.

---

2 You may notice that both "DevOps" and "devops" appear in this book. The choice is intentional. When referring to titles or product names, I use "DevOps." When referring to the practice, I use "devops," the original hashtag. The practice of devops encompasses the underlying efforts to connect people and help them navigate working together, changing conversations from *us versus them* to conversations that enable businesses to implement practices that will be sustainable for people. Organizations can sell DevOps tools, but you can't buy devops.

CHAPTER 3

Storage

Think about any contemporary product website; it's the virtual front door of a business and one common managed system. I have handled many websites over the years with various responsibilities, including system design; the web servers and database servers; backups; all the generated assets, including pictures of products, testimonial videos, and logged user activities like searches and purchases; and updates to any backend inventory systems.

There are lots of hidden decisions for artifact storage. Imagine managing that product website; when someone searches for the product on the website and lands on the product page, the action generates multiple log entries that have to stream somewhere. Every time someone purchases the product, order information, shipment details, and the product's availability need to be updated because your company doesn't want to sell something that it doesn't have. Building out the system you'd need for this website requires planning the appropriately sized computing environment and appropriately sized and scoped artifact storage to drive business decisions.

In the systems you manage, whether websites or some other system, you create strategies and make decisions for storage because you need to optimize assets differently. You don't want to waste money on unneeded storage, or infrequently accessed data on more expensive low-latency storage. And for frequently accessed data, you want your users to have fast responses, which may even include caching data in memory; it's more expensive, but happy users are worth it to your business.

There are many options, and you have to consider the data asset in question in the design of your system. In this chapter, I will focus on framing your storage strategy by laying out the landscape of storage technologies and the associated practices to consider with those technologies.

Why Care About Storage?

Storage is an inextricable part of the systems you manage. Therefore, you need to handle any data assets associated with your systems and minimize the risk they pose to the business.

Decisions you make about data storage have long-term effects on your systems' durability, portability, flexibility, and consistency. Unfortunately, there's a perception that storage has become a commodity business, a cost to contain. But in practice, take a more holistic approach and optimize the storage of assets based on their characteristics. Again, think back to the example product website—pictures shown to customers need to load quickly; the history of activities needs to be stored accurately but doesn't require speedy access.

Cautionary Examples in Evaluating the Value of Data

Often, the data you store is more valuable than the media you use to store it because the information is far harder to replace. Examples of organizations losing invaluable data to negligence, short-sightedness, or disaster abound:

- NASA overwrote its original data tapes for the Apollo lunar landings in the 1980s (*https://oreil.ly/3YvhP*).
- The BBC routinely reused videotapes before 1978, erasing thousands of hours of broadcast programming, notably early *Doctor Who* (*https://oreil.ly/pzefI*) episodes.
- The 2021 OVHcloud data center fire (*https://oreil.ly/dUdSk*) in Strasbourg, France, destroyed one of four facilities, affecting 3.6 million websites (*https://oreil.ly/TkuKG*).

There are many more data loss stories—you probably have some yourself.

On the other hand, there are ongoing costs for storing data perpetually. For example, many people are concerned about how organizations store and aggregate their data. As a result, customers lose trust in organizations that mess up data storage. In addition, legal frameworks such as the European General Data Protection Regulation (GDPR) compel companies to give people control over how their data is stored. So if you mess up and store data against your committed policies, you could have additional fines to pay on top of your storage costs.

Think carefully about what data you are storing and how you are storing it. Then, regularly audit your data assets to ensure that your expectations match the reality, and repair any identified problems.

Some data collection may include personally identifiable information (PII), personal data, payment card information, and credentials and have explicit legislation governing their storage. PII is mainly used within the United States, while personal data is associated with the EU data privacy law, the GDPR.

Your users and their location inform requirements you must follow, including ensuring that you store data in appropriate places:

- The National Institute of Standards and Technology (NIST) defines PII (*https://oreil.ly/cWklx*) as information that identifies or links an individual. An example of PII is an individual's Social Security number.

- The European Commission defines personal data (*https://oreil.ly/ly7lP*) as any information that can directly or indirectly identify a living individual. An example of personal data is a home address.

- Payment card information is data found on an individual's payment cards, including credit and debit cards.

- User credentials are how your site verifies that an individual is who they say they are.

Examining your data can help qualify your liability based on privacy and data retention laws and regulations. When dealing with PII, personal data, payment card information, and credentials, ensure you investigate requirements to comply with all relevant legislation.

Let's look at the key characteristics of storage so you know how to evaluate the options available when designing your systems and how to evaluate improvements to existing artifact storage.

Key Characteristics

Even though you may be all in on cloud computing, the underlying supported data storage media is the same as on-prem computing (hard disks, solid-state disks, flash memory, magnetic tapes, and optical media). And each type has varying performance characteristics, reliability, and costs.

If you're managing physical hardware, you may need to dig deeper into understanding the underlying storage, partitioning it, and getting it ready for use for whichever OS you manage with the appropriate device drivers. On the other hand, providers take care of many low-level intricacies if you've migrated to the cloud.

One of the benefits of cloud computing is that you can characterize and optimize your storage spend by testing the options available because the cloud provider manages the physical storage systems.

You must understand your storage options regardless of your computing environment (on-prem or cloud computing). Critical characteristics of storage include these:

Capacity
: The total disk space for a storage device.

Input/output operations per second (IOPS)
: Measures read and write operations possible; storage devices can be specialized for read or write operations and sequential or random access.

Input/output (I/O) size/block size
: The size of a request to perform I/O operations can vary depending on the OS and application.

Throughput
: Measures the data transfer rate between the application and the filesystem in a specific time interval.

Latency
: Measures the response time an application must wait for a request to complete.

Applications access data with different patterns. So, when deciding how to build systems and what resources to use, you'll review resources with these characteristics and narrow your options based on your needs. The relationship of IOPS to throughput when considering storage performance is *IOPS = Throughput / I/O size*.

Suppose you need to identify what kind of Amazon EBS storage volume to attach to your Amazon EC2 instance. You understand how many requests per second your application needs, the size of requests stored, and how that maps to the throughput of the underlying filesystem. Then, you calculate the minimum IOPS and evaluate what combination of storage solutions will work based on what's available.

In Table 3-1, I've captured some of the characteristics of EBS SSD available in the August 2022 Amazon EBS Features documentation (*https://oreil.ly/6vVPR*). The first two options are similar and share the same cost, but the third option (EBS General Purpose SSD) is quite different.

Suppose you determine that your application needs less than 16,000 IOPS and no submillisecond latency or high durability commitments. In that case, spending less on storage and receiving monthly free IOPS might be beneficial.

Table 3-1. Amazon EBS volume types in table format[a]

Volume type	EBS provisioned IOPS SSD (io2 Block Express)	EBS provisioned IOPS SSD (io2)	EBS general purpose SSD (gp3)
Durability	99.999%	99.999%	99.8%–99.9%
Volume size	4 GB–64 TB	4 GB–16 TB	1 GB–16 TB
Max IOPS/volume	256,000	64,000	16,000
Max throughput/volume	4,000 MB/s	1,000 MB/s	1,000 MB/s
Latency	Submillisecond	Single-digit millisecond	Single-digit millisecond

[a] "Amazon EBS Features—Amazon Web Services" (*https://aws.amazon.com/ebs/features*), Amazon Web Services, Inc., accessed August 15, 2022.

Optimizing performance for your specific workloads and applications is outside the scope of this book. However, if this is an area of concern for you, investigate the particular recommendations for your application, and leverage performance tools to identify and improve performance. For example, on Linux, you can use iostat.

Storage Categories

Current storage categories are block, file, object, or database. Let's examine each of these to better understand the underlying storage abstraction layers and the impact on your system design choices.

Block Storage

For computing environments, block storage is the most direct way to interact with physical storage devices; the other forms of storage are at a higher layer of abstraction. Block storage fragments data into segments of uniform size to write to the storage media. The system uses queues of reads and writes to balance access to the media efficiently. Virtualized block storage uses the same strategy but transparently adds a network layer and stores the individual data segments on different drives, servers, or even data centers.

Redundant array of independent disks (RAID) technology allows you to configure multiple drives as a single logical block device, vertically scaling the capacity and performance while adding a layer of data protection. Storage networks extend this idea to scale across multiple servers horizontally.

Block storage is ideal when you need to interact with raw storage volumes, whether for the boot drive for a computer, the logical volumes used by virtual machines and containerized images, or data drives used for databases or file storage. In addition, block storage generally has the lowest latency.

File Storage

File-oriented storage is the conventional filesystem interface, with nested hierarchical folders containing files, each of which has attributes such as a name, an owner, permissions, and access dates.

File storage may be local through your OS or networked. Examples of networked file storage are Samba shares, NFS mounts, or a cloud-hosted service like Dropbox, Google Drive, iCloud Drive, or Microsoft OneDrive. These network storage services provide ways for your applications and OS to interact with network-hosted storage in the same way as storage on directly attached drives.

File-oriented storage is the approach for your typical "desktop computing" needs, whether that means shared access to an office file server or a subscription to a cloud-based service. This approach is also practical when you need to allow a cluster of servers to have shared access to configuration files, application data files, or software. Examples include media stores or user home directories.

File storage can encounter scaling problems when dealing with large numbers of files. Even as the backend network services scale to support theoretically unlimited capacities, the frontend software interacting with the storage can be a bottleneck. Conventional file browsers can fail when working with directory trees many layers deep, with thousands or even millions of files and subfolders. Organizing the data helps, but with large file hierarchies, people may have different ideas on how best to manage content.

Object Storage

In contrast to hierarchical file storage, object storage takes an unstructured approach. Each piece of data and associated metadata is stored with a unique identifier that individuals can quickly access on demand. Object storage is appealing when you have a considerable quantity of static items to store and you don't need to organize individual items in any particular way. So, use object stores for ordinary files: text, images, audio, video, or any other data.

Note that object storage doesn't organize objects into a hierarchical tree as you would with a traditional filesystem. Instead, you have a list of objects with nonsequential identifiers and annotated with metadata fields. You may adopt a framework that treats objects as files in a structured file tree. Still, interacting with object metadata provides many other ways to explore the data, such as photos taken with a specific camera, on a particular date or location, and using respective descriptive tags. Common use cases for object storage include scalable and flexible storage for modern applications, "big data" applications, backups, and media storage.

Database Storage

Relational databases are systems that often use a SQL dialect to organize and access information in interconnected tables of rows and columns. In databases, atomicity, consistency, isolation, and durability (ACID) are the properties to guarantee data integrity. Think of banking or credit card transactions, where funds must be simultaneously taken from one account and added to another. If the system can't complete the transaction, it must cancel it with no change to either account balance. A database system that promises ACID compliance promises to maintain a reliable data store that can recover from any problems by either committing each state-changing operation or rolling back to the most recent state before the attempted failed update.

Scaling a relational database places pressure on this ACID guarantee. You can scale vertically by adding storage and compute resources to handle the load, but there's only so much RAM, CPU, and disk that you can place into a single server. Eventually, you will have to scale horizontally and add more servers, and your application becomes distributed. Once you have a distributed application, you have to make unavoidable trade-offs.

The CAP theorem explains a set of trade-offs: for a system to continue to function in the presence of a network partition (partition tolerance), the system can either ensure every request receives a response, though not necessarily the latest write (availability), or ensure reads receive the most recent write or an error (consistency). In summary, the system can't guarantee availability and consistency simultaneously.

The PACELC theorem extends the CAP theorem for distributed systems running optimally (without a network partition); a system must choose between low latency and consistency:

- If your distributed application is sensitive to latency (meaning you prioritize the speed of responses over accuracy), you prefer for the response to a request to return before it has been validated to be the latest version. This models *eventual consistency* in a system.

- If your distributed application absolutely must be consistent (meaning you prioritize accuracy of the data), you prefer for the response to be validated as the latest version. This will increase the latency of requests depending on environmental resource contention, concurrency, or total storage requests in flight at a given point.

In other words, your database management system guarantees that the information is always consistent (e.g., Apache HBase (*https://oreil.ly/v9yeR*)), but people might have to wait to get a response. Or, your database management system maintains responsiveness but sacrifices consistency (e.g., Apache Cassandra (*https://oreil.ly/6X6As*)).

For many workloads, responsiveness can be at least as important as consistency. Think of a social networking site where the default view shows a set of posts from your friends, or a search engine that returns a list of results for a query. The person using the site does not necessarily need to see every post when they access that web page, but it is a big problem if the page comes up empty. If the system can make a best-effort attempt to show relevant results, this eventually consistent behavior is acceptable.

NoSQL databases are distributed systems that optimize for availability with eventual consistency. Instead of using SQL to enforce a schema when writing to a database, NoSQL databases enable the application developer to enforce the schema at the application level. This delay solves the long downtimes required for schema updates to a database by creating additional complexity at the application level.

A few NoSQL database types include key-value stores, document-oriented storage, graph, and wide-column databases:

Key-value stores
> Like the associative arrays, dictionaries, or hashes provided by many programming languages, key-value stores associate a piece of data with an identifier key. Examples of key-value databases include Redis and Amazon DynamoDB.
>
> Use cases for key-value databases include workloads with simple requirements to store, get, and remove data, for example, session management.

Document-oriented storage
> Document databases associate keys with a structured format (JSON, XML) known as a *document*. It is not necessary for the individual documents in the repository to conform to a consistent schema. As with object storage, document databases are a particular example of key-value storage.
>
> Use cases for document databases include workloads that require a flexible schema, including user profiles, content management and organization, and real-time business analytics.

Graph databases
> Graph databases emphasize the fundamental interconnectedness of all entities. A graph comprises an entity (i.e., a person or place) and a relationship that enables analysis that is difficult with earlier relational systems. Examples of graph databases include Neo4j and AWS Neptune.

Use cases for graph databases include any system looking for patterns in datasets: social networks, recommendation engines, fraud detection, financial risk assessment, and bioinformatics.

Wide-column databases

Wide-column stores structure data around columns rather than rows to optimize performance with common queries. Examples of wide-column database applications include Apache Cassandra and Apache HBase.

Use cases for wide-column databases include distributed systems with large-scale data requirements.

Many database products and hosted services support a mix of these options. Building a complete solution that meets your organization's needs will involve identifying the type of data and metadata you will need to store and assembling a mix of solutions that meet these needs.

Considerations for Your Storage Strategy

Now that you have a general sense of the storage options available, how do you decide which ones to use?

The standard question at this point is: do you need a cloud, on-prem, or hybrid approach to storage? Next, you'll need to identify solutions that will be appropriate for each niche of the system that you're overseeing, which may have varying needs (as discussed at the beginning of this chapter).

Generally, use whatever solution is appropriate and cost-effective for your needs. More specifically, you need to examine your data and how it flows to make decisions about storage.

Here are a few questions to consider about your data:

- What kind of data are you managing?
- How is it produced, and how is it consumed?
- How much data are you dealing with, and what are you doing with it?
- Who needs access to it, and how is it delivered? Are users internal or external to your organization?
- What are your data retention requirements?
- Are there contractual, legal, or privacy considerations? Remember any constraints both on what you must retain and what you must not retain.
- How frequently is the data being accessed?

- Are users primarily interacting with recent data, or are they analyzing historical data?
- Do the individual users tend to access a lot of data in a single session?
- Are user applications intolerant of latency?

Here are a few questions to consider about the devices you manage:

- Do your computing devices need to be able to boot independently? If so, they each need a boot drive. You can, of course, centralize administration by setting up a netboot server for diskless systems.
- Do your computers need to access shared storage? Maybe it makes sense to put things like config files and user home directories on a central file server on the local network. Or perhaps you have remote colleagues who don't necessarily have ready access to a server at the office, and it makes more sense to use a cloud-backed tool that synchronizes local files to a service provider.

Investing in on-premises hardware solutions can provide high capacity and throughput with low latency to internal users in a single geographic region.

There is a high up-front cost and an ongoing maintenance burden with maintaining backups and monitoring hardware health. Scalability can be a limiting factor, too. If a server runs out of capacity, your options are to delete or offload data or add more servers, which may require significant lead time.

By contrast, cloud-hosted solutions have minimal up-front costs and maintenance requirements as you mix and match block, file, object, and database storage solutions with virtually unlimited capacity to scale out as your needs grow. In addition, you can choose to replicate data to different regions to improve latency for global users.

These solutions require perpetual subscription costs that can unexpectedly spike if you're not placing boundaries on your storage consumption. In addition to storage guardrails, you can migrate data that isn't accessed frequently to "cold" storage tiers with lower ongoing costs to constrain expenses. Finally, you watch the cloud provider's billing dashboards instead of monitoring hard drive health reports.

For some organizations, there may be a strict requirement that you cannot connect critical infrastructure to the internet. Some cloud providers do offer solutions that meet government standards for housing sensitive information. Still, for institutions that cannot even consider this possibility, on-prem solutions are the only viable consideration.

Anticipate Your Capacity and Latency Requirements

Consider a video streaming service that provides a library of thousands of movies and TV shows to their subscribers. Each piece of content gets encoded in a range of quality settings, from standard-definition (SD) to high-definition (HD) formats (720p, 1080i, 1080p, 4K, and 8K). The demands on bandwidth and storage increase rapidly with every technological advance. Encoding formats or codecs can reduce the raw amount of data these formats produce but increase the cost of computational overhead and decreased picture quality.

The customers of video streaming services use various devices, from mobile phones to personal computers to large-screen televisions. Moreover, their connection speeds range from dial-up modem rates to gigabit or faster broadband connections. As a result, services need to store dozens of pregenerated formats to support this range of clients. It's not hard to imagine how keeping a single full-length movie in a range of high-quality formats can require a terabyte of capacity, and a library of a thousand movies would require a petabyte of storage. And that's just for the raw data, not including the overhead storage requirements of the databases and software that manage access to the video library, not to mention backups.

Streaming services use content distribution networks (CDNs) to replicate data to worldwide facilities to minimize customer latency delays in different regions. That petabyte of data for a movie library can end up being duplicated to hundreds of locations. An additional infrastructure layer must be in place to manage it, keeping the replication current and removing any stale data.

Think about your own organization's data requirements. Maybe you're not using data as voraciously as this, or perhaps you're using even more. Whatever the current rate, chances are good that it will keep doubling in the future.

Retain Your Data as Long as Is Reasonably Necessary

Your data has a lifecycle. Some of it is ephemeral, and some is long-lasting. Storage capacity has become inexpensive but isn't free, and retaining data has ongoing costs. Software that has to process more data either runs more slowly or consumes more computational overhead to maintain responsiveness.

Consider the infrastructure required to support the user of a fitness device that records metrics about heart rate and count of footsteps. The sensors record events with precision but don't retain raw telemetry due to capacity constraints. Instead, the device calculates configured rates and discards the original telemetry. Finally, the user syncs their device and uploads the summarized data to their account.

Users typically want to see trends over time but are less likely to look up their step count from an afternoon several years ago. So it's OK for the application to retain summarized data with a granularity of a day, a week, or even a month. Note that the system reduces incoming data to just what the next step in the pipeline requires at each data collection stage.

A similar approach arises when dealing with an organization's internal processes. For example, when working on a project, you'll often keep track of things in tickets, chat systems, emails, and shared documents. Once the project is complete, is it useful to be able to refer to such archived discussions, or is it sufficient to have a summary report to inform future work? Some organizations have policies that disallow retaining such artifacts, while others encourage preserving this institutional knowledge. Both approaches have strengths and weaknesses.

Deletion of Data When Disposing of Equipment

Your data retention policy also needs to extend to the disposition of equipment that is no longer required. Before disposing of servers, personal computers, mobile devices, portable drives, and so on, you should always assume that people may have stored potentially sensitive information on this equipment. Motivated people with access to the right tools can, in some cases, recover "deleted" data from storage devices.

If this risk is a concern, you may want to take additional steps to purge the data, such as writing zeros or random data to the drives. Scrambling the data can be an effective strategy for thwarting data recovery, but it is time-consuming, and even this may not be enough assurance for some organizations. For devices configured to use "whole-disk" encryption, the "deletion" process can be as simple as destroying the encryption key, which can make the data unrecoverable to all but the most committed of adversaries.

When in doubt, you should erase and physically destroy drives to be sure that malicious actions cannot recover the data.

Respect the Privacy Concerns of Your Users

I can't emphasize enough how important it is to respect the privacy concerns of your users. Pay special attention to how you handle PII or personal data. Often, there is a contractual or legal requirement to obtain such information only for a specific purpose and to delete the information as soon as it isn't needed.

Privacy advocates have drawn attention to the problems that arise when user data is collected, bought, and sold, often without fully informed consent. In jurisdictions with "right to be forgotten" laws, people can request that you remove their data, and you have both a legal and a moral obligation to fulfill such requests.

Defend Your Data

Data breaches—privacy violations in which an unauthorized party copies, steals, transmits, uses, or views private data—happen frequently. Such breaches may include financial information, personal health information (PHI), PII, trade secrets, and other intellectual property. These incidents can have significant direct and indirect costs, ranging from remediation efforts to reputational damage.

Data breaches happen for a variety of reasons. Both insiders and external actors can cause them. They can be due to negligence, such as a misplaced device, an easily guessed password, or a failure to use strong encryption, or they can be due to deliberate action, such as hacking, sabotage, or theft. Attack vectors can include malware, phishing, ransomware, social engineering, and theft of physical media.

The principle of least privilege is one way to defend against these problems: "every program and every privileged user of the system should operate using the least amount of privilege necessary to complete the job." This philosophy has guided OS design for decades and is still applicable today.

Think about who needs access to your data at different stages. Consider particular services your software provides. Do developers need full access to everything, or is it sufficient if they merely have high-level metadata access to validate that things are working? Or, to use a concrete example, do admins need access to a user's email account and Slack messages, or is it sufficient to verify that the account is active and the user can access it?

Your system should encrypt data at both motion and rest to reinforce least-privilege policies. Network protocols should encrypt data by default. The days of using open standard protocols safely (i.e., HTTP and SMTP) have been gone for years.

I know I'm repeating myself, but I can't stress enough the importance of giving special attention to how you handle financial, medical, and PII. The easiest way to defend this data is to not collect it.

Data breaches can be costly. Disclosure of personal information can lead to identity theft and other forms of fraud; victims of such crimes have come to expect remediation measures such as credit monitoring, replacement credit cards, and other forms of compensation. Disclosure of intellectual property such as source code or other trade secrets can undermine a company's market competitiveness and give an unexpected advantage to competitors. For example, data breaches at Yahoo in 2013 and 2014 exposed information on three billion user accounts; when Verizon acquired Yahoo in 2016, the company's value was adjusted downward by $350 million to reflect the damage—nearly 10% of the $4.8 billion acquisition price.

Be Prepared to Handle Disaster Recovery Situations

Assume that data loss is a fact of life. Individuals accidentally delete files or reformat the wrong drive. Service providers have outages due to accidents as well as physical hardware failures. Data centers are not immune to natural disasters.

Consider your data availability expectations. Does "everything" need to be backed up? How often? How timely? If a user created a file 10 minutes ago and then removed it 5 minutes ago, could you recover it? What if they need a deleted file from five months or years ago? Would it be acceptable if the recovery takes an hour? A day? A week?

A backup that isn't validated is just an aspiration. You need to simulate various forms of data loss (and repeat this periodically) and prove that you have a tested, documented procedure for getting the data back within a time frame that meets expectations. The worst time to find out that the backups don't work is when someone with a deadline needs their data back.

Case Study: Pixar's Toy Story 2

In 1998, a Pixar employee accidentally deleted the entire film archive after the computer-animated film *Toy Story 2* had been in production for nearly two years. Unfortunately, backups had stopped working due to the lack of available space. Luckily, Galyn Susman, the supervising technical director, had been working from home and had a copy of the data.

The team was able to use her copy, a two-month-old backup, and a variety of cobbled-together assets from failed renders and animators' local storage to painstakingly review tens of thousands of files to assemble a new source tree for *Toy Story 2*.

Pixar later decided that the story wasn't working, intentionally deleted the film, and started over.

Consider the lessons here:

- Guard against deletions.
- Monitor your backups.
- Trust people with the autonomy to tend to their families.
- Sometimes, it's OK to throw it away and start over again.

Wrapping Up

Data is generally your organization's most valuable asset, and in a healthy organization, it is continually growing. Traditional on-premise storage technologies can offer high performance and large capacities but also have high fixed costs and ongoing maintenance burdens; cloud-hosted solutions offer unlimited scalability but incur recurring and potentially unpredictable usage fees. Choose the portfolio of hardware and service solutions that meet your needs.

More Resources

Check out *Modern Data Protection* from W. Curtis Preston (O'Reilly) for more in-depth resources on protecting your data with backups. See Brendan Gregg's *Systems Performance* (Prentice Hall) for more detailed concepts, tools, and tuning for Linux operating systems and applications.

If you are primarily focused on managing databases, check out these resources:

- *High Performance MySQL* by Silvia Boltros and Jeremy Tinley (O'Reilly)
- *Database Reliability Engineering* by Laine Campbell and Charity Majors (O'Reilly)

CHAPTER 4

Network

Let's round out the fundamentals of systems by talking about the network. Networks are the communication bedrock of every system; they connect all your resources and services. Problems with the network lead to system failure. The critical nature of networks led to early specialization and networking admins to manage the networking hardware. Microservices, virtualization, and containerization have brought a tectonic shift to building and managing today's networks. More resources to interconnect, software-defined networking, and latency-dependent applications have all upset prior expectations of network admin skills, bringing some of these administration responsibilities back into scope for the systems team.

In this chapter, I explain the landscape of networking technologies (network virtualization, software-defined networks, and content distribution networks) so you can collaborate with your network and network security teams and build the skills to strengthen the interconnection of your system's components.

Caring About Networks

Let's revisit the example from the previous chapter of a contemporary product website; it's the virtual front door of a business and an example system you might manage.

A user opens up a web browser on their phone to buy a product from your company. Their wireless service provider routes their request to a CDN that operates in a data center physically close to them. If the CDN doesn't have the data to fulfill the request, their request is routed onward. Next, a load balancer routes the request to a physical server on which the hypervisor determines which VM to route to in your cloud-hosted infrastructure. Once the VM's Linux kernel has received the traffic, your application processes the request, and the response follows a similar path back to the client.

A lot is going on here. How many different networks did you count? Each network introduces some processing as a router determines the best path to get to the next destination. More network hops and different network types with varying transmission speeds lead to inconsistent and long response times. How many types of network devices were involved?

Your users generally don't care about these implementation details as long as the traffic gets through reliably. However, when requests aren't making it through, it matters a lot, and you have to figure out what is happening now. Rather than reacting to requests later, it's helpful to understand the context of your system's networks and build and manage them based on that knowledge. Understanding your system's needs enables you to make informed choices, as illustrated in the example of caching data closer to clients with a CDN and routing requests to the appropriate destination with load balancers.

As with all decisions in the building blocks of your systems, the context of what you are building matters. Effective use of the resources and options available to you will improve the cost to the humans on the team to manage the system, the impact on your customers, and the business's overall bottom line.

Key Characteristics of Networks

As with storage, there are a couple of primary ways to think about network options—wired versus wireless—and within each of these broad categories, there are different media (e.g., copper wire, fiber-optic cables) and communication protocols.

Networks have a topology, element arrangement, and data flow. Depending on the medium, network topology will define the layout of the physical cabling, the location of the different network resources, and embedded fault tolerance. All of these factors play into the cost associated with the network.

The key characteristics of networks include the following:

Bandwidth
> The capacity of the communication channel usually described as a rate for a fixed time; i.e., megabits per second (Mbps) or gigabits per second (Gbps).

Latency
> The time required for the signal to travel from one point to its destination, which depends on the physical distance the signal has to travel.
>
> Network latency is more accurately defined by the end-to-end time to transmit the message (transmission time), the time to process the request by all the

network devices along the way (processing delay), and the length of time taken up by the queue of requests to be processed (queuing delay).

Jitter

The variance from the median latency. For a specific request, you can see the network latency. To calculate the expected latency, an average of some number of data points will be used. The jitter is how to describe the variance of that measurement. For workloads that depend on low-latency networks (e.g., audio, streaming), jitter can be helpful to assess the quality of the network in terms of consistency.

Availability

The measure of the probability of the network being available. Different networks are capable of handling different numbers of failures.

Build a Network

Imagine that you're responsible for deploying a system to a data center. The system has a gateway that routes to an application that consists of a database and a bank of web servers. The data center provides backbone connectivity, but you're responsible for everything else. So, what network resources will you need? Here are some that come to mind:

- A firewall to filter ingress and egress traffic
- A gateway router to accept incoming traffic from the public internet, steer it to internal resources that process that traffic, and relay outbound traffic from the internal hosts onward back to remote clients
- A load balancer to distribute traffic among the web servers
- Intrusion detection systems to protect the network from unauthorized external access and other suspicious network activity
- A VPN gateway that grants authorized remote users elevated access to the private network

When factoring in your network's needs, think about the traffic patterns, type, and amount of traffic.

Often networks are described based on the available bandwidth. However, even if two compute environments both have high bandwidth in their connection to the broader internet, their physical separation may limit the quality of interaction because of the latency or jitter.

The Open Systems Interconnection (OSI) reference model is a seven-layered architecture that is used to visualize details about protocol and interface implementation.

For example, traditional load balancing is called Layer 4 (L4) load balancing because it occurs at the fourth level, transport. This type of load balancing occurs by the network device or application distributing requests based on the source and destination IP addresses and ports without deeper introspection into the content of the packets. Layer 7 (L7) load balancing occurs at the seventh level, application. Network or applications that are using application load balancing distribute requests based on the requests characteristics.

But the labels aren't perfectly accurate; they capture enough context to differentiate their use. For example, L4 load balancing could be more accurately described as L3/L4 load balancing because the load balancer uses network and transport characteristics in distributing requests. And L7 load balancing could be more accurately described as L5–L7 load balancing because the load balancer uses session, presentation, and application protocol characteristics to identify the best destination for requests.

Early L7 load balancing was very expensive due to the compute necessary to process requests. Now, with the advance in technology, the cost between L4 and L7 implementations is negligible compared to the benefits of more flexibility and efficiency of L7 load balancing.[1]

Recall the five layers of the Internet model from Table 1-2.

Each layer communicates via the interfaces above and below via a message object specific to the layer. Layering separates the roles and responsibilities, enabling humans to build (and change) different parts of communication protocols, which has fueled much of modern network transformation.

Virtualization

Creating a network comes down to two things: an ability to send and receive data and a mechanism to make decisions about how to do so.

In the past, you would buy a dedicated single-purpose device for each network function. Now you can deploy virtualized versions of these components using techniques similar to your other infrastructure resources. Just as service providers have virtualized traditional server roles (i.e., databases and web servers), providers virtualize network services with anonymous network equipment, so you can run software that manages how the hardware transmits and receives data.

However, you can't virtualize all aspects of networking. For example, communication with remote hosts necessarily involves physical data channels, such as Ethernet cables, transoceanic fiber-optic lines, satellite uplinks, or WiFi adapters. These

---

1 Learn more about layer 7 load balancing from the NGINX documentation (*https://oreil.ly/tFfiK*).

channels are different enough to require specific hardware to handle the data link operations. But that's the advantage of the separation of protocol implementation and interfaces with the internet. As long as the physical layer resources are in place and working, you have the flexibility to set up the transport and network resources as you see fit.

The ability to deploy arbitrary network functionality on generic hardware empowers us with tremendous flexibility. You don't have to acquire specialized equipment and then go to a data center to "rack and stack" it when an API call can fulfill the same need. Instead, network resources can scale vertically and horizontally with the rest of your infrastructure.

Software-Defined Networks

With the proliferation of deployed network resources at scale, your challenge is managing and protecting these resources in a cohesive, holistic way. Early approaches to internetworking used a decentralized philosophy where routers had only a vague sense of how to relay traffic to its final destination. A decentralized philosophy made the internet resilient enough to recover from natural disasters but didn't guarantee network stability. Moreover, this approach didn't account for the evolving nature of security. While early engineers designed the internet to survive network segmentation, they didn't consider malware threats like the Morris worm or the ubiquitous integration of computers into daily life, making everyone much more vulnerable to malicious activity.

Consider the challenges faced by a university network administrator. The institution provides certain computing resources (i.e., servers, workstations, and printers) and allows students and faculty to use their own devices (i.e., laptops, tablets, and phones). While the IT department patches and physically secures the university's equipment, it's much harder to enforce specific security policies on other people's equipment. As a result, it's only a matter of time before there's a problem with malware, ransomware, or viruses originating from unsecured personal devices.

Software-defined networking (SDN) provides tools to help you manage and protect your resources. SDN is an approach to network management that conceptualizes entire networks as a single programmable computer. Just as conventional computers use an OS to orchestrate hardware resources on behalf of high-level applications, SDNs introduce a centralized framework for coordinating the operations of a distributed network, activating resources as needed, automatically adapting to volatile conditions, and allowing you to push out uniform policies.

So a network admin could run a threat intelligence management application combined with shared threat sources (*https://oreil.ly/uetEd*) to compile a denylist for malicious websites. Then when device owners attempt to visit a malicious website, they will be directed to a warning page so that they can take the appropriate actions.

The defining attribute of SDNs is the use of a high-level control plane to govern the operation of the activity on individual network devices. While providers optimize software on the data or forwarding plane for speed, simplicity, and consistency, the control plane provides a flexible interface for defining policies and handling exceptions.

SDN architecture uses a centralized, programmable controller that oversees network operations. This controller uses southbound APIs to push information down to devices such as routers and firewalls and northbound APIs that relay state information to the controller. Most SDN implementations use the OpenFlow protocol to manage network devices in a vendor-agnostic way. As long as the physical or virtual equipment supports a programmatic interface for defining how to route or drop traffic, you can govern it with an SDN controller.

Multiple SDN controller applications can participate simultaneously. For example, some control plane applications focus on deployment and provisioning operations, others may meter traffic for billing purposes, and others can handle various aspects of network security.

Segmentation is another way to protect your networks. Segmenting your network can optimize traffic flow for legitimate uses of the network and classify the damage done in the event of a malware attack or data breach. With machine learning, modern software-defined networks can automatically learn to identify usage patterns and use this information to guide the operation of microsegments. Still, as with all machine learning systems, the outcomes are only as good as their training data.

Content Distribution Networks

A key element of smooth system operation is responsive network services. Users have come to expect near instantaneous response times and assume that things are broken if there are any delays. And yet, no amount of computing power can overcome the speed of light. The further away your users are, the more noticeable this is.

Consider a site operating from San Francisco as depicted in Table 4-1 with the following assumptions:

- All sites are connected to San Francisco with fiber in a straight line at the stated distance.[2]

---

2 In reality, networks don't connect this way. A complex set of partnerships and geographic locations have different levels of network infrastructure. Learn more about internet exchange points and how internet service providers and CDNs connect from the Cloudflare Learning Center post (*https://oreil.ly/Og7DC*).

- The speed of light is approximately 5 ms per 1,000 km for fiber.

Table 4-1. Distance and average latency from San Francisco to other sites

	New York City	London	Tokyo	Sydney	Johannesburg
Distance from San Francisco	4,130 km	11,027 km	17,944 km	11,934 km	16,958 km
Latency	21 ms	55 ms	90 ms	60 ms	8 5ms
Round-trip time	42 ms	110 ms	180 ms	120 ms	170 ms

Now, multiply the round-trip time (RTT) by the request size. The difference between users accessing the site from New York City and Tokyo is markedly different. In the real world, we have to factor in the fact that most places are not connected by fiber in straight lines, media has different latencies, and for every network hop, the network devices add delay for processing the route. Also, there are no guarantees about other traffic on the same network segments.

To overcome the limitations of network latency between sites, you need a copy of your site somewhere close enough to your customers so that these delays are negligible. While you could do this by building out a global network of your own, it's far simpler to outsource the work to CDNs, which take on the burden of operating a global array of data centers called *points of presence* (PoPs). By distributing your site to a local PoP, you can lower the response time for users close to those points to less than 1 ms.

Choose your CDN based on the set of features (e.g., availability, regions served, and routing options) that optimize your expenditure. With a CDN, you can do the following:

- Improve load times by distributing content closer to your consumers.
- Reduce the cost of bandwidth. Instead of making multiple redundant cross-country trips, most requests stay on the edge and pull from cached content.
- Increase availability and redundancy by having numerous global copies of your content.
- Improve security by mitigating the impact of a distributed denial-of-service (DDoS) attack. In a DDoS attack, malicious actors attempt to flood a site with traffic to exhaust a system's resources. Some CDN providers can prevent the malicious activity from reaching your servers, meaning that your system won't experience perceived downtime.

Using a CDN helps solve some of your problems, but it does add a layer of complexity in managing services, the specific configurations provided by your CDN, and your site's caches.

If you are currently using a CDN, check your service provider's documentation to figure out when you should clear cached resources. Consider situations such as these:

- Problems are occurring for a subset of your users. For example, someone pushed a change that had unintended consequences based on existing cached data.
- Problems are occurring for all of your users. For example, you had a bad site build.

In general, avoid purging your entire cache because doing so would cause a cascade of requests to repopulate the cache.

 If you are using caches with a web server, take some time to learn about *web cache poisoning*, an online attack on your cached data where an attacker leverages a vulnerability in your (unpatched) web server that causes a change in your cache that is then served to other users. James Kettle provides a great resource on how caches work and how web cache poisoning occurs (*https://oreil.ly/74vNx*).

Guidelines to Your Network Strategy

With your understanding of the landscape of networking technologies (network virtualization, software-defined networks, and content distribution networks), you can start to build your network strategy. Consider the following:

- Understand your latency needs. Consider bringing necessary systems closer to the end users to improve latency, whether through caching, mirrored systems, or segmented data. This means having a good understanding of how and where your users connect to you; i.e., via phones (unreliable wireless availability), laptops (mostly reliable wireless connections), hardwired connections, and physical distance like global markets.
- Leverage new protocols in your systems:
  - Use HTTP/2 to provide a faster and higher-quality user experience.
  - Use QUIC networking to maintain a seamless connection even when mobile users switch between network connections.
- Keep informed of internet security threats, and monitor advisories related to the software you use.

Wrapping Up

Whether wired, wireless, or virtualized, networks are how the resources and services that you manage exchange data with one another. Just as with the rise of devops, the boundary between system administration and software engineering has become blurred, and so too is the distinction blurring between sysadmins and network admins.

Modern software-defined networks take a centralized approach to route network traffic efficiently while providing network operators with tools to regulate traffic, protect against malware, defend against unauthorized activity, and handle billing for metered users. Similarly, content distribution networks provide a better experience for a global population of users by caching website data at facilities that are physically close to your users.

When you begin to set up and manage your network infrastructure, you need to consider how different resources on your network communicate with one another, how much data they're exchanging, and how tolerant they are of latency delays. Using modern approaches can provide you and your users with a fast, secure, and resilient network.

Practices

In Part II, I share the practices that have emerged to help reduce the impact of evolving technologies on your systems and to improve your systems' reliability and sustainability for the humans working on the systems.

This set of chapters helps you think about the different practices to apply to your systems that will improve maintainability, simplicity, and usability. I want you to feel enabled to adopt the practices to support you in supporting your systems.

CHAPTER 5

Sysadmin Toolkit

A toolkit represents a collection of useful items to support a particular set of purposes. In my early sysadmin years, I had a physical kit in my laptop bag that included various items to support the work I encountered. It varied over time, but essentials included a pen and a Sharpie for labeling, sticky notes (folded over a cable; they were super helpful in tracing gnarly cable issues), a mini screwdriver set to open cases and replace hardware, bootable CDs for a wide spread of operating systems, and a lot of different cables and dongles.

The modern sysadmin toolkit focuses more on nonphysical essential tools. Your working environment is your first managed system and part of your kit. This chapter shows you how to build your digital kit by adopting a codified development environment so that you can automate everyday tasks and improve collaboration with your users and colleagues by sharing your kit or adopting tools or practices from theirs.

What Is Your Digital Toolkit?

As a system administrator, you are responsible for the reliability of systems. Whatever your specific role is, whatever the system is, you need a safe way to simulate a realistic model of your production environment to tinker with and figure out workable processes. Ultimately, you want to identify resilient and sustainable ways to operate.

Your digital toolkit is a development environment that helps you minimize the risk to any customer-facing system by giving you the set of tools and technologies to develop code isolated from a live environment. Your environment can be on your laptop or workstation, and it can also be a private sandbox on a remote system with a cloud provider.

Your toolkit may enable the following:

- Working offline

- Debugging code/configuration

- Onboarding new employees or team members with the relevant context necessary to do a specific task

- Embracing policy compliance and recommended practices through codified standards

---

How I Learned to Stop Worrying and Love My Development Environment

By Chris Devers

My work involves supporting broadcast production systems where downtime can be massively disruptive, so I need to feel confident before deploying the fix when problems arise. I might have ideas about how to proceed with a solution, but conducting experiments in production usually isn't acceptable. So I need access to an environment that meaningfully replicates production to try things out without disrupting anyone or jeopardizing data or services.

For example, the software I deal with can back up material to LTO tape media for cold archival storage. But all sorts of problems can arise with the tape libraries: someone might have removed the necessary tape, or the tape might be unreadable. Sometimes, a tape is physically OK, but it's unlabeled, so the library can't scan the barcode. Or, the label jams the robotic mechanism for shuttling tapes. Or the tape hardware is working fine, but the data cable is not fully seated, so the hardware intermittently disconnects from the server. Virtualized tape software is available for "happy path" scenarios when the hardware is running. But, if I need to be sure that the software will behave for hardware anomalies, then I don't feel confident deploying a fix I haven't tried.

To deploy changes to production systems, I need to prove that the changes work correctly in conditions comparable to where they will be running and without introducing unwanted side effects. Local development environments that replicate production provide me with a way to prove that the changes I'm working on will work as expected without putting the production system at risk.

The Components of Your Toolkit

Your toolkit will be specific to the set of tasks and projects that your work requires, including some combination of the following elements:

- An editor
- Programming languages
- Frameworks
- Libraries
- Applications

And, of course, any configurations specific to any of these components. Let's review these components in more detail.

Choosing an Editor

Sysadmins write code, scripts, infrastructure, documentation, and tests. The correct text editor reduces your overhead, helps you catch problems in your code early, suggests code completions based on language semantics, formats your code based on team expectations, and integrates with other tools.

For example, you could manually craft a Dockerfile, the text file containing the build instruction for a Docker container, looking up each build instruction. With a contemporary editor, you get suggested snippets corresponding to valid Dockerfile commands to quickly build out a new Dockerfile to ease the creation of a Dockerfile as you compose the file. For an existing Dockerfile, hovering over a command will give you a detailed description of what that command is doing.

What should you look for in an editor? While you're probably already familiar with one or more text editors, there are features that can make it worth learning another, such as these:

- Integrated static code analysis
- Code completion
- Indented code to match team conventions
- Distributed pairing
- Integrated workflow with Git

Be open-minded about others trying and adopting different tools. For example, while vi or emacs may have all the features you want and need, they may not be the right choice for others. Building and learning the necessary editor context from scratch with all the unique mechanisms to operate the editor may not be the best use of their time, especially when there is so much more to being an effective system administrator than your editor.

Integrated static code analysis

You can speed up development and reduce potential issues by adding static code analysis or linter extensions for the languages used. For example, you can install `shellcheck` and the `shellcheck` extension for writing bash scripts. Then, as you write shell code, the editor will alert you of potential problems. In the following example, I wanted to find all the files with a *.png* extension in the current directory, so I wrote some shell code:

```
#!/bin/bash

for file_name in $(ls *.png)
do
  echo "$file_name"
done
```

My editor warned me that "iterating over `ls` output is fragile." So I updated the code, removed `ls`, and used globs as recommended:

```
for file_name in *.png
do
  echo "$file_name"
done
```

Running a linter as you write code allows you to catch and fix problems. There are linters for many files, from YAML to specific languages. Within the editor, you can customize the options for how the lint runs, allowing you to run linting as you type code or, if that is too distracting, after you save your updates.

Code completion

Code completion improves the coding experience by providing educated guesses about what you are trying to do. As you type, autocomplete options will pop up. Some languages have better completions automatically; you can add extensions to improve others.

Establish and validate team conventions

Many organizations use code linters to help enforce a consistent coding style, making it easier for teams to maintain a shared code repository. For example, the team can standardize the text indentation rather than debate whether spaces or tabs are more readable. Each individual can customize their editor to display their preferred indentation. Additionally, you can convert the amount of spacing currently used within a file to conform to new requirements.

Integrate workflow with Git

As you work on a project, it's helpful to see your changes and whether you've committed them. Seeing your intended changes can prevent unfortunate surprises, such as forgetting to share your fixes for bugs back to the shared source control repository.

Choosing Programming Languages

While you might not develop applications, honing development skills in shell code and at least one additional language helps you collaborate better and build the functionality that improves your team's productivity. In addition, automating work—from opening JIRA tickets with prepopulated meta information to scanning compute instances for systems out of compliance with required standards—frees up the team's time to focus on areas that need human thought and creativity.

Bash and PowerShell are reasonable choices in most environments, are available on current versions of both Linux and Windows, and will be handy daily. Once a shell script starts getting longer than 50 lines or needs complex data structures, it becomes more difficult to understand, leading to a fragile mechanism for managing a system. No one wants to break the script. Reimplementing a script as a utility in a general-purpose programming language can help in those cases. Languages like Python, C#, Ruby, and Go can provide these benefits:

- Better error handling
- A rich community of libraries
- Additional debugging tools and utilities

So how do you choose a specific language? Think through these concerns:

What languages are already in use within your organization or team? How much code in a specific language do you already have?
> Learning how to read whatever language(s) your development team uses can be beneficial. When the system isn't working as expected, it can be helpful to check whether the problem is with the code or tests of that code.
>
> You can also leverage the fact that multiple people can support debugging or feature implementation.

Sometimes the right choice is to go along with popular opinion; sometimes, the right choice is to buck the trend. For example, it's OK to choose languages and technologies based on existing skills on the team.

Are there tools and technologies that you or your team would like to adopt, but they're implemented in a language that nobody on your team is familiar with?

You could adopt an alternative technology that uses a language your team already knows or take it as an opportunity to broaden your skill set by learning a new language. And teams that don't develop new skills will stagnate, limiting their choices in software adoption because new software often leverages contemporary languages.

Include the overall cost of using and supporting the tools in your decision. For example, some teams value the collaboration possible from the worldwide community of open source technologies. In contrast, other teams benefit more from access to commercial training and support. Of course, neither of these options is inherently better, but choosing one that goes against your team culture will add to the complexity of successful adoption.

Consider the impact of different kinds of changes:

- New language versions can break backward compatibility with existing codebases.
- New libraries may simplify previously complex chores but require refactoring legacy code.
- Security patches require cessation of vulnerable features that need legacy refactoring with urgency. Any language popular enough to have an active development community will be in flux. Therefore, your options will include alternatives when planning what your team wants to work on in the future.

 Documenting the reasons a team has chosen a language creates helpful reference material for the future.

What languages are widely used by your industry peers?

Widely adopted languages within the industry will have more support resources with documented example code in community forums.

What challenges are you facing with previous decisions about language implementation?

Sometimes even though a particular language is widely used within your organization, it has associated challenges that may hinder a new project. Identifying and documenting your thinking process in your decision is part of proposing and adopting a new language.

It takes time and energy to refactor a tool to a new language, and the refactor could require you to support two different tools simultaneously. Even if your team is sticking with one primary language, languages evolve. It can be necessary to refactor legacy code to keep working with new versions of the language or libraries. For example, organizations trying to migrate from one infrastructure automation tool to another often end up with both technologies rather than a clean migration. In addition, applications with overlapping concerns add confusion and complexity to the environment.

In the end, there is no right language to learn as a system administrator. So instead, balance your experience with the features and the rest of the team's skills.

 Sometimes, your operating system will include a version of the language. Often this is an outdated version, and you'll need to update it to leverage the language's latest features. Changing the system-included language isn't a recommended practice. Instead, install the desired version separately and set execution paths appropriately to prefer the later version. The explicit external installation will help prevent system instability due to modifying the software the system might use. It also helps eliminate undefined dependencies in environments.

Frameworks and Libraries

Your organization's service providers and languages will define what additional frameworks or libraries you need. Some examples include the following:

- AWS SDKs for specific languages,
- PagerDuty API client libraries to manage your PagerDuty configurations
- ChatOps automation frameworks in a specific language

These will be highly specific to your environment and needs and potentially problematic if functionality changes across library versions. Documenting versions of these frameworks and libraries and codifying them into environments prevents lost time debugging different outcomes.

Other Helpful Utilities

Beyond your editor, languages, frameworks, and libraries, additional applications round out your toolkit. Different tools will be helpful in your organization:

- Ticket or bug tracking
- Infrastructure and application monitoring

- Alerting
- Config management, container orchestration, and infrastructure provisioning
- Pipelines
- Artifact repositories
- Builds
- Source code
- Chat
- Knowledge management

You can codify all of these tools with infrastructure code into prebuilt containers or virtual machines or leverage a remote system provided by a cloud provider.

Additionally, you can customize your command line with shell customizations. *Dotfiles* are files that generally (but not always) start with a dot and help us back up and customize our systems. You can share dotfiles with other engineers to improve their productivity with new tools. Some organizations use dotfiles to configure aspects of a new system for productivity. While dotfiles may feel more familiar on Unix-like systems, they are also available on Windows systems.

 Be aware that you shouldn't just adopt someone else's dotfiles into your environment without understanding all the code. Also, configurations that work for one person may not function optimally for someone else.

Over time, you'll also build out sets of tools that you rely on regardless of your environment. I want to share some of my favorites. Many of the following recommended tools are cross-platform, although some are UNIX-specific:

The Silver Searcher
The Silver Searcher (*https://oreil.ly/Km2em*), or *Ag* for short, levels up searching through code repositories. Ag is fast and ignores file patterns from *.gitignore*. It can be integrated with editors as well. When debugging errors or other "needles in the haystack" of code, it can be super helpful to search for a specific string to understand how it's called.

bash-completion
Modern shells provide command completion by allowing you to start typing the beginning of a command, hit Tab, and see potential completions. *bash-completion* extends this feature and enables you to add completion features. Extensions are shareable across the team.

cURL

cURL is a command-line tool and library to transfer data. For example, you can use it to verify whether you can connect to a URL, which is one of the first validations when checking a web service. You can also use it to send or retrieve data from a URL or retrieve HTTP headers to see specific server response codes.

Docker

Docker provides a mechanism to create isolated environments called *containers*. A Dockerfile encapsulates the OS, environment files, and application requirements. You can add a Dockerfile to a project and commit it to version control.

With Docker installed and access to a Dockerfile, onboarding a new collaborator to a project can be as straightforward as running docker run to get a working test environment up. This test environment would match even more closely to a production environment if running production on containers.

gh

Using Git as version control and GitHub as the project repository, gh (*https:// oreil.ly/dSBI3*) extends Git functionality that helps with GitHub tasks from the command line.

For example, if I want to test a pull request (PR) submitted to a project, I can use gh pr checkout <issue-number> to check out that specific pull request and do local testing in my environment before approving the PR to be merged.

Git

Git is a distributed version control system. Look for more information about version control in Chapter 6.

HTTPie

HTTPie is a command-line HTTP client to test, debug, and interact with APIs with JSON support and syntax highlighting.

jq

jq is a lightweight and flexible command-line JSON processor. Combined with cURL, you can process JSON output from the command line.

mkcert

mkcert (*https://oreil.ly/T8R4i*) makes locally trusted development SSL certificates.

ShellCheck

ShellCheck is a utility that shows problems in bash and sh shell scripts. It can identify common mistakes and misused commands. You can ignore specific checks if they are not checks your team wants running against your code with a configuration file.

---

tmux

tmux (*https://oreil.ly/Qrkny*) is a terminal multiplexer that allows you to switch between several programs in one terminal.

tree

tree is a utility that's a part of most OSs and lists the contents of a directory in a tree-like format. It can be helpful to visualize the structure of a filesystem, especially for documentation to show others what to expect to see. Sometimes, showing that expectation rather than just saying "in the current directory" can help uncover missed assumptions.

Wrapping Up

A sysadmin's toolkit is a collection of codified tools and technologies to minimize your cognitive load and maximize your efficiency by enabling you to automate and manage the installation and configuration of your system to have a consistent and repeatable base.

An excellent local development environment provides the right text editor, programming languages, frameworks, libraries, and other applications to experiment with, learn about, and evaluate changes to your production environment.

Adopt what works for you, share with those working with you, and improve the foundations required for collaborative work by collectively reducing the load on any individual to get started on daily tasks.

More Resources

Check out Thomas A. Limoncelli's article "Low-Context DevOps" (*https://oreil.ly/OtR64*) to learn more about creating environments that support your productivity regardless of your existing background knowledge.

And check out these resources on dotfiles:

- Dotfiles on Github (*https://oreil.ly/KwzW2*)
- Lars Kappert's Medium post "Getting Started with Dotfiles" (*https://oreil.ly/I1zwu*)

CHAPTER 6

Version Control

Imagine you are running a small business with a partner who lives in another location. You share a business bank account to pay the bills. While online banking lets you log on at any time to see the state of your finances, it doesn't tell you about planned changes or provide insight into your finance management. As a result, you often receive late fees from unpaid bills and the occasional overdraft fees due to duplicate payments to the same vendor.

You adopt a system that allows you to schedule your bills and track the accountability of planned changes. The new system improves your collaboration and enables you to do the work you want to do. Ultimately, what differentiates your business from others isn't how you manage your money.

Now replace "shared bank account with a business partner" with the system you need to manage. Your business partner is the rest of the team you have to work with (including the future you at 2 a.m., who has to deal with the system's state and occasionally makes mistakes). Every individual on a team could have different preferences for managing the system. Unless you all agree on a common way of working with the system, you will experience the pain and frustration of trying to fix it whenever there is conflict. Instead, suppose you adopt version control and leverage the tools already in your organization (e.g., Git, Artifactory, GitHub, and GitLab). In that case, you get visibility, accountability, and alleviation of the pain of conflicts.

In this chapter, I want to help you think about version control and enable you to move your work into version control to manage and track changes with reproducibility, accountability, and conflict management.

What Is Version Control?

Version control is confusing, partly because we use the same words and abbreviations to mean different things. It's an overused term with many meanings.

Deploying a system requires the source code or binary packages, configurations, deploy scripts, and all the processes to get everything in place and monitored from end to end. The method of backing up and minimizing risk to your system is version control.

Because we (mistakenly) use the terms *source control* and *version control* interchangeably, we think of version control, the *practice*, as the domain of (only) software developers to maintain source code. But the practice of version control—managing and tracking change to configuration files, scripts, and build images—is crucial to a system administrator's ability to create multiple environments with the same configurations, replicate and restore systems to original states, and apply published recommended practices to meet compliance standards.

Take a look at Figure 6-1. In the broadest sense, as depicted in the largest rectangle (and the one I'm going to focus on in this chapter), version control is the *practice* of managing and tracking data changes. It can apply to text files like source code or configuration files and build artifacts and images.

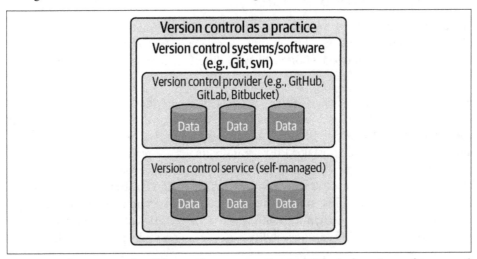

Figure 6-1. Examining the difference between version control as a practice, software, and service

The middle rectangle contains version control *systems* (VCSs). VCSs—such as Git, a distributed system, and Subversion (svn), a centralized system—are specific implementations of version control *software* that handle the features of repositories and branching differently.

Artifact management systems are another type of version control system not pictured in this figure. Artifact management systems manage repositories of compiled binaries instead of text files.

Finally, the two inner rectangles represent the implementations of VCSs—provider-managed (e.g., GitHub and GitLab) and self-managed.

Benefits of Version Control

Early into my first official job as a system administrator with the keys to the kingdom in hand (aka the root password), my coworker walked me through how to update a configuration. The first step was to make a backup copy of the file so I could get back to a known good place if I needed to. Next was to make the edits to the file. On some systems, that meant using **ed**, which doesn't have all the conveniences of modern editors. Making mistakes was easy, and I often relied on the backup file to try again. Next, I restarted the service and validated it was in a good state. As I got used to all the various intricacies of managing the systems, I noticed a lot of old backup files sitting in the service directories with random naming patterns from *.bak* to *.bak.date*, *.date.bak*, *.name.date.bak*. Knowing which extraneous files to save and which I could remove was difficult.

Today, you don't have to configure systems directly. Instead, you can adopt VCSs without having to create a unique backup naming scheme. And even if you haven't moved to a system that automatically handles your version-controlled system configuration, you can still deploy version-controlled configurations to your special snowflakes to maintain them in a systematic, repeatable, and documented manner.

With a VCS, you get management and accountability for change with the following:

- A copy of each version
- Access controls for creation, deletion, and modifications
- History of changes, including who is responsible for a change
- A process to prevent or handle conflict
- The ability to document changes

As a sole administrator for a given system, you can leverage version control to track the system's state over time and document decisions about changes. In addition, practicing version control is the foundation for collaborating with others on your team and within the organization to help them understand how you manage your systems using standard practices.

Leveraging version control with your infrastructure code, configuration files, and system tools in addition to source provides important benefits:

Reproducibility
> You can deploy a specific version of a system or an environment with the scripts, configuration, and software artifacts.

Enculturation
> You facilitate the onboarding of new team members with version control change-logs, which can increase productivity and efficiency.

Visibility in change management
> You can grant read access to your team's repositories to non-team members who want to view or discuss your projects. As a result, people can see what changes and any work in progress. Additionally, you can grant permissions that allow individuals to approve changes, which would enable interaction without granting access to modify the repositories.

Accountability
> You use a VCS to track changes. The history of system changes provides an audit trail, making it possible to answer questions about who created each system and its intended purpose. In addition, accountability can decrease costs because you can audit systems to ensure they are still needed.

Organizing Infra Projects

There is no single right way to do project organization when choosing between one project per repo (multirepo) or all projects within a single repo (monorepo). Each approach includes a set of trade-offs, including code organization, dependency management, and configuration control:

Code organization
> With multirepos, you agree to one project per repo, but there is no holistic definition of a project. As a result, some projects line up well with the project definition, but other work might not be so clear-cut. For example, think about this scenario: where would a single helper script for configuring a laptop reside? You could put it in a single repository. Or you could group it with other random helper scripts or all of your workstation-related code.
>
> So, how does your team find this helper script or identify whether the script exists already? In a monorepo, the search is limited to one repo. With multirepos, the team would need to know about all the repos to search.
>
> As projects grow in size in a monorepo, you can experience performance impacts when checking out and building the project. For multirepos, projects don't

impact one another. Multirepos can lead to duplication of code or a complex web of dependencies.

Whichever model you follow, ideally, you have a standard practice across the organization to reduce the cognitive load on humans to figure out what to do when organizing a new project.

Versioning
With multirepos, versioning can occur separately for each project.

Dependency management
With a monorepo, you can lock your dependencies down to specific versions, which can be helpful when your projects need the same software version. However, if they require different versions of the same software packages, you can run into problems trying to navigate requirements, forcing one project to upgrade any code so that it can use the latest version.

With a multirepo, each project can have dependencies locked to the version needed without conflicts.

Configuration control
When separate functional teams need to collaborate on different projects and to work on the monorepo in different ways, work preferences can cause personal conflict between groups, causing problems in code reviews and merging code.

Questions can also arise as to who "owns" the contents of a repository that multiple teams contribute to and is therefore responsible for making changes and verifying that these changes do not break things for other teams.

Organizing material into smaller repos can minimize this problem but steepen the learning curve for understanding which repos to work in for a given change requirement.

This list of trade-offs is not comprehensive. Your team will have to decide whether a monorepo or multirepo is more appropriate. It would be best to document your preferences so that when it comes time to work with other teams or onboard new contributors, your collaborators will understand the agreed-upon approach.

Wrapping Up

Version control is the practice of managing and tracking changes to data. Your system infrastructure and how you manage it is critical data. Adopt version control to improve managing your system infrastructure. VCSs ease management with the following:

- Accountability for change with an *audit trail* (information about each change and version of the project)
- Access controls to regulate who can change data
- Mechanisms to handle conflict and provide visibility

These capabilities provide you and your team with a flexible toolkit for collaboratively maintaining and extending your infrastructure.

CHAPTER 7

Testing

In many conversations with other sysadmins, I get the sense that they don't think of themselves as testers. Whether we think of ourselves as testers or not, the reality is that we are using tests to give ourselves information on the state of tasks and to explore our environments so we can understand them better. We want to prevent those terrible 2 a.m. pages or at least learn to remedy problems quickly. In this chapter, you'll learn what tests to write to leverage automated testing, evaluate the effectiveness of tests, and change them to suit your needs. You'll need these foundational concepts to apply testing to infracode (Chapter 11) and infrastructure management (Chapter 12).

You're Already Testing

Have you ever run through installing a set of software on a nonproduction or nonlive system, watching to see how the system responded and whether any gotchas could impact users? This manual testing approach is known as *exploratory testing*. The goal of exploratory testing is to help discover the unknown by experimenting with the system and looking at areas that may need more subjective analysis as to whether they are in a good state. In "Exploratory Testing Explained" (*https://oreil.ly/BZEa1*), James Bach defined exploratory testing as "simultaneous learning, test design, and test execution." In contrast to scripted tests, exploratory testing is executed based on your knowledge and perspectives, so it's vulnerable to your personal biases.

You can level up your manual exploration and add some objectivity by adopting more rigor in your analysis—defining testing objectives with short feedback loops to inform your next steps. Then, working with software engineers and testers, you can help shape the testing to eliminate some manual testing for their scripts and infrastructure code (infracode). These scripted tests provide the following benefits:

Increase your team's confidence in your code
Tests help you reduce the fear of repercussions of making change. Rather than expecting everyone to execute flawlessly, build safety nets that help them make change confidently.

Speed up delivery of working tools and infrastructure
With tests in place, you can iterate on releases rapidly, confident in the knowledge that if the tests have passed, then the release should be reliable, too.

Tackle new projects
Other people can take on the responsibility for work you've completed when automated tests exist. You've created a safe space for individuals to learn and make changes.

Document the expectations and context of the code
Good tests can describe expected functionality well.

Testing helps you deliver a working product that includes the infrastructure and scripts that will help your system run effectively, eliminates single points of knowledge, and increases confidence that problems won't easily make it to end users.

 Having new team members explore products and processes during their onboarding is helpful. They can bring unbiased insight to level up quality to correct problems with the product and processes and clear up misunderstandings and inconsistencies that may already exist within the team.

Let's explore other common types of tests that you can script and leverage to build out automated testing: linting, unit, integration, and end-to-end tests.

Common Types of Testing

You can write more effective tools and infracode with testing. Understanding the different types of testing, including their benefits and drawbacks, helps you create appropriately leveled, maintainable tests. As there is no exact definition of these test types, there may be different interpretations of these tests depending on the team. For example, some Google teams frame tests by size instead of type (*https://oreil.ly/ EgVgm*).

Linting

Linters are a basic form of static analysis to discover patterns or style convention problems. With linting, you can identify issues with code early, and you don't have to write specific tests. In addition, it can uncover logic errors that could lead to security vulnerabilities. Linting differs from formatting changes to code because it analyzes how code runs, not just its appearance.

 You may get several warnings if you run a linting tool on an existing project. Modifying functional code with stylistic changes may frustrate your team, especially if there are reasons for those particular styles or conventions. Instead of immediately making changes, bring up the results and document the conventions explicitly by configuring the linter.

There are three key reasons to adopt linting in your development workflow: to discover bugs, increase readability, and decrease code variability.

Discover bugs

The best time to discover a bug is right after you create it, when your code is fresh in your mind and you have clarity about what you intended to write. Linting while you code allows you to fix it with that known context. While you can lint manually, many editors have linting plug-ins to receive near-instantaneous feedback about potentially problematic code. You fix issues as they arise instead of after you have committed your code and submitted a pull request for review.

Increase readability

Consistent, readable code is easier to maintain, fix, and extend functionality. When you need to work on an existing codebase, chances are high that the original author will no longer remember the context, but if they wrote clear code, it is easier to get up to speed. Linters help enforce readability.

Decrease variability

Consistent standards and practices ensure that code is cohesive. Encoded style prevents arguments over team conventions so you can focus on discussing the changes that have an impact, for example, specific architectural design or security fixes.

You configure your linter with a configuration file to implement the team standards and ignore or modify default rules. For example, the default line length configuration for RuboCop, the Ruby language linter, is 80 characters (*https://oreil.ly/9pvRX*). Contemporary displays are much larger than traditional 72-character TTY displays, and your team may want to enable more characters per line. As depicted in Example 7-1, you can set the check for line length to 100 by creating or updating the RuboCop configuration file, *rubocop.yml*, within the project source code repository. This ensures that everyone checking out the project will run linting without getting a warning for the line length less than 100 characters.

Example 7-1. RuboCop configuration to update characters-per-line test

```
Metrics/LineLength:
  Max: 100
```

While individuals may prefer using two or four spaces and tabs instead of spaces within their code, your team can validate their code and configurations against the team standards within their editor. This way, code reviews can focus on implementation details rather than stylistic concerns.

Here are some linters for common languages that sysadmins use in their daily work:

- ShellCheck for shell scripts (*https://oreil.ly/saNSu*)
- jsonlint for JSON (*https://oreil.ly/U3XTU*)
- yamllint for YAML (*https://oreil.ly/Nvqgm*)
- Black for Python (*https://oreil.ly/QmFPJ*)
- Prettier for CSS, HTML, JavaScript, Markdown, and other languages (*https://oreil.ly/tfMFe*)

Unit Tests

Unit tests are small, quick tests that verify whether a piece of code works as expected. They do not run against an actual instance of code that is running. Any resources that depend on calls to external resources are stubbed (i.e., database requests or calls to specific services). Stubbing makes unit tests super helpful for quickly evaluating code correctness because they are fast (generally taking less than a second to run). With unit tests, you aren't checking code on actual system instances, so you don't receive insight into connectivity issues or dependency issues between components.

Unit tests are generally the foundation of a testing strategy for a project because they're fast to run, less vulnerable to being flaky or noisy, and isolate where failures occur. They help answer questions about design, regressions in behavior, assumptions about the intent in code, and readiness to add new functionality.

When you write unit tests, ensure that they are testing your code. For example, when you write infracode to configure a file or create a directory, your unit test should validate that you wrote code to configure a file or create a directory, not that your infracode platform knows how to execute those tasks. Write tests that describe your desired outcomes and validate your code.

Examples of a unit in infracode might be a managed file, directory, or compute instance. The unit test to verify the example units would describe the file, directory, or compute instance requirements, including specific attributes. The unit test describes the expected behavior.

Integration Tests

Integration tests verify the behavior of multiple objects working together. The specific behavior of integration tests can vary depending on how your team views "multiple objects." Integration tests can be as narrow as two "units" working together or as broad as different, more significant components working together. Integration tests run against an ephemeral environment and don't test every project element; they give insight into the project's behavior at a broader scope.

Because integration tests don't test everything, problem determination isn't precise. For example, it would help if you understood the environmental conditions of what went wrong and what caused the failure. In addition, integration tests run in minutes due to the increased complexity in setting up potential infrastructure dependencies, including other services and software.

You might test whether a database successfully installs, configures, and starts up appropriately, allowing for connections, for example.

End-to-End Tests

Finally, *end-to-end* (E2E) tests verify the flow of behavior of a project function as expected from start to finish in a temporary environment with realistic test data. E2E tests validate the applications and services defined by the infracode work as intended. As you can imagine, it could take quite a while to provision and configure new instances and run them through the testing suite. In addition, an E2E test failure is not isolated and deterministic to a single component. E2E tests check specific function output and require more frequent changes to the test code. For example, a test environment in an Amazon availability zone with network issues may have intermittent failures. The flakier the tests, the less likely individuals will spend effort maintaining those tests, which leads to lower quality in the testing suite.

Even with these challenges, E2E tests are critical to a testing strategy. They simulate a real user interacting with the system. Modern software can comprise many interconnected subsystems or services built by different teams inside or outside an organization. Organizations rely on these external systems rather than expending resources to build them in-house (which incidentally has even higher risk). System administrators often manage these boundaries where systems need to interconnect.

Identifying and reading the tests in your services product may help you identify tools or patterns that can help you eliminate manual processes in your testing of infrastructure for those services.

Explicit Testing Strategy

One of the ways that the industry describes testing strategy is through the metaphor of the test pyramid. In 2009, Mike Cohn coined the term *test pyramid* (*https://oreil.ly/jmisr*) in his book *Succeeding with Agile* (Addison-Wesley Professional). This pyramid serves as a visual representation of how to think about and plan a system's testing strategy.

As shown in Figure 7-1, the pyramid stresses the importance of the different types of tests while recognizing that tests have different implementation times and costs. As you move down layers, tests run faster because there is a decrease in the scope and complexity.

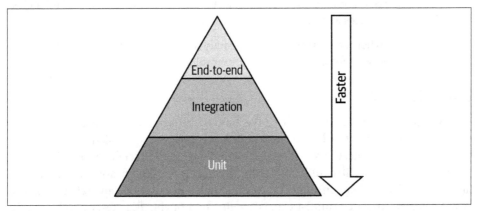

Figure 7-1. Test pyramid framework

A good rule for writing tests is to push them as far down the stack as possible. The lower in the stack, the faster the test will run, and the faster it will provide feedback about the quality and risk of the software. This is because unit tests are closer to the code testing specific functions. In contrast, end to end is closer to the end-user experience; hence, the pyramid shape is based on how much attention and time you spend writing the particular type of test.

You can examine the tests for a project and qualify the strategy based on the number and type of tests to inform you of areas to add or eliminate tests.

Think of your tests as building blocks. For example, a unit test is 1 × 1. An integration test will test multiple components and range in size, for example, from 1 × 2 (to test 2 components) to larger. Your E2E tests will vary in size, but you don't have to get down into each component's nitty-gritty specifics, especially if you test the piece in an earlier (and faster) test.

In Figure 7-2, you can visualize the shape of your project's testing strategy based on the number and type of tests. On the left, in a healthy approach, you use mostly unit tests, with integration tests bridging components and a few end-to-end tests. On the right, in an unhealthy situation, you've got many overly specific, E2E tests that will take longer to run.

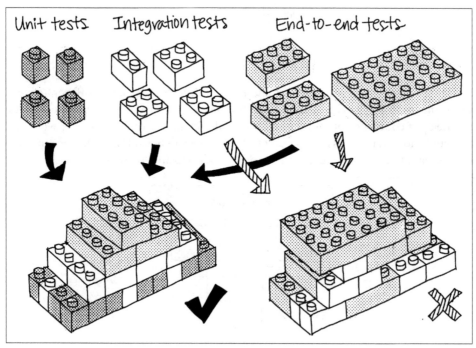

Figure 7-2. Assessing automated testing (image by Tomomi Imura)

Let's model some different testing implementations to understand what could be wrong and the steps to take, adding or removing tests. Examining testing implementation can help you know how much invisible work is being passed on to your team.

In Figure 7-3, having an approximately equal number of tests at every level indicates that there are overlaps in testing; in other words, you're testing the same thing at different levels. This may mean longer test times and delayed delivery into production. Identify the duplication in tests, and reduce those testing areas within the E2E testing cycle.

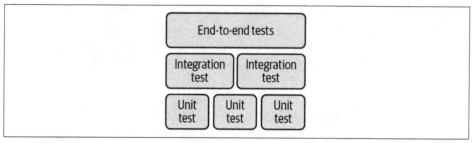

Figure 7-3. Testing square

In Figure 7-4, having more E2E tests and fewer unit tests indicates insufficient cover-age at the lower levels of unit and integration tests. This may mean longer test times and delayed code integration because it will take longer to verify that code works as expected. However, increasing the unit test coverage will boost the confidence in code changes and reduce the time it takes to merge code, leading to fewer conflicts!

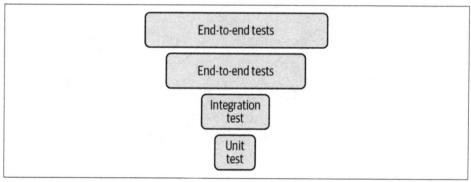

Figure 7-4. Testing inverted pyramid

In Figure 7-5, having full coverage but having more E2E tests than integration tests may indicate insufficient integration coverage. You could also have more E2E tests than needed. E2E tests are more brittle, requiring more care and maintenance with changes.

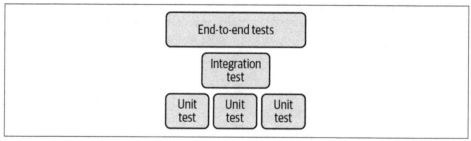

Figure 7-5. Testing hourglass

These different strategies may also indicate that the team spends more time maintaining tests than developing new features. That said, infrastructure code testing does not always follow these patterns. Specifically, infrastructure configuration code testing does not benefit from unit tests except when there may be different paths of configuration. For example, a unit test is beneficial when there are differences in platform requirements due to supporting different operating systems. It can also be beneficial when there are differences in development, testing, and production environments or when you need to make sure that production API keys don't get deployed in development and testing.

So, as shown in Figure 7-6, while you want to push tests as far down the stack as possible, due to the nature of infrastructure code, integration testing might be as far down as it makes sense to push tests.

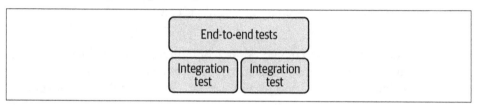

Figure 7-6. Modified testing pyramid for infracode

Improving Your Tests; Learning from Failure

It's easy to write tests; it can be difficult to write the right test. As with any skill, you should practice writing tests. To improve the quality of your tests, reflect on failures and apply what you learn. Passing tests tell you that you haven't found a problem—yet. So let's talk about how you leverage the feedback you get from testing.

To assess and understand how to adopt tests into automation, you must understand how tests fail. Failing tests tell you more than "found a problem with your code." Examining why tests fail and the different kinds of feedback you are getting allows you to plan a roadmap and automate responses as possible.

It would help to think about these as you create and update your test automation. Automation without the ability to act on the feedback you get from the tests adds work, which detracts from the value you could be bringing to your customers and frustrates the team. You can plan how to assess the different outcomes of tests and implement controls around what can be automated versus what needs human intervention.

There are four main types of test failures to plan for:

Environmental problems
> These are the most likely and fastest to resolve. Some environmental issues include file permissions, network connectivity, hardware, or variance between the testing and live environments.

Flawed test logic
> This arises when the test isn't testing the code correctly, whether due to evolution in specifications or initial miscommunication about the intent of the code.

Changing assumptions
> Are issues in the test implementation due to your beliefs about how something works? For example, you change the time when the tests run, and all of a sudden, the tests fail, and there has been no change in the code.

Code defects
> These tend to be the least common source of test failures but the most complex to identify and resolve. When you believe you've ruled out the other possibilities, it may be time to fire up a debugger and start looking for problems in the code.

Test Failure Analysis Case Study

By Chris Devers

My team discovered that our test framework was reporting that web services weren't enabled when the deployment tool ran. However, it was unclear why the error was suddenly showing up—we hadn't changed the code for the web service setup.

After investigation, we discovered that a broader system setup script unconditionally ran the web service setup script, followed by a second tool to set up other services. The second tool re-enabled the web service, masking a bug in the setup script for the web service itself. Unfortunately, when we reorganized the system setup script and reordered the steps, the web service was shut down by its configuration script and never restarted.

Think about how this shows different types of test failures. Fixing the broader system setup script introduced an environmental problem that hadn't existed before. The rationale for fixing the dependency was good, but we assumed that the individual steps were idempotent. Ultimately, we traced the defect to the web service setup script we might have discovered earlier with unit tests. On the other hand, even without unit tests, the integration test framework detected the problem before a customer noticed it, so this layered testing approach was still a win.

It's easy to blame code defects for test failures in an established project, but code defects can be the most costly to uncover. Instead, rule out environmental problems, test implementation, or changes in assumptions to avoid wasting time changing code.

Next Steps

Testing comes in more varieties than I've covered in this chapter, such as burn-in, performance, compliance, longevity, security, penetration, and capacity testing, to name just a few. And you can continually improve code. However, depending on your use case, you may need to adopt a different testing strategy. For example, long-lived monolithic databases can be prone to subtle resource allocation errors due to memory leaks. Unfortunately, these problems can be hard to detect in shorter tests, leaving your live production vulnerable to service outages. In this case, you'd run a simulated workload on the testing environment for days or even weeks to hopefully uncover problems before they arise in production.

If your production environment is ephemeral, where resources are short-lived and regularly restarted, you don't need to spend money on testing in a long-running environment. As your testing skills evolve, you'll discover ways to understand the quality of your systems and potential vulnerabilities. There are many resources dedicated to each of these different types of testing; seek out information resources to address your specific context as you need it.

Finally, you don't need to start with a perfect testing strategy. Instead, iterate and improve as you uncover the specific problems in your environments.

Wrapping Up

Testing is one way to learn about your systems, work with new things, and evaluate that changes will work as expected. When testing systems, use the test pyramid model to organize your test efforts based on unit, integration, and end-to-end tests.

Test frameworks that skew toward many high-level end-to-end tests are labor-intensive and make it difficult to identify specific causes of failures. On the other hand, a test suite that emphasizes unit tests lends itself to automation; provides clear, rapid feedback; and is easy to extend.

When writing tests to validate your code, consider how to evaluate your tests to understand the right tests to write. A passing test could mean that a code change is good, but it could also mean that the test isn't thorough enough. Failing tests can have many root causes, from external environmental factors that generate errors, as well as flaws in the tests themselves, to outdated assumptions that cause errors with code that used to work. These factors should be evaluated and eliminated before concluding that the code has a defect.

CHAPTER 8

Infrastructure Security

Early in my career as a Unix system administrator, I felt total dread when I saw many failed login attempts coming from external IP addresses outside of the US because we had only two people focused on security, covering everything from the physical network to network and host intrusions for our Unix systems. Seeing the failures made me wonder about other malicious activity we weren't detecting. Talking through these concerns with the security team helped me better understand the risk and motivations of the attackers, learn about the patterns of behavior and resources, and build up the relationship between groups.

You can't have perfect security, but you can collaborate with other parts of the organization to establish acceptable levels of security. The amount of security work that every organization needs to do to achieve "acceptable levels of security" cannot be distilled and assigned to one team, especially as the attacks evolve and become more costly to detect or repair. In this chapter, I focus on sharing general security principles so you can define security, explain threat modeling, and have a few methods for communicating security values during architecture planning.

What Is Infrastructure Security?

Infrastructure security protects hardware, software, networks, and data from harm, theft, or unauthorized access. Unfortunately, many people view security as being at odds with desirable features and user convenience, which can exacerbate implementation resistance even though the ultimate purpose of security is to reduce the risk to people.

Your vulnerabilities may include risks to your networks, physical or virtual machines, applications, or stored and processed data. When the pager goes off, you don't want to discover compromised systems, data corruption, or defaced websites. So, how do you increase the security of your systems and services?

Tackle security like you do other difficult problems. Break up the immense task of "security" into smaller achievable tasks that the team iterates on. Allow feedback and learning to inform and modify the team's practice of working in collaboration with software and security engineers.

Security incidents are not a matter of *if* but *when*. They impact companies financially and reduce users' trust. It's fundamentally impossible to release or manage a perfectly secure application or service when dependencies like underlying libraries, operating systems, and network protocols can have security issues. Whether you are building or deploying open source or commercial software, plan a layered strategy to minimize vulnerabilities and reduce an attacker's opportunity to exploit them.

Share Security Responsibilities

When you choose hosted compute, you also choose to share the security responsibility. The more operational burden you hand off to the cloud provider, the more levels of security are taken care of for you. For example, a cloud provider offering dedicated servers purchases the hardware, connects it to the network for your access, and manages the physical access to that server.

Let's revisit computing environments from Chapter 2 from a security perspective.

Starting from the bottom of Figure 8-1, if you manage dedicated physical hardware, you are responsible for everything listed in the security responsibilities column. As you move up the stack, your service provider takes on below-the-line responsibilities.

> Different roles exist within security. An organization's "security team" doesn't necessarily own all security responsibilities. You shouldn't do security work without recognition, especially if you are the one sysadmin managing and maintaining the systems. That's a path to burnout. Instead, make necessary work visible so that your team and management can assess and prioritize as necessary.

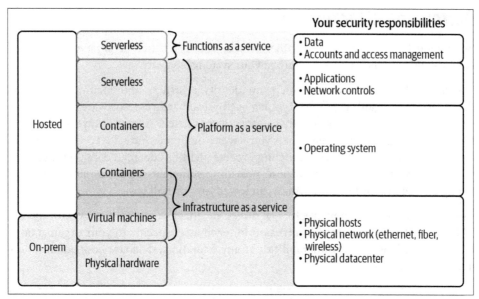

Figure 8-1. Security responsibilities for different compute environments

Whether you use infrastructure as a service (IaaS), platform as a service (PaaS), or functions as a service (FaaS) from a provider, you are still responsible for parts of your security. You may assume that your service provider takes care of all the infrastructure security when using their services. But, at minimum, you must configure account and access management, specify and configure endpoints, and manage data. For example, it doesn't matter if your cloud provider encrypts all data on disk if you configure it to have worldwide public access.

For any service provider, ask and understand their security posture. When someone leverages a vulnerability of your provider, if you tell your customers, "It was our provider's fault," you will lose their trust and bear the financial hit of the compromise. At a minimum, find out how the provider handles notifications and the appropriate escalation path for discovering security events.

Borrow the Attacker Lens

Borrowing the attacker lens, in other words, taking a different perspective on the systems you manage, can help improve your systems' security.

Threat modeling is a process by which you identify, prioritize, and document potential threats to your organization's assets, such as physical hardware, software, and data, to help you build more secure systems. Unfortunately, assets are not always well understood or recognized, especially when you haven't designed or deployed the system or service. Sometimes, the threat modeling process identifies detailed data that increases the risks to your organization without providing sufficient value; therefore, they are strong candidates for removal, which can lower your overall costs.

Next, consider the different vectors of attack or attack surfaces. *Attack surfaces* are all the potential entry points of intrusion for each asset specific to your organization. For example, look at the vulnerabilities of any endpoints, database connections, and network transports.

Threat Modeling Tools

Various threat modeling tools are available to help surface and examine problems in your systems:

- NIST Common Vulnerability Scoring System Calculator (*https://oreil.ly/MWlE6*)
- Microsoft's Threat Modeling Tool (*https://oreil.ly/lT8Ml*)
- Process for Attack Simulation and Threat Analysis (PASTA)[1]
- OWASP Threat Modeling Control Cheat Sheet (*https://oreil.ly/QS72x*)

If you aren't using a threat modeling tool now, consider using one to help understand vulnerabilities and areas for improvement. There is no right way or tool; instead, learn from instigating the necessary discussions.

Ask yourself these questions:

Who are your attackers?
> Attackers can be anyone. They may be internal or external to your organization. Based on the statistics from thousands of security incidents analyzed in the yearly Verizon Data Breach Investigations Report (DBIR) (*https://oreil.ly/pWfl7*), most attacks are external. There are occasionally internal rogue system administrators,

---

1 Check out the presentation (*https://oreil.ly/GgZfR*) from the OWASP Foundation on threat modeling of banking malware-based attacks that introduced PASTA.

but internal security issues often stem from system configuration errors or publicly publishing private data. In Chapter 11, I'll cover some tools and technologies to help reduce the number of errors resulting in internal security incidents.

What are their motivations and objectives?

Attackers have different motivations and objectives for their activities. The major motivations can be categorized into the following types:

- Amusement. Some attacks are carried out for no other reason than for fun.

- Personal beliefs. Insiders might have personal agendas outside of the organization's values and interests.

- Ideology. People with social or political ideological differences from the organization might want to harm your organization's reputation or deny services to your customers.

- Revenge. An insider with a grudge against your organization might want to cause harm.

- Financial gain. Some organized attacks use PII or personal data to apply for credit cards, sell to spam campaigns, use existing payment card information fraudulently, or gain access to an individual's resources and services.

- Espionage. Nation-state attacks are a growing threat. Numerous breaches to gain intelligence about state secrets, intellectual property, and influence politics have occurred (*https://oreil.ly/BVku1*).

What kind of resources do they have to attack?

The attacker's resources include time, money, infrastructure, and skills. Tools are evolving that reduce the knowledge required for an individual attacker to obtain their target assets. While you can't necessarily prevent every attack, you can make each attack more expensive to the attacker.

What are their opportunities to attack?

Opportunities are the windows of access to a particular asset. For example, when a vulnerability or flaw in software is discovered and released, there is a window of time to exploit that vulnerability on unpatched systems and services. Therefore, successful mitigation requires awareness of necessary patching and adequate time and authority to complete the work.

In some cases, there may be assets outside of your responsibility that attackers leverage to get into production systems. Minimize these opportunities by tracking all assets and promptly patching OSs and software.

Check out Ian Coldwater's talk from KubeCon + CloudNativeCon 2019, "Hello from the Other Side: Dispatches from a Kubernetes Attacker" (*https://oreil.ly/KsOSO*) for more on what you can learn by borrowing the attacker lens.

Another good resource is the yearly Verizon Data Breach Investigations Report (DBIR) (*https://oreil.ly/g77MX*), which analyzes thousands of security incidents and breaches and provides insight into evolving security trends.

Design for Security Operability

Layer your strategies to reduce risk to services and applications, limiting the attacker's opportunity and the scope of damage of a potential breach. This approach is known as *defense in depth*. Layering defenses means that if one defense in your system fails, you can contain the blast radius of the compromise. For example, build defenses at the edges of your networks with firewalls, and configure subnets to limit network traffic from approved networks. Locally on systems, lock down elevated-privilege accounts. Additionally, recognize that 100% secure software is impossible and assume zero trust. Zero trust means having no implicit trust in any services, systems, or networks, even if you leverage cloud services.

Participating in the early architecture and design process with a security operability mindset provides early feedback on the system architecture, reducing the risk of needing a refactor to incorporate security later. Case in point: I once joined a relatively new team building a multitenanted service for an internal audience. I reviewed the architecture and realized that the code relied on having no MySQL root password. With hundreds of backend MySQL servers planned for this service, many unsecured services worried me.

The following lists some of the potential attack vectors:

- A misconfigured subnet could make these servers directly accessible to the broader internet.
- Malicious attackers that breached systems on the internal network could easily compromise unsecured systems.

Working with the security engineering team, I managed to prioritize the work to repair this design defect. Identifying the issue before deployment to production felt great. However, if we'd started in a more collaborative place with the design, we could have avoided the development cost of repairing the assumptions that depended on a completely open database.

Often, product decision makers forget to invite system administrators to design meetings. By fostering and building relationships with the people designing and building the software, you can create opportunities to get those invitations. Having early access means you can influence decisions about the system's operation before it exists. And when you need changes implemented, you'll have developed the necessary relationships to prioritize your work.

One way to collaboratively uncover security requirements and prioritize work is to use the CIA triad model. This model provides a way to establish a shared context and align values for feature work. CIA stands for confidentiality, integrity, and availability:

Confidentiality
> The set of rules that limits access to information to only the people who should have it

Integrity
> The assurance that information is true and correct to its original purpose and that it can be modified only by those who should be able to modify it

Availability
> The reliable access to information and resources for the individuals who need it when it's needed

In the case of the root password for the MySQL issue I described earlier, anyone with access would have been able to log in to the database management system (compromised confidentiality) and look at and edit any available data stored (compromised integrity). Sysadmins can flag CIA issues as part of the software acceptance criteria and incorporate operability stories to prioritize them appropriately. Having intentional conversations about the design and tracking those conversations helps inform the development and product teams' decisions.

For web applications and web services, the Open Web Application Security Project (OWASP) (*https://oreil.ly/CuLHL*) provides a set of requirements and controls for designing, developing, and testing called the Application Security Verification Standard (ASVS) (*https://oreil.ly/rZ7gf*).

 If you find it challenging to get executive support for your efforts to design and implement quality continuous integration and deployment mechanisms, reducing the impact of security vulnerabilities is an excellent use case.

Categorize Discovered Issues

No matter how much effort the team makes to examine software and services from the attacker's perspective and to design systems to incorporate a security mindset, there will still be security issues. People may find issues with your company's software, or the problem may be with software you use directly or indirectly. As a standard, organizations track vulnerabilities in publicly released software packages with Common Vulnerabilities and Exposures (CVE) Identifiers (*https://oreil.ly/UrrSp*).

When quantifying the cost and potential impact of a discovered issue, categorize issues through labeling (i.e., bug or flaw) to convey additional context.

Implementation bugs are problems in implementation that lead to a system operating in an unintended way. Implementation bugs can sometimes cause serious security vulnerabilities, for example, Heartbleed.[2] Heartbleed was a vulnerability in OpenSSL that allowed malicious folks to eavesdrop on presumed secure communications, steal data directly from services and users, and impersonate those users and services.

Design flaws are issues that prevent the system from operating as intended; the problem is with the design or specification. Design flaws can be super costly to repair, especially if other tools are built on the system as currently designed or depend on its implementation. Thus, sometimes flaws are too expensive to change and carry specific warnings about use.

While you don't want metrics that incentivize discovering flaws and bugs over other types of sysadmin work, you need to surface the work in progress, especially when the work prevents a compromise or security incident. Measuring the prevention of an incident establishes a clear signal about your intent and the outcomes of the work, even though the event that didn't occur isn't measurable.

By categorizing the work, you can better identify the different types of appropriate and valuable work. You build stronger relationships and trust as others have more visibility and context of the work that you've done and how it relates to the business's bottom line.

---

2 "The Heartbeat Bug," Synopsis, Inc., last modified June 3, 2020, *https://heartbleed.com*.

Check out these examples of implementation bugs:

- MS17-010/EternalBlue
- CVE-2016-5195/Dirty COW

And check out these examples of design flaws:

- Meltdown (*https://meltdownattack.com*)
- KRACK (WPA2 key reinstallation)

Wrapping Up

Infrastructure security is the practice of protecting your systems from threats. Of course, perfect security doesn't exist, but with careful vigilance and a layered approach, you can reduce your systems' risks.

Infrastructure security is a shared responsibility; if there aren't already practices in place, you can lead the establishment of recommended practices in your organization. A good strategy for establishing practices is to consider who might want to attack your systems, what they might hope to gain by doing so, and what resources they can bring to bear. Each of these can suggest lines of defense to use. Then, when building and deploying your systems, leverage the confidentiality, integrity, availability triad model to identify security requirements for implementation.

Categorizing infrastructure security issues provides additional context around cost and potential impact. For example, one label set is "bugs" and "design flaws." Implementation bugs result from programming errors that usually lend themselves to patch fixes. Design flaws are architectural problems that may be more challenging to mitigate without fundamentally redesigning parts of the system.

CHAPTER 9

Documentation

It was the early days of my first sysadmin job, and everything felt so new. Every step I took felt vital to system availability and performance. All of the rote sysadmin tasks I learned quickly by reading a book didn't tell me when to use some root privileged commands. Thankfully, experienced sysadmins had adopted a culture of sharing knowledge. Our docs site was a wiki with a theme derived from the Cheapass Games card game "Give Me the Brain" (GMTB) (*https://oreil.ly/u2f04*). GMTB's basic gameplay was that you were a zombie working at a fast-food restaurant with one brain to pass around. Only one person could "have the brain" at a time. Associating the documentation to this game embedded the behaviors expected of the team, especially with the idea that your documentation was setting your future 2 a.m. zombie self up for success during an incident.

In this chapter, I want to help you think about documentation. I want you to feel enabled to adopt the practices that support quality documentation that is accurate, available, accessible, organized, and maintainable because documentation is part of the system.

Know Your Audience

People need insights into the information relevant to their responsibilities, ranging from "nuts and bolts" details of the operation of a specific system to "bird's-eye" overviews of the activity in an overall environment.

Presenting people with relevant, accurate, and timely information helps them carry out their duties effectively. If individuals aren't taking everyday actions, this may be because their data is stale, vague, or inapplicable. If teams overfocus on short-term speed and execution at the expense of long-term strategy, this could indicate a broken feedback loop.

In Figure 9-1, the writer of the documentation tries to help everyone, leading to extraneous information that might not be useful to a specific user. In Figure 9-2, the writer of the documentation targets the user and provides just the information to do the tasks the user needs when needed.

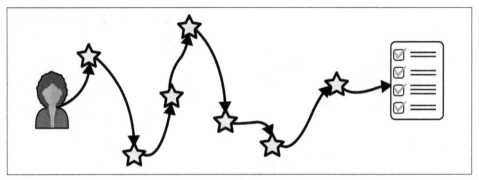

Figure 9-1. Documentation with extraneous information

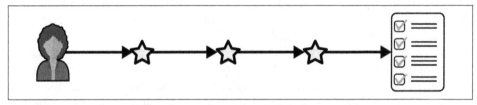

Figure 9-2. Documentation with user-focused specific information

Observe that of the two paths, the user-focused path is shorter and follows a direct route to the goal. One path isn't better than the other. Again, consider your audience and what they need when you are writing. For example, consider the needs of someone debugging a specific problem. They need task-oriented documentation with a very specific set of information. Extraneous information is frustrating. Here are a few prompts to help you reflect and connect with your audience:

- Who is your audience?
- What is important to them?
- What do you want them to know or do?
- What do they already know?
- What is their preferred method of consuming information?
- How does your data make your point?
- Does documentation already exist?
- Do you know what your audience needs?

Audiences need different levels of detail. Depending on where people are on their journeys, their needs may change. And the documentation they encounter will bring them to the next stage on their journey and affect what further documentation they need. If they have a lot of experience, they may need direct-to-the-point information. If they have little to no experience or knowledge, they may need a longer, more detailed, conceptual explanation in addition to the relevant context. If you don't know what your audience needs, interview them to identify what is useful.

Dimensions of Documentation

You may write documentation for yourself, your team, your broader organization, or wider groups of people outside of your organization. You may read the documentation online (e.g., monitor or mobile) or on print media. You'll write different documents, including records, conceptual documentation, task documentation, reference guides, and planning documentation:

Records
> A reference to decisions, actions, or discussions. Records include meeting notes and decision records. They provide a historical resource and can help you figure out why choices were made and inform future decisions.

Conceptual documentation
> Explains general information. Conceptual documentation includes topic introductions. Use this documentation type when the reader needs to understand the terminology, ideas, or abstractions.

Task documentation
> Guides readers through steps to accomplish a specific goal. Examples of task documentation include how-to guides and tutorials. Use this documentation type when the reader needs to know how to do something or understand what happens. Sometimes, you can use this documentation to guide the automation of tasks.

Reference guides
> Detailed documentation, often in the form of a list or a table. Examples of reference guides include operation and troubleshooting manuals. Use reference guides when you have a lot of information to organize and group.

Planning documentation
> Provides the shape of larger projects to be done. This documentation type often includes a project's scope or objective and provides necessary background information, the plan, and potentially time estimates and any necessary resources to support the plan. Reviewing project plans with the rest of the team can help surface potential concerns and areas that might need further refinement.

Finally, effective documentation summarizes experience and knowledge integrated across many people collaborating. Collaboration requires a shared understanding of the goal, a style guide to inform a consistent writing style, and a set of procedures to follow.

 Creating and sharing templates allows individuals to quickly spin up the required type of documentation following expected style guides.

Organization Practices

Information architecture is the structural organization of your information. Quality organization of information supports the following:

Reuse
You can reuse documentation in different ways to support the axes of inclusivity, the levels of knowledge, and the way people learn.

Change management
You can add, update, version, and deprecate documentation.

Governance
Documentation has clear roles and responsibilities, enabling contributions and enabling ownership.

Connectedness
Documentation can show connections between topics.

Organizing a Topic

When structuring a topic, have a clear and specific title. However, titles should not be too general. You organize information into sections with liberal use of headings and subheadings. Once you write the text, revisit the headers to check the flow of information. Ideally, reading the table of contents created from the headings makes sense to your reader. Write your introduction and conclusion last because the content will have changed from when you initially thought about the topic.

Topics follow a (documented) and defined lifecycle to enable change management and provide a framework for governance. Figure 9-3 depicts a possible document lifecycle, where you research and analyze a topic, create (or update an existing) document, verify that the information is correct, version the topic, and release the document. Feedback on the topic or change in systems continues to drive the lifecycle until analysis identifies that it's time for the document to be deprecated and eventually archived.

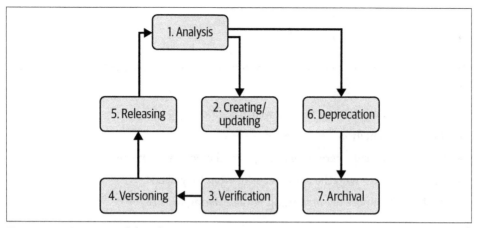

Figure 9-3. Document lifecycle

Organizing a Site

Organize the information for discoverability and connectedness when structuring all the information topics. The site should inform the standard structure of the topics. Consistency in the topic organization supports the reader in understanding how to find relevant information that reduces the cognitive load.

Depending on the team's culture, there may be a preference for a single long document or many small pages for organizing the team's knowledge base. There is no one right way. A single lengthy document may take time to download from a remote system and readers may have inconsistent experiences depending on their browser. But by providing documentation in one page, the reader can scan for information and know that it's missing if it is not found.

Small pages will load quickly but require a search and indexing system to improve discoverability. Readers may not find the information and either spend more time searching or mistakenly conclude that information is missing.

Whichever your team chooses, be consistent so that the team knows what to expect from the documentation and when to ask for help or contribute documentation.

Recommendations for Quality Documentation

So you've' bought in on the need for quality documentation, but it doesn't feel like people are reading or contributing to the documentation. Instead of assuming that people are not reading the documentation, consider the following:

- Are you giving them time to read the documentation?
- Are you using terminology without defining it?

- Is the information too vague?
- Is the information too scattered?

Instead of focusing on people not creating or updating documentation, reflect on these questions:

- Are they given sufficient time to write the documentation?
- Does documentation need to be written?
- Are they given sufficient time to organize the documentation?
- Do people know who the audience is or what they need?
- Do the tools support contributing in the existing workflow?

Then, assess your documentation for the following qualities to identify areas of improvement:

Accuracy
Accurate documentation is current, complete, and correct. The documentation contains what the reader needs to do their task promptly. It increases the successful completion of the job and reduces the risk of errors.

Available
The available documentation is accessible when you need it. So make sure to print out any relevant emergency response guides in case there is a network or power outage that would limit access to online manuals that help you get the systems back up and running.

Accessible
Accessible documentation is inclusive and meets the reader where they are. You may need to present the same information in multiple ways based on the reader's level.

Organized
Organized documentation enables readers to find the document they need.

Maintainable
Maintainable documentation supports the writer in adding, updating, and deleting documents effectively. Storing documentation in a version control system provides change management and accountability and enables you to leverage the same workflows already in use in your organization.

Regularly review documentation to measure the quality of your documentation for these characteristics. Codify documentation hygiene so it becomes a regular part of the team's processes.

Wrapping Up

Effective documentation requires knowing your audience, understanding the dimensions of your documentation (e.g., online or print media, and records, conceptual, task, and reference guides), and organizing your documentation for reuse, change management, governance, and connectedness.

In the next chapter, I'll extend some of the concepts from this chapter to distilling and presenting information in different formats.

More Resources

In *Docs for Developers: An Engineer's Field Guide to Technical Writing* (Apress), Jared Bhatti et al. provide detailed practices for all stages of the documentation lifecycle specifically around software development but applicable to sysadmins managing systems as well.

In *Living Documentation: Continuous Knowledge Sharing by Design* (Addison-Wesley Professional), Cyrille Martraire offers up Documentation 2.0 and explains how to use well-crafted artifacts and automation to improve documentation.

CHAPTER 10

Presentations

Stories are the fundamental way that humans organize and make sense of information. Stories provide structure and purpose to data. Effective system administrators recognize the power of a good narrative and use different mediums to share messages effectively. They organize their information and communicate beyond text to tell a story with images, photos, graphs, charts, audio, and even video. So often, when mentoring other sysadmins trying to make a change in their organization, I share some key concepts about data organization and presentation.

Show 5 clever people the same data, and they'll develop 10 interpretations. You can't assume that others will draw the same conclusions unless you put in the effort to craft a narrative that will lead and influence people. In this chapter, I want to help you learn how to distill information and present it compellingly to tell the necessary stories to influence people regardless of authority.

Know Your Audience

Just like when writing documentation, you need to assess your audience to make custom and specific visualizations when preparing and presenting the information.

In the movies, the protagonist can often determine the next right step based on a single query or dashboard that integrates all the necessary data. They glance at this digital display of information and have the right context to make a fast decision.

And in the real world, while your management may request a "single pane of glass" to distill and manage your complex systems into a single dashboard that provides all the context needed to support all decision-making, a single view of all the data is not possible. Of course, you can dump all the possible options into a single console, but the cognitive overload affects the efficiency of accessing the necessary and timely information you need now.

If your manager asks for a "single pane of glass," figure out what question they are trying to answer or what problem they are trying to solve and provide them with that set of visualizations. It's OK to give each person a custom dashboard and have your own that reflects the context you need.

You are competing for attention and acknowledging that you have the supporting data for your conclusions, so make sure you reflect on the audience prompts in Chapter 9. No single graphic or dashboard can aggregate information in a way that is useful for everyone. So instead, tailor each graph and dashboard to narrowly focus on the needs of a specific audience.

I sat in yet another meeting as a coworker tried to convey the importance of a new project. He read sentences directly off his slides describing tedious maintenance work that could save money already spent. Unfortunately, the large numbers from his measurements didn't alleviate the boredom or compel me to participate in the additional toil to achieve his project goals. It wasn't clear why this would be the team's highest-priority work or whether we had the right tools to eliminate the toil.

Don't Bury the Lede

Instead, when you need help, tell people what you are asking for so that they have the necessary context when listening to your pitch. For example, sysadmin and author Thomas Limoncelli (*https://oreil.ly/UcJF8*) offers the following examples of some of his introductory sentences:

- I'm here to ask for funding [or resources or money].
- I'm here to ask for a policy decision.
- I'm here to ask for advice [on how to do something or who to talk to].
- I'm here to give a status update.

Executives have several stakeholders that they are responsible for and busy schedules. They also have limited levers to control outcomes: providing resources, clarifying policy, and referring you to different resources.

This kind of experience reminds me of a Mark Twain quote: "Often, the surest way to convey misinformation is to tell the strict truth." It's not enough to give people the cold facts and trust that you'll inspire them to action; you have to demonstrate why those facts are compelling and how they relate to larger goals and then create an emotional connection so people want to help your cause.

As shown on the left in Figure 10-1, if you have a bunch of text on the screen, your audience will read the text and potentially shut down. On the right, if you distill the data into charts, your peers are more likely to be inspired and motivated to take the actions that you need them to promptly.

Figure 10-1. Presentation styles (image by Tomomi Imura)

And, if you craft high-level scorecards for your technical director, they are more likely to fund your initiative. Don't bog them down with all the details and minutiae.

 Sometimes you can't land the change you seek regardless of how you modify your message. This lack of action signals that people aren't taking time to reflect on how their work aligns with the organization's goals or a systemic problem in the environment due to broken feedback loops.

In that case, consider letting it go. Constantly chasing after an unachievable outcome is going to exacerbate any potential burnout. And it might be that if you wait, the system will change, and you'll be able to achieve what you initially set out to do.

Choose Your Channel

Once you've reflected on the questions about your audience, think about what you want them to do. Then decide if verbal or written communication is best—this will depend on your objective and message type.

Verbal communication mostly happens in real time and allows you to convey feelings along with facts. It's most valuable when there is a component of emotion or sensitivity you want to communicate or if you need immediate feedback.

Tips for Speaking

The more you present information through public speaking, the better you will get at it. Beyond practice, there are a few tips that I've learned over the years that may help you level up your speaking:

Breathe

Especially if you are nervous, you may find yourself breathing faster or holding your breath. Altered breathing can impact your speech and pace, affecting how well people understand you. You can prepare by adding cues to your speaker notes to remind yourself to breathe and leverage explicit pauses for emphasis or laughter as appropriate for your content.

Vocabulary

Your speech needs to sound like conversation and use clear and natural words, especially for technical talks. The environment of the room and the listener's experience and knowledge will affect how they parse and understand what you are saying. Avoid jargon and acronyms, and make sure the audience understands any technical terms you need to use, taking a moment to define any potentially unfamiliar concepts.

Pitch

Modulate your voice to create inflections to drive interest in your message. Practice this on different words to see how it changes the message. When you find the right fit, make notations to your presentation.

Pace

The right pace for your talk varies depending on your audience. In general, for simple, straightforward topics, it's OK to speed up the pace. For more complex topics, you want to slow down. When you have a mixed audience of beginners and experts, this is where you can enter the dreaded middle ground of expectations where beginners may feel you went through the material too fast, while experts may feel you went through it too slowly. Be thoughtful and consistent in your delivery, and you'll satisfy at least half of your audience.

Authenticity

Match your expression to your words. Your body language and expressions convey information. For example, smiling can give energy and engagement to your topic. However, if your message and manner don't match, it brings a dissonance that your audience generally interprets as dishonest. For example, when someone says, "I'm so excited to share" in a dull and disinterested voice, do you believe them?

Setting

Finally, in-person presentations are very different from virtual ones. When presenting to people, there can be an energy feedback loop that you tap into as you respond to the audience responding to your content. In front of the camera, it can feel draining. You can level up speaking to a camera by creating a virtual audience—set up a side channel with live supporters to whom you can direct your attention rather than just looking at a camera.

Often, written communication is asynchronous, whether through proposals, design documentation, code, or reviews. However, some communication, like chat and messaging, can be either real-time or asynchronous. Written communication is a better choice when you want to focus on facts or need time to think before responding and have less urgency about getting a response. However, for more complex messages, written communication *with* verbal communication may be necessary and more meaningful.

Either of these communication methods can benefit from visualizations to complement the words you use. Choose your specific visualizations based on the type of information that you are sharing and the stories you want to leverage. And both methods require time and effort to get right.

Choose Your Story Type

You can use stories to reflect on the past, explain what happened, and provide future direction. Each type of story reveals information slightly differently, and choosing a compelling story to present information drives your reader's reaction toward your desired outcome. Some example story types include the following:

Factoid

Factoids distill data into interesting data points, highlighting the most common trends or notable outliers. An exciting story may drive interest in exploring the rest of the data. For example, you can show the total number of community members using a specific technology or unique visitors to a website; marketing commonly uses factoids in dashboards for website stats or product newsletters.

Interaction

Interactions show relationships between different datasets. Positive correlations between datasets move together: when one set moves up or down, the other trends in the same direction. Negatively correlated sets move in contrast to each other, with one moving down when the other moves up. Identifying a positive or negative relationship is helpful but doesn't explain why datasets move together. Be mindful that correlations may be spurious, where the connection is just a coincidence. A compelling story shows the correlation and establishes that the data is meaningfully linked.[1]

For example, you can show a graph of MySQL query times and end-to-end request latency to observe better whether the performance is related to the workload or if an increase in end-to-end latency is due to a problem in the database configuration that has become a bottleneck.

Change

Stories about change are a way to describe how something evolves over time. For example, you can use change stories in capacity management and problem detection. You can use a graph to show the growth of your current used capacity as it approaches the total configured capacity over time. In addition, it can show the velocity (change in use from one point of time to another) and acceleration (slope between the lines) to illustrate how urgent it is to plan or increase capacity.

Comparison

Comparison stories are a way to show the impact of data that tells different stories. For example, you can show the various performance characteristics of rolling out a managed relational database from a service provider versus a self-managed MySQL instance in a scorecard. It could aggregate essential metrics like cost (including the cost of in-house support), performance, scalability, and reliability.

Personal

Personal stories connect to real-world experiences. For example, you show an incident summary that contextualizes technical issues with individuals' experiences and choices based on their understanding.

Storytelling in Practice

I want to share a few scenarios from my career where presenting data to teams has been worthwhile. I shared a visualization in the first case to inform and change

---

1 Check out "Beware Spurious Correlations" (*https://oreil.ly/qU688*) from Harvard Business Review, which shares more about why you want to be careful with correlations.

assumptions about my team's work. In the second case, I shared the data that different audiences needed.

Case #1: Charts Are Worth a Thousand Words

It was the dreaded quarterly planning, a time for the team to assess the accomplishments of the previous quarter and commit to projects in the next. I was new to the team, and I had few expectations. My coworkers expressed frustration because "they never had time to work on team projects to resolve technical debt because of customer interruptions."

An undisclosed motivation for joining the team was that I had heard that there were challenges with visibility into the work queue and that requests were often delayed or incomplete with no notice. The manager had sought me out explicitly to bring engineering excellence and follow-through execution to the team.

After the planning meeting, I figured out what data to collect around the goals. I worked with the team to categorize the work based on incoming requests and operational debt. I wrote some Perl code to query the internal bug API and, based on the classification of requests, created a few different dashboards to visualize the work. In the next meeting, I presented the image in Figure 10-2, showing that contrary to assumptions, we focused primarily on the work we chose rather than customer interruptions or requests.

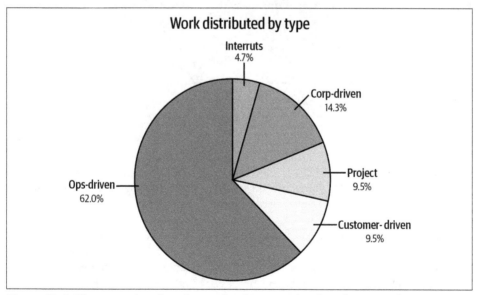

Figure 10-2. The categories of work completed in a quarter based on tagged associations

I could have written up a report, but this simple graphic was easily understood and, combined with access to the underlying data, influenced changes in how we prioritized work as a team and led to further improvements for customers in visibility into the work.

Case #2: Telling the Same Story with a Different Audience

Before I get to a story in this example, there is some important context to consider. For projects where you need to focus on data analysis and presentation, think about who you are presenting information to and how to frame the data, especially around the language used. Figure 10-3 may better illustrate what I mean here, but remember that your team and organization may differ.

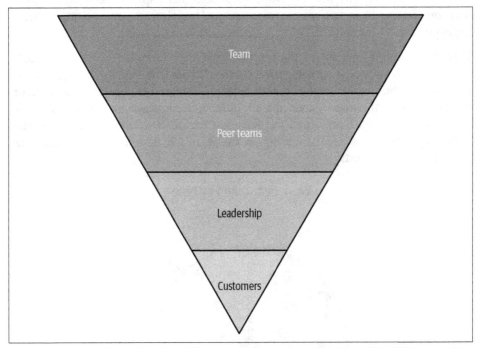

Figure 10-3. Visualizing the shared language when communicating with different audiences; the larger the slice, the more shared context

Let's examine the layers in Figure 10-3:

- The team is the largest layer with a lot of shared language and context. They work together closely, sharing tools and processes. They might even have team slang or reuse specific terminology to mean something special in the context of their systems. As a result, they benefit from having all the information available when managing their systems. Improvements may help any individual's workflow when handling on-call or touching production systems.

- Peer teams may share some common terminology, but it's helpful to establish a shared context and understand their expectations. In some cases, talking through jargon may reveal incorrect assumptions about concerns.

- Leadership may understand some terminology depending on their background. Still, the broader their scope and responsibilities, the more vocabulary may need to be translated to set the appropriate context and risk level.

- Finally, customers may share language, but it will be much harder to scale translation across all customers. Customer communication requires the most care and diligence to communicate and set expectations correctly.

So when presenting information to each of these different audiences, customize what you share so that you provide them with the right level of information at the right time. A single dashboard or set of visualizations might be too broad.

Now let me share a personal story from my experience. First, senior leadership announced the closure of several colocation facilities (colos) to cut costs. As a result, we needed to migrate data to the closest regions and minimize customer latency and availability impacts. As a result, I needed to think through what actions we could take as a team to limit the impact on day-to-day activities (i.e., upgrades to software and hardware maintenance) and customer activities (i.e., onboarding new customers and increasing capacity). Part of the data that needed to migrate was customer data. We provided a NoSQL, multitenanted database made up of a number of tables. We managed the database tables for the customers so they could focus on their applications. So, I also needed to think about how to limit the impact on our customers' data.

Based on the different timelines for each colocation, I could aggregate where each customer had data and the best configuration to minimize latency impacts in addition to new projects and capacity constraints of the overall system. I spun up a plan of migrations that balanced out speed, performance, and capacity. Then, I wrote some Perl to query the different service APIs and some JavaScript using the *D3.js* library to create charts.

For each customer table in each region that required a move, we needed to do the following:

1. Issue a table copy.
2. Monitor the table copy progress.
3. Verify the table copy completion.

Multiple table copies and other administrative activities on that table could not coincide.

For each region, we needed to do the following:

1. Wait for all customers to migrate their service over to their new endpoint (minimize latency issues).
2. Update table configurations to drop the tables in the region .
3. Shut down all the servers in the region.
4. Notify SiteOps to shut down and deprovision servers.

Team dashboard

The team dashboard looked like Figure 10-4. The table contained an ordered prioritized list of tasks with regions, jobs in progress (P), unaffected regions, and completed work (C). This information allowed the ops team to quickly identify whether new customer requests to change a specific table required stopping a task or waiting until the job was complete.

	Region1	Region2	Region3	Region4	Region5	Region6
Task1	C	C	C	C	C	C
Task2	–	C	–	P	C	C
Task3	C	C	C	C	P	C
Task4	C	–	–	C	C	P

Figure 10-4. Shared context for the team of planned work, locality of the work, and state of the work

Looking down the table row, any SRE could quickly see which regions were completely done and which had work in progress. For a region that had work in progress, we knew when we needed to take extra care with upgrades, either pausing data migration or redirecting customer traffic to the next colo to minimize disruption.

Finally, with minimal coordination, everyone could complete upgrades, compute, and table deployments for a completed region. And ultimately, deprovision and request SiteOps to shut down equipment when all customers had completed their migration work.

Manager dashboard

The manager dashboard looked like Figure 10-5. They didn't need to know all the specifics about every single task. They just needed to know what work was in progress, if we were blocked, and whether we would finish on time.

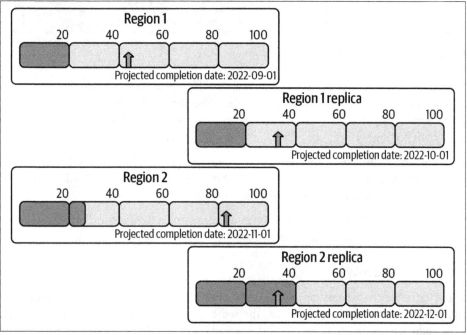

Figure 10-5. Manager-specific context showing planned work state, current work state, and projected work state

This dashboard shows a gauge for each region and replica, showing all the effort in a colo. The graphs updated daily based on the work completed. For example, with a glance at this dashboard, management could see that three of the regions were within the scheduled completion time and one was not. Then they asked crucial questions of the team and had the updated information to provide to stakeholders.

Since this was a long-running project, it provided management with the necessary information to reprioritize any work and assign additional interrupt work because they could immediately see the impact to the timeline for this project.

Customer dashboards

Finally, in Figure 10-6, the customer dashboards let customers know where their database tables were available, what we had planned for their tables, estimated completion dates, and where their tables were unavailable.

	Region1	Region2	Region3	Region4	Region5
Table1	Ready for use	Ready for use	May 1	May 15	Ready for use
Table2			Ready for use	Ready for use	
Table3	Ready for use	Ready for use	May 15	Ready for use	
Table4	Ready for use	Ready for use	Ready for use	Ready for use	

Figure 10-6. A simplified customized customer view

Note that customers didn't need to know about the region replicas. The replicas were in place to handle low-latency backups within the same colo. However, management cared about this detail because it impacts whether they are meeting the success metrics of getting services shut down in time within a colo.

Each customer didn't have to reach out to us for updates on their tables. Instead, they could proactively migrate when they were ready and ensure they didn't add latency to their requests by deploying services to the wrong regions.

I did send out email summaries when we completed all activities for their tables. With the updated visualization, they could prioritize their colo-migration work.

The Key Takeaways

These different visualizations reduced the number of support and status requests, allowing team members to focus on the work. Adapt your message based on what your audience needs. Everyone doesn't need all the data collected. Instead, focus your message on the information that matters to the individuals. Tell your audience what data is missing and what they can learn from the information collected.

Know Your Visuals

> *The greatest value of a picture is when it forces us to notice what we never expected to see.*
> —John W. Tukey

I showed a few ways to visualize data in the previous two scenarios. Still, there are many more visualizations to choose from to transform your data into compelling stories. You can also use design principles to help your audience see what you want.

Visual Cues

Visual cues can help you display information that others can process without conscious thought. The four basic visual cues are color, form, movement, and spatial position:

Color

You can imply relationships between two metrics or points in time by varying the hue. You can indicate quantity or strength by varying the saturation. You can adjust the temperature or the perceived warmth or coolness of color to focus attention. Warmer colors advance into the foreground, while cooler colors fade into the background. Use color to show important data points, but don't rely on it as the sole expression of that data.

Form

You can change length, width, orientation, size, and shape. For example, increase the size of something or use space to emphasize its importance.

Movement

Flicker and motion can call attention to specific areas of importance but can also be distracting or annoying. You can imply motion through the other visual properties rather than using motion directly.

Position

You can use a 2D position and spatial grouping.

Sometimes cues are inappropriate if they mislead or hinder your audience's interpretation of your visualizations. For example, don't use different-sized circles for categorical data if the magnitude difference of the categories doesn't hold any significance.

 Learn more about design principles from Robin Williams's *The Non-Designer's Design Book* (Peachpit Press).

Chart Types

Instead of just sharing lines of data or sticking to the pie chart, choose your chart based on your data.

Data tables

Data tables organize data into rows and columns. Tables can be a valuable tool to do the following:

Plan
> For example, you can itemize a list of requirements for a proposal, brainstorm quarterly projects, and elaborate on details that apply to each identified element, such as the proposer or length of time.

Document
> For example, to lay out a list of options or provide comparisons between different tools and services.

Define
> Lists as a quick periodic review for tactical direction. Examples include top pages or sources for websites.

Explore
> Large sets to filter, display data, and drill down into individual queries.

Tables can be an overwhelming way to present a large volume of data, so complement them with other visualizations to draw attention to trends, outliers, and different patterns in the raw table data.

In Table 10-1, the table format is used to compare the on-demand and provisioned Amazon DynamoDB throughput limits. The format works because there isn't a lot of data, and it's clear what is different.

Table 10-1. Amazon DynamoDB throughput limits in table format[a]

	On-demand	Provisioned
Per table	40K read request units and 40K write request units	40K read request units and 40K write request units
Per account	Not applicable	80K read capacity units and 80K write capacity units
Minimum throughput for any table or global secondary index	Not applicable	One read capacity unit and one write capacity unit

[a] "Service, Account, and Table Quotas in Amazon DynamoDB" (*https://oreil.ly/M2cjV*), Amazon, last modified December 15, 2020.

In Figure 10-7, from an excerpt of data on the Honeycomb Play with Live Rubygems.org data playground (*https://oreil.ly/hmGNE*), the table format is used with visual cues to the raw event logs in the data table. Rows have alternating backgrounds to make it easier to read the table.

Timestamp (UTC)	cache_status	client_ip_hash	content_type	geo_c:
2021-01-18 21:15:25	HIT	0a8b1069f217aed3f6f3307136f2e0a59d351ded15f339428af10cd011fb0a52	binary/octet-stream	cambr:
2021-01-18 21:15:25	HIT	dbdb4a3a06785feaa5e29dd1bf2466bb187ff3f967ddfe0e6027a5e5c92bf78e	application/octet-stream	ashbu:
2021-01-18 21:15:25	HIT	4dbc8a020963bf0553e087fea64e85c875b4cdf1156e38141c27d67379629a40	application/octet-stream; charset=utf-8	louis:
2021-01-18 21:15:25	HIT	769a0fe4eb80fa5e2685ea60ac6a061ef8717eaa543fe17e3029113ba7c8dd12	text/plain; charset=utf-8	ashbu:
2021-01-18 21:15:25	HIT	cbf0ab785c36706715ff57c25996a39327f49bf2add13d78a99030070f45ebef	application/octet-stream; charset=utf-8	dubli:
2021-01-18 21:15:25	HIT	afca926e07a90d729928645dbfb566dda787599478a6b248c4c1ea506750c1c1	binary/octet-stream	londo:
2021-01-18 21:15:25	HIT	61cba6bf0089bcd8273eb5ca78245f636171ba83948cb30795b17130ed2aa962	application/octet-stream; charset=utf-8	san j:
2021-01-18 21:15:25	HIT	794e7164d2f423d2a10173106e2b9c87601c2bea9b91fb78a1209c81881fdca5	text/html	pavas

Figure 10-7. Raw data in table format for Rubygems.org[2]

Bar charts

Bar charts are useful for quantified categories of data that you want to compare when you have more than two or three categories. Compound bar charts extend the idea of visualizing how the proportion of elements within a category contributes to the total for each bar. Bar charts are often displayed vertically, primarily when representing time-series data, but a horizontal orientation can work better when using long category names.

For example, I've used bar charts to visualize system audits across multiple colos to see the number of nodes running out-of-date operating systems. Other uses for bar charts include displaying the disk consumption of a list of directories, partitions, or servers to help explain the use of storage capacity.

Line charts

Line charts plot changes in value and show patterns over time or relationships between two variables. Add lines to the chart to show trends between series. These are often the go-to for showing time-based trends and differences between series.

---

2 "Honeycomb's Play with Live Rubygems.org," Honeycomb (*https://honeycomb.io*).

Often the vertical axis will represent a statistic like the count, sum, or average of a measured attribute across a dataset. Use a continuous interval on the horizontal axis, for example, time.

Figure 10-8 is another example from the Honeycomb live Rubygems.org data playground (*https://oreil.ly/AzouI*). The line chart shows the counts, and the table provides the legend in addition to the total count of cache hits, misses, errors, and passes over time.

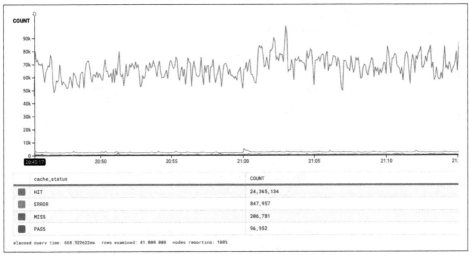

Figure 10-8. A line chart depicting Rubygems.org results

Area charts

Area charts are based on line charts and show quantitative data over time. Stacked area charts help show part of the whole or cumulative values.

Heat maps

Heat maps show data patterns through shading or color. One of the challenges of these kinds of graphs is ensuring that the color schemes are accessible and don't create artificial gradients. Heat maps can also be problematic when there isn't a discernible pattern that can hinder comprehension.

Flame graphs

Flame graphs are a way to visualize profiled software and help debug resource exhaustion problems.

Treemaps

Treemaps use tiles of varying sizes to illustrate proportions; they are, in effect, two-dimensional compound bar charts. Treemaps help show how a total value is composed of many smaller elements. In addition, tiles can be color-coded to convey additional information.

For example, use a treemap to show space on a hard drive with large rectangles for files using a lot of disk space and clusters of rectangles for directories. Color-code individual tiles to indicate attributes such as file types, ages, or ownership.

> ## Additional Resources for Chart Visualizations
>
> To learn more about information visualization, check out Edward Tufte's books *The Visual Display of Quantitative Information*, *Envisioning Information*, *Visual Explanations*, and *Beautiful Evidence* (*https://oreil.ly/YgGks*) (Graphics Press).
>
> For more on other charts, see AnyChart's "Chart Type: Chartopedia" (*https://oreil.ly/S7dVS*).
>
> Learn more about Flame graphs (*https://oreil.ly/tHfqS*) from the inventor of Flame graphs and system performance subject matter expert, Brendan Gregg.

Recommended Visualization Practices

In presenting information, you control the narrative and provide a way to interpret the data. Modern tools allow us to explore the data and interact, verify, or provide alternative narratives to explain what is happening.

Imagine you manage a cluster of load-balanced web servers. You might have a line chart of total errors with a different color line per server. Multiple lines can be visibly noisy but quickly show outliers in error types.

You might also have server graphs showing different shapes per error type. Using different shapes shows at a glance when a particular server serves more errors and whether the errors are associated with a specific type of error.

Apply these recommended practices when presenting visualizations:

- Distill your key points. Don't rely on text alone. Instead, choose the right visualizations to support your key points.

- Use consistent colors in a dashboard with multiple charts and within a chart. Color directs focus. Lower the saturation for supporting or less-critical data. Limit the number of colors in use. While color can be helpful, charts must be understandable even when reduced to grayscale.

- Graphs should always have labeled axes and a legend. Eliminate duplicate information within the graph, though. For example, a legend isn't helpful if you use bar charts with labeled categories.

- Include references to the sources of data. Then, if something looks off about the chart, people can go back to the data to verify and dig deeper if needed.

- Design for the format. For presentations, lots of words will be hard to read and might obscure the most important message. You'll appreciate more detail with clear and specific steps on your on-call dashboard for those 2 a.m. pages.

- Point out key observations using annotations and highlighting when visualizing a specific dataset.

- Construct dashboards so that charts can explain each step of discovery, especially if you rely on that dashboard for on-call support in the middle of the night.

 See different visualizations of one dataset and how they change the message with Nathan Yau's "One Dataset, Visualized 25 Ways" on FlowingData (*https://oreil.ly/DmUGO*).

Wrapping Up

An effective presentation provides audiences with the interpreted data and the context to understand and make decisions promptly. Tell a compelling story tailored to the needs and interests of your audience. Consider the nature of your data, the message, and the expression of the data interpretation. Remember that stories are at the heart of effective communication. So when you're preparing to present information—to fellow sysadmins, to leadership, to customers—ask yourself:

- Who is your audience? What do they care about, and what do they need?

- What is the nature of the data? What kind of story are you telling?

- What format will be most effective in reaching this particular audience? Should you present your information in writing, verbally, graphically, or as a multimedia presentation?

- What interpretation do you want the audience to understand? What context do they need to reach the conclusions you have in mind?

- What information does the audience need to understand your story? What information should you omit because it distracts from the story? What information should you include, even if it might undercut your narrative, to allow the audience to reach conclusions you might not have considered?

- Visualizations can be an effective way to convey meaning concisely. What type of visuals would be effective for telling your story?

You'll know your presentation is successful when your audience understands your message and can promptly make decisions based on your information.

Assembling the System

In Part II, you learned about the practices that support maintaining reliable and sustainable systems. In Part III, I'm going to focus on assembling the system, which pulls together all the practices from Part II along with the fundamental building blocks (computing environments, storage, and networking) from Part I. Infrastructure is vast and varied. It's a widely accepted practice to eliminate snowflake servers (*https://oreil.ly/zWuZ4*) with infrastructure as code. Yet, every organization has its unique methods, which leads to challenges in solving infrastructure management and needless arguments about the one way to do it.

I've seen a number of tools, techniques, and practices to manage infrastructure advocated for in my years in the industry. Some have weathered time and some have not. Ultimately, you need to build reusable, versioned artifacts from source. This will include building and configuring a continuous integration and continuous delivery pipeline. Automation of your infrastructure reduces the cost of creating and maintaining environments, reduces the risk of single points of critical knowledge, and simplifies the testing and upgrading of environments.

CHAPTER 11

Scripting Infrastructure

I talked about baking in Chapter 1 when reasoning about your systems. Let's use another baking metaphor because baking is a really useful way to explain systems. Cookies are a delightful small, sweet treat generally composed of some ratio of sugar, fat, and flour. You might buy ready-made cookies, bake them from prepackaged cookie dough, or assemble them from scratch from the ingredients you have in your kitchen.

Likewise, with your infrastructure, you can use services, buy prepackaged resources, or pull your own from what you have available. All the problems that can occur with your infrastructure (the process, resource state, or environmental conditions) can be remediated by scripting your infrastructure with infracode and creating the necessary recipes for your infrastructure. In this chapter, I will explain why you need to script your infrastructure regardless of your infrastructure choices and the different infrastructure lens to plan your infrastructure project.

 This chapter will focus on infracode, the literal Ruby, YAML, or other language used to describe your infrastructure. In Chapter 12, I'll discuss the Infrastructure as Code model and the practices applied to your infracode.

Why Script Your Infrastructure?

I've seen organizations where the pace of change in practices was stagnant because there was always so much urgent and interrupting work that there was no time to invest in scripting. Sometimes there is fear that automation will somehow take away the job. To manage infrastructure automatically, you can write infracode, human- and machine-readable language to describe the hardware, software, and network resources to automate consistent, repeatable, and transparent management of resources.

Regardless of the type of infrastructure management automation tools you adopt into your organization, you can do the following:

- Increase your speed at deploying the same infrastructure
- Reduce infrastructure risk by eliminating errors introduced through manual configuration and deploys
- Increase the visibility across the organization to governance, security, and compliance controls
- Standardize configuration, provisioning, and deployment tools

These outcomes might not map to specific business values, so it is sometimes difficult to secure a sufficient budget or support for an infracode project. And on some level, this makes sense: it takes time to automate what you do manually, and there may be complexities that are not automatable.

So, to motivate your team and inspire stakeholder alignment, especially when there are competing priorities for the team's time, try the following:

- Think about and document the manual resource provisioning, configuration, and deploys (the what, how, and any corner cases handled).
- Identify small projects that can successfully be completed and support your vision.

Let's look at a few ways that you could describe a vision with goals that align with business values:

Consistency

You deploy and configure systems uniformly that have been tested and documented. This aligns to business values because consistency can increase the productivity and efficiency of the team.

Scalability

Infracode streamlines the provisioning and deprovisioning process, allowing you to activate and deactivate fleets of systems as required with minimal effort. This effort can take the form of easy manual scale-up and scale-down, fully automated cloud management, or any combination, allowing the system to dynamically respond to peaks and troughs in demand while also giving humans the authority to govern the operation of the automation system. This aligns to business values because scalability can increase revenue, add product differentiation, reduce always-on infrastructure costs, and increase user satisfaction.

Empowerment

You define layers of responsibility to allow different teams to have autonomy over their resource governance. You represent how to share responsibility between infrastructure, security, and application teams, enabling self-service within negotiated boundaries and maintaining overall visibility.

This aligns to business values because empowerment can decrease the friction of deploying new products while keeping spending within acceptable boundaries, enabling operational teams to review resource usage to ensure departments are using their budgets effectively. This autonomy leads to increased revenue and differentiation in product development.

Accountability

Tracking infracode changes with version control gives you a history of system changes and an audit trail so that anyone can answer questions about systems created. This aligns to business values because accountability can decrease costs because you can deprovision systems that should no longer be in use and revisit decisions where assumptions have changed and a different solution may be a better alternative.

Enculturation

Version control changelogs facilitate onboarding new team members. They can see how you do the work and can copy the same processes. This aligns to business values because enculturation can increase productivity and efficiency.

Experimentation

Infracode can allow people to spin up test environments easily, try new technologies, and quickly push them to production when such experiments are successful. This aligns to business values because experimentation can increase revenue and help the team focus on market differentiation.

You know your organization and its leaders best. Based on the company and larger organization objectives, define a project scope and goals that align with those objectives. Once you've got your project scope and goals, you can use a specific perspective to model your infrastructure to successfully land your project and goals.

Three Lenses to Model Your Infrastructure

Think about the infrastructure that you are managing. You may have the physical hardware or compute instances with various dependent services. Each compute entity will have an OS and may have several containers or virtual machines. Networking connects different entities with access control lists or policies that allow or restrict communication. Now, think about how you describe your infrastructure.

At a high level, you may provision in a cloud-first manner with each resource over their whole lifecycle, from provisioning to removal from service, as shown on the left in Figure 11-1. Or you could focus on a low level, as depicted on the right, and configure a single compute instance to match up to a specific set of policies to build machine images in a repeatable, consistent, and reusable fashion.

Figure 11-1. Deciding on an approach to infracode; all are valid (image by Tomomi Imura)

 Technological advancement is like a biological ecosystem with various habitats, niches, and species. With technology, some new tool comes along and fulfills a need. The community adopts the practices, if not the technology, leading to collaboration and communication pattern changes. Other technology platforms change to mirror the community's new needs.

I hope to show you general patterns in this book because books reflect a point in time, and at the moment you read this book, newer tools, technologies, and practices will exist. Look at the documentation for the specific version of your chosen tool for up-to-date recommended practices.

With this perspective in mind, when choosing a tool, think about what lens fits your immediate need for infrastructure management, encoding your infrastructure to do the following:

- Build machine images
- Provision infrastructure resources
- Configure infrastructure resources

Code to Build Machine Images

Early in my career, I deployed and maintained many physical systems. Thankfully, at one job, I had a hard drive duplicator that allowed me to clone multiple drives simultaneously from a single hard drive to speed up the deployment process. Of course, I still had to update the configurations for each system after installing the newly cloned drive, but it saved hours of OS installation and update time. This process was manual but faster than building the physical machine, installing the OS via CDs, and then figuring out how to update the system while it was still potentially vulnerable.

This pattern is known as building from a *golden image*: a perfect, known good mold from which you create more imaged systems. Workflows today conceptually descend from this approach, where a *machine image* (e.g., Amazon Machine Images or VMware templates) serves much the same purpose as golden images. With machine images, you automate system builds, harden the OS to reduce vulnerabilities, preinstall any necessary and standard tooling, and ultimately provision your compute resources from a more secure and robust base.

An essential task for system administrators has been deploying physical computers, but what this entails has evolved; the compute infrastructure you manage could include physical machines, virtual machines, and containers.

 Because technologies reuse many of the same concepts, infrastructure automation developers tend to reuse terminology, but this can create confusion when you need to be specific about the level of abstraction that you're using. For this explanation, I'm going to refer to *machines* and *machine images*, with the understanding that, in practice, machines have a spectrum of meanings, from physical systems and virtual machines to containers.

Take a look at Figure 11-2, a machine image for a server that will run a specific OS and a set of containerized applications.

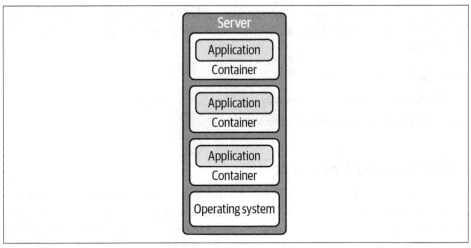

Figure 11-2. Building machine images

Examples of tools that build machine images include:

- Packer for multiplatform machine images
- EC2 Image Builder for Amazon Machine Images
- Buildah to build Open Container Initiative (OCI) container images

You may want to write code to build machine images if you need to:

- Ensure systems have a standard updated base image
- Install a set of common tools or utilities on all systems
- Use images built internally with the provenance of every software package on the system.

Code to Provision Infrastructure

When providers introduced cloud architectures, I relished the opportunity to quickly access complex infrastructure with simple APIs. No more racking and stacking, tracking cabling, and configuring network ports in addition to installing the application. Instead, the installation of provider SDKs and tooling allowed me to quickly provision and configure the necessary infrastructure. Provisioning cloud resources through infracode enables you to:

- Specify the virtual machines, containers, networks, and other API-enabled infrastructure needed based on your architecture decisions
- Connect the individual infrastructure components into stacks
- Install and configure components
- Deploy your stack as a unit

Take a look at Figure 11-3, depicting provisioning individual resources (e.g., servers and databases).

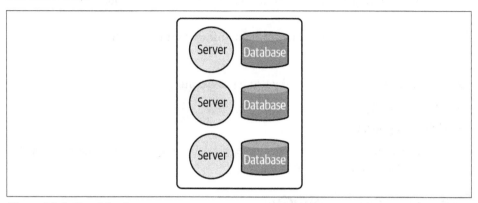

Figure 11-3. Provisioning resources

Examples of tools that provision infrastructure resources include these:

- HashiCorp Terraform
- Pulumi
- AWS CloudFormation
- Azure Resource Manager
- Google Cloud Deployment Manager

Writing valid infracode requires a lot of knowledge to successfully provision and configure infrastructure resources. Additionally, while cloud providers often offer fundamentally similar services, there are subtle differences in capabilities. Trying to map one-to-one functionality between providers, especially with infracode, can be frustrating because syntax and abstractions vary widely. If you have a multicloud architecture, you most likely will benefit from leveraging frameworks like Pulumi and Terraform, which can deploy to multiple platforms.

Infracode obfuscates the underlying "how does this work." Humans work with these systems and must understand more than just deployment automation. When problems occur (and they will), you need to know where to debug.

For example, suppose you write infracode to manage your DNS records for mail and forget SPF and DKIM records. In that case, this misconfiguration could disrupt mail delivery from your domain to most providers. Unfortunately, checking for valid syntax doesn't prevent operability mishaps in the code. In addition, redeploying the infracode won't catch the missing configurations.

You may want to write code to provision infrastructure if you have or need the following:

- Systems that are already partially using provisioning
- Multicloud support
- Multitier applications
- Repeatable environments, for example, a testing environment that is a smaller clone of the production environment

Code to Configure Infrastructure

Configuring infrastructure resources through infracode allows you to handle software and service configuration once hardware infrastructure is available. Take a look at Figure 11-4, depicting the configuration of the OS and applications to be consistent, repeatable, and reliable.

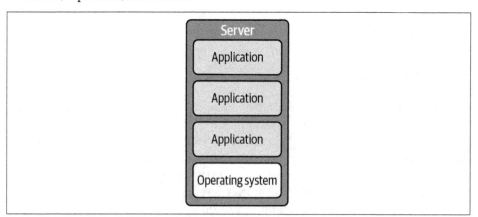

Figure 11-4. Configuring infrastructure

Here are some examples of tools that configure infrastructure resources:

- CFEngine (*https://oreil.ly/8v4HK*)
- Puppet (*https://oreil.ly/dTIk8*)
- Chef Infra (*https://oreil.ly/n62da*)
- Salt (*https://oreil.ly/BfTSD*)
- Red Hat Ansible (*https://oreil.ly/olg8H*)

Each option implements configuration management slightly differently with different terminology to describe the building blocks that represent the abstractions of configuring infrastructure.

You may want to write code to configure infrastructure if you're going to do the following:

- Manage installation and configuration of software installed on systems
- Configure OS parameters
- Repeat installation and configuration of a system
- Automate repair of manual changes made directly to systems

Getting Started

I've shared three lenses that can help you narrow your infracode research. Different tools have supporting features depending on the infrastructure you want to manage, which may lead you to reconsider your underlying technology choices, too!

If you aren't using infracode, consider how the tool fits within the context of your environment. For example, apply the decision framework for choosing a programming language from the Sysadmin Toolkit (Chapter 5) to determine your infrastructure management tools.

Selecting and implementing infracode platforms has long-lasting impacts on the team, if not the entire organization. It's difficult to retire technology that's still in use—difficult, but possible. The field is evolving quickly, and some tools may lock you into using a specific vendor's toolset, which may not be an acceptable trade-off.

Deploying your chosen tool depends on whether you're adopting it for a new environment (*greenfield deployment*) or need it to solve struggles in an existing environment (*brownfield deployment*). In a greenfield deployment, try to use the selected tooling for all the workflows where it is relevant to encourage the adoption of infracode habits and highlight any workflow issues. You may solve the problems by changing processes and tools or find that you need to rescope the project.

In a brownfield deployment, prioritize workflows and gradually apply the new tool. Focus on one area for improvement at a time. For example, you might manage all SSH configuration with Puppet or Chef and then move on to other parts of the web server configuration for a single server. If the automated process asserts reasonable defaults, then the team will see this as a labor-saving improvement and will likely get on board with finding other automation opportunities. On the other hand, if folks are manually configuring systems, they will view the automation as counterproductive and seek ways to bypass and undermine efforts to automate processes.

Additionally, be wary of taking on projects that are too complex or try to force one tool to fix everything. For example, if you have numerous platforms but mostly Linux, focus on the Linux platform before trying to adapt your infracode to multiplatform and support Windows. You may find that you need entirely different workflows and tools rather than trying to force a single tool for all platforms.

Often your infracode solution is a multiprong approach that accommodates the complexity of your infrastructure. A multiprong solution is OK. It's perfectly reasonable to adopt Packer to build machine images, Terraform for immutable ephemeral containers in the cloud, and Terraform with Chef for longer-lived instances; you can devise a cohesive approach that weaves together these tools into a sustainable solution.

Wrapping Up

The purpose of infracode is to enable you to manage your infrastructure collaboratively as a team in a consistent, reliable, and scalable way. Current widely used infracode tools generally focus on three main use cases: building machine images, provisioning infrastructure resources, and configuring existing infrastructure. With these guidelines, you can create an infracode journey customized to your organization or team's needs, technology, strengths, and weaknesses.

You may have an existing brownfield environment with pain points that you're struggling to deal with, or you may have an opportunity to set out on a new greenfield project where you have wide latitude to select the latest and greatest tools. In both cases, you need to think about the relevant workflows people need to handle and find tooling that can best meet the needs of these workflows. With these guidelines, you can assemble an infracode toolbox customized to your team's needs, technology, strengths, and weaknesses. In Chapter 12, I'll share ideas for sustainably managing at scale by looking at how to use infrastructure as code and infrastructure as data.

Managing Your Infrastructure

Contemporary computing environments range from managed compute to container orchestrators like Kubernetes with virtualized storage and networking. As discussed in Chapter 11, you can choose a variety of tools to define these critical resources with infracode.

Once, I discovered 11 different active ways of managing parts of the configuration and deployment for a single service. I'd completed an upgrade with a shadow, so I attempted the next upgrade solo. Except, this one process wasn't automated and depended on a developer-generated package that didn't exist. So, while I followed the extensive checklist and executed the various shell scripts leveraging the 11 different configuration systems, I had upgraded only part of the thousand-node system, which put the entire system in a precarious state.

It's not sustainable to manage systems even with a thorough checklist and infracode. This chapter introduces infrastructure models to improve and modernize infrastructure management and provides getting-started recommendations. You can navigate thorny infrastructure scenarios and incrementally adopt more contemporary (and sustainable) practices.

Infrastructure as Code

Let's start with the more well-known model: infrastructure as code (IaC). IaC is taking time-tested recommended practices from software development and applying them to improve quality and visibility in infrastructure management.

IaC is all the software development practices applied to infrastructure code, while infrastructure code is the Ruby, YAML, or language used to describe your infrastructure.

The industry will adopt new practices as software development evolves. Current approaches include storing infrastructure code (infracode) in version control, code reviews, automated testing, and deployment automation:

Infracode
> In Chapter 11, I introduced infracode, the human- and machine-readable language, to describe the hardware, software, and network resources to automate consistent, repeatable, and transparent management of resources.

Version control
> In Chapter 6, I introduced the fundamental practice of version control; you can store infracode in version control for reproducibility, visibility (how have resources changed and when), and accountability (who made what change).

Code review
> Storing infracode in version control is great because it gives you insight into the changes made. How do you introduce change and decide whether you want to incorporate it into the system systematically and repeatedly?

> Code review is the process of a peer looking over code (and, in some cases, before merging into the main branch of a version control repository). The goals of a code review include the following:

> - Verifying the implemented solution
> - Verifying that the problem was understood and solved
> - Sharing knowledge about the requested change
> - Providing opportunities for mentorship as the code creator or the reviewer
> - Supporting the enforcement of coding standards and finding bugs earlier

>   Ultimately, code review is one of the ways that your code becomes the team's code and is a practice in navigating disagreements. Therefore, your team's code review practices will evolve as you learn from each other.

Automated testing
> As discussed in Chapter 7, tests help to build confidence and eliminate some of the fear of making a change. The goals of testing infracode are to help you assess risk, respond to and recover from problems quickly, and improve your delivery processes.

Executable automated testing is the only way to manage the needs of contemporary work supporting systems with the rapid pace of deployment, dependency vulnerability announcements, and evolution of infrastructure.

Continuous integration (CI)
CI is the practice of automatically merging multiple contributors' work into a single branch of a shared code repository. CI platforms enable teams to automate testing and get rapid feedback about the quality of potential changes prior to merging the code.

Continuous deployment (CD)
CD is the practice of automatically deploying tested software releases. CD platforms enable teams to automate deployments, enabling faster feedback from customers about new features and improvements.

Deployment automation
With the appropriate tests as validation gates, you can set up a build or continuous integration/continuous delivery or deployment (CI/CD) pipeline, describing the method of automated integration code and automated builds. The steps or phases in a pipeline will be distinct subsets of tasks grouped by different stages.

Figure 12-1 illustrates an example of deployment automation, with a build pipeline that has distinct phases and grouped tasks.

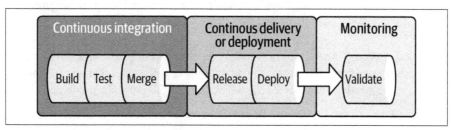

Figure 12-1. The different phases of a build pipeline

Within the CI phase, there are three steps:

1. Build
The project is compiled with the proposed changes.

2. Test
Scripted tests run against the project.

3. Merge
Changes are merged into the main branch.

Within the CD phase, there are two steps:

1. Release

A version of the project is published to an artifact repository.

2. Deploy

A specific project version is deployed to a live environment, either upgrading an existing system or deploying to newly provisioned resources.

Finally, within the monitoring phase is the last step:

1. Validate

The production environment is validated against expectations. While this final phase monitors the artifact deployed to production, monitoring occurs to validate each task within each of the other phases as well.

Applications built to run on serverless compute have significantly different architecture demands for local development, testing, and monitoring. You can use whatever CI infrastructure to promote change in the application through the various phases of the development lifecycle.

Additionally, because sysadmins aren't managing the hardware, promoting the application between environments is faster. Finally, serverless relies on underlying cloud-provided services, so your application may run differently when those services change.

Realistically, your pipeline should model your build processes, which may mean not having these exact phases. Instead, you may have different pipelines per project or specific configurations that direct the flow based on the part of a single project.

Let's follow the path of your pull request after you write, lint, and test your code on your local development environment (Figure 12-2).

You submit a pull request, and the deployment automation software is triggered, which sends a notification to the team chat, a Slack channel, and triggers a build of the software with your proposed change. At this stage or in a later stage after tests, your team may review the code and approve or reject the pull request.

The automation runs unit tests and sends the outcomes to Slack. On a successful code build that passes unit tests, automation kicks off a container build that builds, tags, and pushes the container image to an artifact registry.

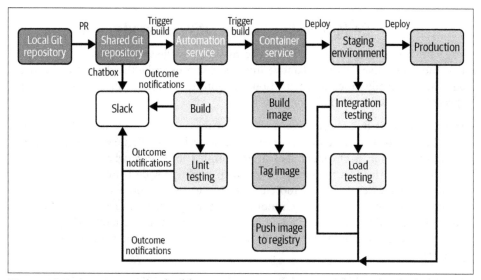

Figure 12-2. A more complex build process incorporating integration of code changes and deployment to production

A successful container image delivery to the registry triggers the provisioning of a staging environment, an ephemeral environment that emulates production, to start the second round of testing, which may include integration, load, and other tests. Finally, after successful testing, the image is deployed into production, where further validation testing may occur.

At any point, failure triggers a signal to the team chat.

Following are examples of tools that support automated testing and deployment automation:

- GitHub Actions
- CircleCI
- Jenkins
- Azure DevOps
- Google Cloud Build
- AWS CodePipeline

 Often IaC is conflated with IaaS, but these are two different concepts. You can use IaC with on-prem hardware and cloud computing environments. IaaS is a service a cloud provider offers and a service delivery model.

Declarative Versus Imperative Infracode

Infrastructure management tools take two main approaches with infracode: declarative and imperative. With declarative infracode, you describe the desired end state, and the tool handles the implementation. In contrast, with imperative infracode, you specify the procedure for achieving a task.

In practice, tools that confine you to either of these extremes are difficult to work with because of your resources. For example, a declarative framework might work for most common deployments but be too limited to express what has to happen for other scenarios. An imperative framework might provide better expressiveness for those edge cases. Still, it is too cumbersome for when you just want to deploy a standard image with only a few minor tweaks through custom variables. The infracode tools that find widespread adoption tend to balance the declarative-imperative axis, providing straightforward and flexible ways to implement many deployment pipelines.

Treating Your Infrastructure as Data

In a 2013 blog post for the O'Reilly Radar, "The Rise of Infrastructure as Data" (*https://oreil.ly/n2xUH*), Michael DeHaan, creator of Ansible, wrote, "Infrastructure is best modeled not as code, nor in a GUI, but as text-based, middle-ground, data-driven policy." He coined the term *infrastructure as data* (IaD) to expand on the concept of declarative infracode.

So, should you think about infrastructure as data or as code? There is something compelling about modeling infrastructure as data with a data model and as code with infracode and all of the respective practices, much like light can be modeled as a wave or a particle. Instead of choosing one or the other, choose both.

Reflect on what you learned in Chapter 3 about the importance of data and its value to a company. Your job is to keep data safe, managed, and available. When you create an infrastructure data model, you recognize the strategic value of all the fundamental resources required for your system to function. Consider the following:

- Where is your data model stored?
- Where is the metadata about your data model kept?
- How do you keep track of the changes in the data model?

What About GitOps?

GitOps is a newer infrastructure management model (compared to IaC and IaD) that arose from managing Kubernetes clusters in 2017. OpenGitOps (*https://opengi tops.dev*) is the community-driven set of standards that describes the recommended practices and principles around GitOps. The v1.0.0 principles are as follows:

- Declarative infracode
- Versioned and immutable state
- Resources pull approved configuration from the central repository
- Resources continuously reconcile the actual state from the desired state

The principles of GitOps are not new; GitOps is a repackaging of components of the existing models (infracode, version control, deployment automation from IaC, and immutable state from IaD). Regardless, there is value in GitOps if it helps you adopt improved infrastructure management practices in your organization.

Getting Started with Infrastructure Management

With IaC and IaD models in mind, you can now think about adopting practices to improve and modernize your infrastructure management incrementally. In an organization with few to no current practices, adopting and modernizing your infrastructure is a significant technical change that requires process change and skill updates in addition to the practices and technology. For example, if you're not creating and managing your infrastructure with code now, it can feel overwhelming to identify a place to start. In an organization with current practices, it may be challenging to understand all of the systems in place, let alone how to make improvements.

A key component of success is ensuring that your team and stakeholders have a shared vision of the specific proposed parts of infrastructure management you want to improve. If you don't have alignment, you will be hard-pressed to complete your project.

Additionally, ensure that your project isn't "automate all the things." Instead, scope your project to a specific goal. Automating everything is a multiquarter, potentially multiyear, project, which means an extended time to reach success criteria. Examples of potential well-scoped infrastructure management projects include the following:

- Improving time-to-deploy for development environments
- Helping a geographically distributed infrastructure team collaborate asynchronously by turning real-time system configuration tasks into scheduled code changes at optimal times

- Streamlining onboarding, making it easier to accept part-time assistance for specific projects while facilitating cooperation among different teams
- Considering the pain points that arise during on-call rotations and how automating chores can make these shifts go more smoothly

Identifying the challenge is key; infracode is not an end unto itself, even if that is what your leadership is saying and attempting to measure.

Once you have a goal, break it down into smaller measurable objectives or milestones: version control, code reviews, automated testing, and deployment automation for your infracode, leveraging whatever is in place as necessary:

Start with version control
In a team that has already adopted version control software, decide where infracode will be located (with the project or in its dedicated code repository). If your team isn't using version control yet, revisit Chapter 6, and learn more about how to get started with version control.

Implement code review processes
In a team already doing code review, assess and document the current process.

Identify or choose your infrastructure management tool(s)
In Chapter 11, I introduced three infracode models to help you identify and assess tools in use and choose additional infrastructure management tools.

Implement single points of authority over elements of infrastructure
Eliminate areas where multiple tools are updating the same resources. Conflicts in updates will cause pain, frustration, and needless paging.

Don't sacrifice collaboration
The long-term success of an infrastructure management project requires considering the workflows the tool will encourage and how those workflows will change the dynamics of your team. Once your team adopts an infrastructure automation tool, that tool makes the future relevant system changes. So, everyone on the team needs to understand the adopted mechanism well enough to use it daily.

If the infrastructure management project feels like it belongs to only a subset of the team, those people will become a bottleneck when the rest of the team asks them to make changes they used to make themselves. Everyone gets frustrated in this scenario. Be sure to build adoption by inviting the whole team to give input and get targeted demos that make real day-to-day struggles easier.

Check for single points of failure
Remember that infrastructure includes the software to be deployed. So make sure a single person understands the application definition and the context of when and why the application runs. For example, cloud applications leveraging

serverless infrastructure should be defined in source control and deployed automatically to the cloud provider. Creating a standard project skeleton can be an
example for engineers to start by encapsulating specific security patterns and
preventing the ad hoc creation of resources without oversight.

Identify the necessary skills required to be successful

Even the most experienced among us need some training to bootstrap the successful adoption of technology. If you haven't used version control before, that's
the first skill to obtain, along with creating accounts on whatever version control
system is in use. For example, for Terraform, you may need a combination of
training in HashiCorp Configuration Language (HCL) (*https://oreil.ly/6sgXp*),
Terraform, and Terraform implementation within your organization.

Build quality with automated tests

Think about the infracode practices in use or planned. You can integrate testing
into your initial plans or add them afterward for existing infracode. Many times,
automating infracode tests (infratests) at all is a big step.

Tips for Code Reviews

Navigating the perils of reviewing others' work is not an easy task. When you reach
that special flow state with another human, you develop language that communicates
more than what is said. But, outside of the flow state, words can be taken so many
different ways, and adding more words won't necessarily solve the problem.

Here are a few tips I've learned over the years:

- Code doesn't need to be perfect. Before you assess someone's code, establish
  some understanding of the review process. Maybe you'll adopt some form of
  conventional comments (*https://oreil.ly/P3gM1*) that enable a consistent format
  to improve expectations. Then when reviewing, you can apply labels that signal
  whether your feedback blocks the merge of a proposed change or if it's a preference. This way, you can share your feelings and not slow down progress. It's OK
  to integrate code that improves the system's state even if it's not 100% perfect.

- Don't forget to review the comments. Comments in the code should explain why
  code exists and not what the code is doing (except for complex things like regular
  expressions).

- Don't forget to praise the good stuff. So often, reviews focus only on what's
  problematic; encourage appreciation for recommended practices.

- Don't use hyperbolic words like *always* and *never* because generally there will be
  some context that breaks the rules.

- Most important, be kind. I'm not saying that you shouldn't address problematic
  code—honestly, it's not especially kind to avoid saying the hard things people

---

need to hear. Instead, especially when there are problems, take the extra time to deliver the feedback thoughtfully.

If you have deep concerns about code, consider whether an "out-of-band" approach, such as an in-person conversation or a private Slack message, might improve the outcomes of your concerns. Sometimes, people interpret written reviews more harshly due to the lack of contextual clues. If you use a more personal approach like pairing over the revised draft, your team members can learn from you and not misinterpret intentions.

 Recall from Chapter 7 that the challenge of writing tests for infracode is that it can be straightforward to test the infrastructure platform in use rather than your code. Think about whether you are verifying your code as written or testing that the infrastructure management software is working. Unless it's an in-house developed system, trust that the software does what it is supposed to do. Even if you are working with an in-house configuration system, test that platform in its Git project separately from your infracode project.

Let's revisit the four testing types from Chapter 7: linting, unit, integration, and end-to-end testing, specifically with infracode.

Linting

Because of the nature of linters and the evolution of recommended practices, linter versions can be especially sensitive to change. If one person has one version of lint software on their system and someone else has a different version, the linter will influence their code, causing needless conflicts when working on the same project. As with other tools in the environment, ensure that everyone uses the same version of linter software.

When your linter returns an error, it doesn't necessarily mean that the code needs to be changed. Instead, examine the issues and identify whether you have a real problem or an area where you can customize the project's lint configuration.

Writing Unit Tests

With infracode unit tests, there generally is a specific package that maps out to testing the platform you are using. For example, Chef has Chefspec, and Puppet has rspec-puppet. Infracode can get complicated when you have specific customizations, for example, different operating systems, compute instances, or the environment in which the system exists in test or production. Valuable unit tests will test those inputs that change how the code runs so that you can have deterministic outputs. They help future sysadmins modify your code and see issues early.

Generally, very simple infracode doesn't require unit tests because we can assume that the infrastructure management system manages the individual resource blocks as intended. I know, that's shocking advice that contradicts the premise of the testing pyramid, but the reality is that for infracode, only complex patterns require object-level testing. It's helpful to assess the value of tests regularly because you must maintain them. Crufty tests can inhibit folks from collaborating!

Writing Integration Tests

Recall from Chapter 7 that integration tests are defined differently within organizations. Integration tests may be narrow (testing two components) or broad (testing multiple components). Before you implement tests against infracode, align on the implementation goal. For example, given infracode to configure a third-party service, would you test an active configuration or mock out a connection to the service and assume it would work in different environments?

 Think about scripts containing system commands that have different responses depending on external factors. For example, when integration testing, you might want to control the system command output because you aren't testing the system command; you are testing the script you are writing that includes the system command. Mocking is a crucial technique you can leverage to ensure reproducibility and focus your test.

Writing End-to-End Tests

E2E tests verify that a project's behavior functions as expected from start to finish on a production-like ephemeral environment, which means that there is some non-negligible cost associated with running them. Therefore, there is a danger that if the CI system doesn't clean up the testing infrastructure, you will spend money on unnecessary resources.

Managing Your Testing Infrastructure: Shoring Up the Test Levee

By Chris Devers

When it comes to maintaining and extending a product line for years, I've found that an organization's test environment (the tests, framework, and testing infrastructure) is equally as important as the system maintenance for your product. The good: my team's test framework notices most problems before customers do so that we can get fixes out early and prove new ideas. For example, helper tools for spinning up integration tests helped my team consider new ways to deploy and manage production systems, making our products work better for current and future customers.

The problem is when the test framework itself becomes unmaintainable. The same test framework that is catching problems early and allowing us to experiment with new ideas is also suffering from these problems:

A *"tragedy of the commons" problem*
> It's a benefit to many developers, but no one person or team is genuinely responsible for the maintenance and quality of the framework itself. So it suffers and becomes unmaintainable as even more people make heavier use of it.

A *"who watches the watchers?" problem*
> For a given reported test failure, it can be difficult to determine if the problem was an error in the test itself in trying a scenario that "can't happen in production" or if the problem is an actual defect in the production software and the "can't happen in production" scenario might not be so implausible.

A *"boy who cried wolf" problem*
> Alerts are being triggered for issues that have already been fixed, because the alerts themselves are misinterpreting the test runs, and developers are having to second-guess the test results to figure out which problems are real and which ones are artifacts and echoes from the earlier defects.

Avoid this trap by expending time and regular resources to keep the documentation about the systems in use, including your testing systems, up to date. And see Appendix B for information about how to expend time and resources to resolve the four types of failures that can occur with your testing environment so that you can keep it in a good state.

Follow these guidelines, and you can adopt IaC and IaD practices customized to your organization or team's needs, technology, strengths, and weaknesses; manage your infrastructure more efficiently; and collaborate more effectively.

Wrapping Up

In an era where you manage resources with software, IaC and IaD practices are a customizable framework for building, testing, deploying, and managing your systems' infrastructure. Practices such as version control, code review, and automated testing have been standard for software development teams for many years. And these practices are helpful to adopt in managing our infrastructure.

Adopting IaC and IaD into an organization without these practices may require an incremental approach. Look for specific areas where advancing practices can help your team be more effective in making early progress and iterate on specific improvements.

More Resources

Learn more about the IaC practices from Kief Morris's updated *Infrastructure as Code* (*https://oreil.ly/xxTX8*) (O'Reilly).

CHAPTER 13

Securing Your Infrastructure

Your organization may have security professionals dedicated to securing infrastructure. Or, you may have no one with "security" in their job title or someone with little to no subject-matter expertise. Whether you have the opportunity to collaborate with others or need to figure out what to do on your own, you can improve your infrastructure's security by adopting a security mindset.

Ideally, securing infrastructure starts when you plan and build out your system's required resources. But how do you figure out where to start when dealing with existing infrastructure? *Defense in depth* tells you to apply security practices at different layers to deter harm to your infrastructure, but it doesn't mean it's possible to do everything simultaneously. However, by adopting a security mindset, you can improve the reliability, robustness, and general operability of the specific systems you manage, including your applications, tools, and services (i.e., desired attributes of your particular baked goods).

In this chapter, I model an approach for securing your infrastructure. First, assess attack vectors of a generic build pipeline to find your vulnerabilities, and adopt different lenses to narrow your mitigation efforts (i.e., managing identity access and secrets and securing compute and network) so you address the most frequent attacks. Then, I finish with a set of recommended guidelines for your infrastructure management. This chapter by no means provides an exhaustive method to secure your infrastructure. It barely scratches the surface. But, it does offer you a way to think about breaking the critical security work into smaller achievable pieces.

Review infrastructure security (Chapter 8) for more details on underlying security practices.

Assessing Attack Vectors

While figuring out how to fully assess attack vectors in your environment is well beyond the scope of this book, improving your infrastructure security starts with thinking about the potential entry points of intrusion for assets specific to your organization.

Let's examine the generic build pipeline from Chapter 12 for areas of vulnerability in Figure 13-1.

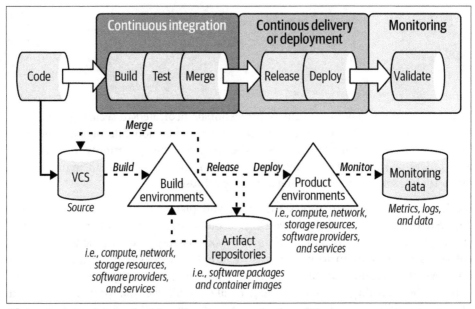

Figure 13-1. Examining build process for areas of vulnerability

At each point, there are different vectors of attack. Here are just a few:

- Your version control system
- The resources in your build environment
- The build platform
- The software packages and container images in your artifact repositories
- The resources in your production and other environments
- The data about all your infrastructure and what is happening

Risks to resources early in the process can impact all the resources built later. Following are some common attacks on these resources:

- Compromised credentials (e.g., a site getting compromised and exposing the username and password pairs and a user who reuses a username and password pair across multiple sites, including the compromised site)

- Weak credentials (e.g., an easily guessable password, like "123456")

- Misconfiguration (e.g., a service configuration that doesn't require authentication and authorization)

- Vulnerabilities to the software packages and container images (e.g., unpatched Docker images)

- Unpatched operating system and software (e.g., installing an OS and not updating to the latest patched version)

How do you improve your security posture to resolve these challenges? With infra-code, you can minimize errors and misconfigurations, compartmentalize your architecture with zero trust, and limit the exposure of resources to the broader internet that aren't needed. As with IaC and IaD, incrementally adopt practices to improve the security of your infrastructure management. Let's look at different lenses to focus your attention:

- Manage identity and access (supports 1, 2)

- Manage secrets (supports 1, 2)

- Securing your compute (supports 3, 4, and 5)

- Securing your network (supports 4)

Manage Identity and Access

Depending on the length of time you have been administering systems, the OSs in your environment, and the use of hosted services, you may have managed users and access in a variety of ways, including the following:

- Synchronizing */etc/passwd* and preventing duplicate user IDs

- Managing an LDAP server, Kerberos services, or Active Directory

- Managing identities in an *htpasswd* file

- Running SQL scripts to add users and grant roles to MySQL databases

Some of these processes may remain valid methods of managing user access. However, new techniques and technologies can facilitate automation, transparency, and compliance.

How Should You Control Access to Your System?

Identity and access management (IAM) is how you configure roles and privileges for users, groups, and services and the underlying technology and processes that support the allocation and revocation of privilege. There are three core elements of IAM:

Authentication
A user is who they say they are.

Authorization
A user has the privilege to do the requested action.

Activity logging
User actions are recorded via logging.

In addition to in-house solutions you manage, external services implement IAM with different terminology and concepts. Unique IAM implementation can occur across services offered by a specific provider (e.g., compute instance versus database authentication and authorization). You'll need to read the service documentation you plan to use to understand how to authenticate, authorize, and log activity. If you are starting a new position, migrating to a different cloud, or using a new web service, don't assume that identity implementations are the same.

Examples of service providers and their identity services include Amazon AWS Identity and Access Management, Google GCP Cloud Identity and Identity and Access Management, and Microsoft Azure Active Directory. Because of the differences between services and providers, you can accidentally weaken your system with misconfigurations.

Listed here are some examples of changes in modern infrastructure identity practices:

- Instead of a single factor of authentication such as a password to log into a system, use multifactor authentication (MFA), which requires multiple pieces of evidence. With MFA, individuals verify who they are with something known (e.g., a password or PIN) and something held (e.g., a security token or card).

- Instead of synchronizing and centralizing */etc/passwd* across many Unix systems or binding them to an LDAP directory, you might rely on configuration infra-code to ensure users have accounts only on the systems they need.

IAM can get complex. For example, in a hybrid scenario where you manage identities with a corporate user directory separate from your service provider, you might have to manage trust relationships and federation between different services. This allows you to share authentication methods across services so that users can use existing credentials.

Complexity is also increased by the need for IAM in different domains, such as corporate identities within an organization, service identities to enable communication between applications, and consumer identities to access customer-facing services.

Most likely, the set of tools you use for IAM for the variety of services you manage is more complex than it used to be. Leveraging infracode allows you to have consistent, repeatable, and testable configurations. You'll also need transparent processes, especially around the on-boarding and off-boarding of employees, to configure anything that doesn't integrate with automation.

Creating more developer-friendly ways to manage the provisioning of resources will require additional guardrails and audits. For example, one of the most common access misconfigurations with object storage services like AWS S3 is configuring full anonymous access to a bucket or allowing anyone to read or write to the bucket. How does this happen? Many how-to guides illustrate the concepts behind services by having developers immediately open up access to make it easy to focus on learning the service and don't explain what those configurations do. Unfortunately, these patterns then get copied into live environments and create vulnerabilities. Providing example infracode snippets that reflect best practices can help make it easier for others and keep settings uniform across your organization.

You may need to audit environmental issues and educate engineers within your organization to use specific technology. For example, you may want to ensure everyone has MFA enabled for their accounts. You might set up an automation that regularly scans for accounts missing MFA and notifies the account holder to remediate by adding MFA or deactivating the account.

You can leverage your infracode tools of choice to track, audit, and modify corporate and service identities to your systems as part of your provisioning process. Using infracode tools ensures the settings you encode are applied uniformly and updates pushed out as needed.

Who Should Have Access to Your System?

Once you figure out how you control access to your variety of systems, then it's a matter of figuring out who should have access to your system. When reviewing application or service documentation, you can often find guidance about expectations on running the systems, including what accounts are needed and any associated permissions. You should also ask yourself:

- Are elevated privileges required for individual or service accounts?
- Should there be time boundaries around access?
- Do users who have logged in require a different experience from a casual, anonymous user?

You can minimize possible harm to your system by applying the principles of least privilege and segregation of duties when granting access to your systems. Using these principles ensures that a user or component has access and authority only to what they need, versus having root or administrator accounts. In other words, with a compromised account, harm is limited to components of the system that the account has access to or authority.

You can examine what application programming interfaces (APIs) are available. Often, people see APIs as the realm of developers, but they are a critical vector of attack. Most modern web applications expose APIs to users in some form. For example, in hosted services, you configure and manage access to all of your systems and data via a provider's API gateway. Check what your service grants by default with open access.

IAM and logging are analogous to the door locks, security cameras, and other physical controls of an on-premises data center or server closet. Infracode is a practical necessity to ensure these "doors" remain appropriately "locked" and access monitored.

Manage Secrets

Engineers want to get work done as quickly as possible with the least amount of barriers, sometimes trusting the privacy of applications that don't have any notion of privacy or accidentally adding them to source control. However, often you have incomplete visibility of the risks from exposed secrets because there may be secrets embedded in code, and different services require different processes. Secrets include passwords, mTLS certificates, bearer tokens, and API keys.

Secrets are subject to a bootstrapping problem: how do I access a particular resource? If I need a password, how do I get that password? Early in my career, I remember being handed a carefully written sticky note and informed that it was critical to memorize the password and then destroy the note. Resetting the root and administrator passwords when anyone left the team while ensuring everyone remaining had the password was problematic.

In contemporary environments, you also need to keep more than host passwords secret from people who shouldn't have access to them. Using infracode to establish best practices around secret management can help you increase adoption and track your progress. However, infracode also introduces new challenges for secret management, as the infracode tools require access to the secrets. Let's examine the concerns to help you manage secrets.

Password Managers and Secret Management Software

Sometimes secrets need to be accessed or used by humans, automated processes, or both. These access patterns dictate what type of interface is best, so secret management software is usually tailored mainly for one use.

When the primary concern is interactive use by humans, secret management software is usually called a *password manager* or *privileged access management application*. You can generate and store strong, unique passwords using a password manager. Password managers reduce the risk of reused passwords and enable sharing secrets across the team without resorting to insecure methods like writing them down or sending them over collaboration services or email. Some well-known password managers include the following:

- 1Password (*https://1password.com*)
- LastPass (*https://www.lastpass.com*)
- KeePass (*https://keepass.info*)
- Bitwarden (*https://bitwarden.com*)
- pass (*https://www.passwordstore.org*)

Secret management software for other applications is a key-value database with authentication and auditing features. Vendors add value to their secret management solution by integrating with different software ecosystems or supporting specific usage patterns. The primary purpose of a secret management platform is to allow you to decouple the storage of secrets from the code or configuration that consumes the secrets. Besides the ability to support that decoupling, you should evaluate secret management software for other concerns, including these:

Centralization
> All secrets are stored in one place, reducing the risk of leaking secrets via storing them in the code or forgetting about their existence.

Revocation
> Marking a secret invalid and no longer trusted.

Rotation
> Updating credentials for an identity. This may include versioning the secrets allowing for the progressive rollout of a new secret so that you don't create brittle interdependencies between secrets and applications.

Isolation
> Ability to assign secrets to individuals or roles so that you grant the least amount of privilege. A single application doesn't need full access to all project secrets.

Inventory
Visibility of secrets being stored (separate from access to secret data) to eliminate secret sprawl.

Storage
Visibility and configuration of how and where secrets are stored and replicated.

Auditing
Interactions with secrets are logged and monitored.

Encryption
Secrets are encrypted at rest and during transit. Secrets shouldn't be written to disk or transmitted over networks in clear text.

Generation
Creation of new secrets.

Integration support
Usability with other services and ability to integrate with your software.

Reliability
Secret access needs to be reliable. How do specific services and systems work if the secret store is down?

Defending Secrets and Monitoring Usage

Monitoring access to and using credentials and other secrets is essential to your defense-in-depth strategy. Secrets can leak in many ways, so it's important to have mechanisms to detect and respond when that happens. Some ways that secrets get revealed include command history, debug logs, and the use of environment variables. Environment variables deserve special attention because they are available to the process, and secrets may be exposed through a process listing with no audit logs to trace exposure.

In 2020, Ubiquiti engineers detected rogue activity (*https://oreil.ly/g42C5*) within the network traced back to the misuse of an IT administrator's credentials that had been inside LastPass. The lack of logging made it impossible to track what had been done by malicious attackers while they had access to the systems. Even if you assume that anyone who has access to your system should have access to all secrets at any time, think about the risk from third-party services that ingest logs that may contain the secret in plain text. Consider the journey of a logged secret during a problem; for example, it may be ingested by Splunk, included in a PagerDuty alert, and sent through email and text messaging.

You want to know what systems are available (and should be!) and be able to detect the use of credentials in unexpected ways (from different source IPs or at other times). Many applications and services provide account anomaly detection through machine learning to enable you to see unexpected behavior.

To identify the breadth and depth of compromise, you need a comprehensive and clear data management strategy for audit logs. Use separation of privileges so that system administrative activities are separate from audit logs' activities.

In traditional environments, you have to worry about managing user access. Now, you need to worry about service access as well. Tools and techniques have evolved, yet secret management is still problematic, especially for machine-to-machine communication. Often you have incomplete visibility into risks from exposed secrets because there may be secrets embedded in code, and different services require different processes. Access logs from secret management software can help with this problem: services that access secrets will have a certain pattern, which can help make anomalous access more visible. Also, you can audit which services or applications don't use the chosen secret management software as a potential risk. Infracode can help close those gaps.

Securing Your Computing Environment

Securing your computing environment minimizes your systems' attack vectors by ensuring the confidentiality, integrity, and availability of your systems' OS, services, and tools. Your efforts to secure your compute infrastructure depend on your service types. For example, part of the cost you incur from using managed services includes the service provider's responsibility of securing the infrastructure.

For virtual machines and containers you choose to build and run, the service provider provides only the physical security and operating environment (hypervisor or container host) for your running workload. Managing your infrastructure configuration with infracode can make it easier to secure your responsibilities to your stack.

Operating systems and applications often default to open configurations prioritizing ease of use over security. As a result, you reduce the exposed attack surface if you secure the configuration for services requiring OS and application management. This is a common compliance requirement under many regulations and standards, including the Payment Card Industry Data Security Standard (PCI-DSS), ISO 27001, and the US Sarbanes-Oxley Act (SOX) and Federal Information Security Management Act (FISMA).

For guidelines, see the following resources:

- The Center for Internet Security (CIS) implementation guides (*https://oreil.ly/4Ises*)
- The Security Technical Implementation Guides (STIGs) (*https://oreil.ly/4aLd3*)

These peer-reviewed standards are available for many OSs, popular applications, and network devices. They have detailed instructions for tightening all sorts of security-related settings, some of which may not be appropriate for your situation. Review standards and implement recommendations that make sense for your industry and environment.

Document Deviations from Standards

By Chris Devers

My team had a new manager who wanted us to update our company's offerings to comply with CIS recommendations. One of their recommendations was that Linux hosts follow certain practices for isolating standard top-level directories on different partitions. What this new manager didn't realize was that we had found that in practice, a far more common source of instability was that when one partition filled up, logs stopped updating and databases stopped appending new records. We had already weighed the pros and cons of this partition scheme versus just consolidating to a more straightforward layout and decided that unifying most of the partitions would be a net-win.

It was important for us to understand the rationale behind industry-standard guidelines, evaluate our systems and conformance to standards, and decide whether it was worthwhile to adopt a recommendation that might cause more problems than it solves.

If you decide to deviate from a "best practice," consider whether an alternative approach solves a problem that might be more critical to your needs than the situations the standard is meant to address, and document that decision in policy and its outcomes.

Another crucial part of managing the security of compute infrastructure is patching the OS, installed packages, and applications. Unfortunately, patching can be complex because of many reasons, including application dependencies on specific versions of OS or other packages, unsustainable deployment practices, or fear of compatibility and stability problems.

Again, infracode helps address these concerns. Application dependencies can be documented and ensured in infracode. The automated, repeatable nature of infracode encourages frequent deployment and can enable testing of patches for critical systems. You can implement automated tests of different versions of dependencies to expose the risk to patching and provide peace of mind to proceed with patching as needed.

You need to update a containerized application the same way you would need to update it if the application were running directly on a server. Most container images include a significant number of OS packages that will require periodic updates. You can use infracode to build new, patched container images and then test and deploy them.

A popular software methodology, the twelve-factor app,[1] recommends that you *explicitly declare and isolate dependencies (https://oreil.ly/45S4A)*, which eliminates the implicit dependence on system-wide packages. By including a manifest with specific versions of applications, you can reproduce builds reliably without impacting the underlying OS. Additionally, it provides a path to test builds with new versions by updating the manifest rather than relying on available upgrades from your OS vendor. If you isolate dependencies, remember that in addition to OS patching, you need to plan to keep your dependency manifest up to date as well, which includes rebuilding, testing, and redeploying your application.

Securing Your Network

Network controls provide defense in depth for networked services. If an attacker is unable to communicate with a service, they can't attack that service directly regardless of vulnerabilities or misconfigurations it may have. This basic insight led to the development of the classic standard networking topology; sysadmins would create a trusted core network to contain most of an organization's systems and configure firewalls to limit incoming access to that core from outer, less-trusted network zones. In this topology, publicly accessible systems such as web servers would go in the outermost zone, often called the *demilitarized zone* (DMZ). Everything outside the core and DMZ is not trusted and must be vetted before passing to the core.

This topology has been described as "candy bar network security": crunchy on the outside, chewy on the inside. The idea is that attacker's attention is focused on the perimeter and assumes that anyone accessing internal resources is doing what they need to and needs a minimal-friction experience.

The shortcomings of this trust-based network become apparent when that network isolation starts being used as the primary defense for insecure systems or protocols,

---

1 Learn more about the twelve-factor methodology (*https://12factor.net*) that emerged from Heroku engineers who "witnessed the development, operation, and scaling of hundreds of thousands of apps."

for example, an attacker who can gain access to one system in the trusted core, then enters a playground of insecure systems.

An early method for improving network security might be to implement virtual local area networks (VLANs) to segment the network. Ultimately, while this provides some additional layers, it's still effectively a flat network that depends on some amount of varying "chewiness."

A more advanced approach would be to adopt a software-defined firewall, pushing firewalls to each of the compute and storage nodes. Now, not only does a system have to be internal to the network, but it also has to be configured to have access. Software-defined networking products are designed specifically to adapt their configuration quickly and easily as you add and remove servers and services. When new systems are being added, consider what services they need to communicate with and restrict network communication to only those services. The initial effort of mapping these network dependencies is rewarded later by an easier-to-understand architecture with data flows explicitly documented in the infracode.

Overall, the industry is moving toward an approach that adopts the zero trust architecture model. The key principles of zero trust are as follows:

- No implicit trust is granted between entities based on their location.
- The model requires resources to have valid authentication and authorization.
- Protection is oriented around resources rather than network segments.

In other words, it's less about securing the network and more about enabling each authorized and authenticated entity on the network (such as a server or a person's workstation) to communicate only with the services allowed based on established policies.

The dynamic nature of containerized and serverless workloads presents further challenges and opportunities for network segmentation. Most products and services have built-in or add-on features to enable zero-trust-style networking integrated with the workload orchestration. For example, Network Policies in Kubernetes can target specific pods according to the familiar selectors admins and developers use for everything else. If you want to use Network Policies in Kubernetes, it's important to make sure your chosen Kubernetes network plug-in supports the features required to achieve your network security goals.

Security Recommendations for Your Infrastructure Management

If your organization currently has little to no adopted IaC/IaD practices, start with understanding what is in use or planned. Integrate security into your initial plans or add them to your overall strategy.

Here are my general recommendations (regardless of the state of your infrastructure management):

- Verify who has the access to run automation and infracode. Make sure that this privilege is limited to only what is necessary to perform those tasks and is isolated from modification of the logging of those tasks.

- Generate and store credentials safely.

- Don't reuse user or service credentials. With IAM, it's possible to generate and revoke the credentials to be used as needed.

- Check that provisioning infracode grants only the necessary privileges required to users and resources (e.g., VMs).

- Check for resource configurations that can strengthen the integrity of the resources you are using.

- In cloud computing environments, limit the impact radius of compromises by associating one account per workload.

- Automate policy compliance against your computing environments. For example, if you were using Google Cloud Storage as an online file store, you might consider addressing only access concerns as identified earlier in this chapter. For this specific resource, it's possible to encrypt the objects in the bucket, which adds another layer of security if someone managed to obtain access to the bucket directly. With this Terraform snippet, you can enable uniform bucket-level access (*https://oreil.ly/imioB*) and provide the key used to encrypt objects in a Google Cloud Storage bucket:

  ```
  resource "google_storage_bucket" "static-assets" {
    name    = "static.example.com"
    uniform_bucket_level_access = true
    encryption {
      default_kms_key_name = "static-assets-key"
    }
  }
  ```

- Add static code analysis to scan your infracode for security misconfigurations or missing best practices. This can be added directly into your deployment automation tool as one of the gating factors for automated deployment. For example, checkov (*https://oreil.ly/mzuBD*) is an open source tool to scan infracode.

Running a scan on the previous Cloud Storage bucket Terraform example returns the following:

```
terraform scan results:

Passed checks: 2, Failed checks: 0, Skipped checks: 0

Check: CKV_GCP_5: "Ensure Google storage bucket have encryption enabled"
    PASSED for resource: google_storage_bucket.static-assets
    File: /gcp_bucket.tf:1-7
    Guide: https://docs.bridgecrew.io/docs/bc_gcp_gcs_1

Check: CKV_GCP_29: "Ensure that Cloud Storage buckets have uniform
    bucket-level access enabled"
    PASSED for resource: google_storage_bucket.static-assets
    File: /gcp_bucket.tf:1-7
    Guide: https://docs.bridgecrew.io/docs/bc_gcp_gcs_2
```

- Scan your version control repositories for secrets. For example, gitleaks (*https://oreil.ly/6tnYR*) is an open source tool that detects hardcoded secrets within Git repos. Hosted source control services like GitHub (*https://oreil.ly/6wck4*) have started providing secret scanning services that alert repository admins and organization owners about potential leaks.

- Finally, you can use infracode to help enforce security policy for your organization. Consider ways to harden the tools you're already using, employ automation to validate that policies are being followed, leverage change control systems to simplify preparing documentation in tandem with policy updates, and provide visibility by making your security policies and compliance auditable.

Wrapping Up

Whether or not *security* is part of your job title, maintaining the security of systems you oversee is a major aspect of your job as a system administrator. Think about the potential attack vectors that could harm the systems you manage and the reasons these vectors exist: mishandled credentials, misconfigured software, and uninstalled patches. To counter these risks, you need a multipronged approach to protect accounts, secrets, and infrastructure resources.

Traditional network security topologies focus on gateway firewalls, but this leads to a "candy bar" syndrome where the network perimeter was crunchy but the interior was soft and chewy. In a zero-trust model, the focus on the perimeter is dropped in favor of a "never trust, always verify" approach that places the emphasis on validating that each attempt to access any resource must come from a verified account on a trustworthy device, regardless of where the traffic originates. This also has the virtue of moving away from godlike root administrative accounts that have full control over things and toward a model of delegating accounts just enough access to perform the tasks they need to accomplish.

The zero-trust approach to security relies on an identity access management framework that allows you to audit the users and services authorized to access your resources, which in turn depends on a secrets management approach to protect the passwords and other access tokens used to gain access to resources.

When considering bringing a security mindset to your work, as with infrastructure as data and infrastructure as code, take an incremental approach, looking for specific areas where you can develop consistent, maintainable, and scalable security standards.

More Resources

You can learn more about zero trust from the following:

- John Kindervag's "No More Chewy Centers: Introducing the Zero Trust Model of Information Security" (*https://oreil.ly/7Nuaa*) published by Forrester Research.
- Google's implementation of the zero trust model: BeyondCorp (*https://oreil.ly/CLGm7*).
- If you are looking for a formal reference, check out NIST SP 800-207 (*https://oreil.ly/GiQXj*).

To learn more about securing your infrastructure, see the following resources:

- SLSA (*https://oreil.ly/AmWmy*), an effort to create a set of industry standards on improving infrastructure resources
- *Container Security* from Liz Rice (O'Reilly)
- A wide variety of security topics from experts in the industry with the book *97 Things Every Information Security Professional Should Know* edited by Tobias Macey (O'Reilly)

PART IV

Monitoring the System

You may be running any number of different systems. The following four chapters introduce a framework for identifying effective monitoring strategies, evaluating current monitoring tools and frameworks, and managing your monitoring data and your work through monitoring your career.

Complex systems monitoring adds application insights and deeper observability into the components of your system. In the past, system administration focused more on system metrics. And as you scale to larger and more complex environments, system metrics are less helpful and, in some cases, unavailable. In addition, individual systems are less critical as you focus on the quality of the application and the impact on your users.

CHAPTER 14

Monitoring Theory

Monitoring is measuring, collecting, storing, exploring, and visualizing data from infrastructure (including hardware, software, and human processes). Monitoring helps you answer the "when" and "why" questions of your work, and it informs business decisions that support humans working sustainably (e.g., hiring so that your sysadmins are not constantly working at total capacity).

In this chapter, I will help you think about monitoring by providing a framework for identifying effective monitoring strategies. I will differentiate monitoring from observability and explain the elements and steps of the monitoring process and how they work together. Understanding these mechanics at a high level will help you prioritize the other desirable outcomes monitoring makes possible, decide how and what you monitor, and increase visibility into your workflow, systems, and teams, regardless of the tools you choose.

Why Monitor?

There are many reasons to monitor and increase system visibility: to bring attention to weakness, fragility, or risk and to help you make better decisions. Some reasons for visibility include the following:

Problem discovery
> You are identifying problems and understanding issue resolution. For example, you could discover problems by monitoring latencies of web requests and identifying when slow MySQL queries are impacting customers.

Process improvement
> You are continuously improving team processes to increase accuracy and speed of task resolution, automate toil work, and improve overall efficacy while not

overworking the team. For example, you could improve processes by monitoring work queues to identify the impact on the team.

Risk management
You are identifying, evaluating, and prioritizing potential problems. For example, you could manage risk by monitoring software deployments and adjusting automation or processes to reduce the frequency and severity of surprises.

Baseline behaviors
You are indexing typical system behavior under a standard load. For example, you could establish baseline behavior by monitoring data over an extended period to see your service trends and analyze the impacts of special periods like holidays, weekends, and predictable news events like elections and sports.

Budget setting
You are identifying, evaluating, and prioritizing infrastructure investment and enforcing spending accountability. One way to set a budget is by monitoring infrastructure spending to identify areas where different solutions may be more cost-effective or set up constraints that enable engineers to test new solutions without worrying about a surprise bill.

Capacity management
You are building sustainable capacity based on business demand. For example, you could manage your capacity by monitoring infrastructure to identify when reserved instances will save money over ad hoc instances.

Monitoring is much more than implementing a single tool; it's identifying what you're trying to learn and desirable outcomes, assessing available tools, and implementing practices that best help you get there. In addition, thinking about why you are monitoring and establishing specific monitoring objectives encourages critical thinking around your business context so that you avoid copying a service provider's monitoring practices if they aren't a good fit for your goals.

Be Your Own Authority

Many practitioners tell us what to monitor and why, but I'm here to tell you that you are the best authority on the systems in your environment. Imagine, for example, that you are running a web service for your company. While it might be the same software in use at other organizations, the specifics of your web service will vary from other organizations. You know the risks of failure in different parts of the service and who is accountable for the live running of that service, from development to support. Software, configurations, processes, and people all affect your monitoring strategy to derive the most business value while helping the humans who run the software.

How Do Monitoring and Observability Differ?

Rudolf E. Kálmán introduced the concept of observability for linear dynamic systems in the '70s. Observability measures how well you can see inside a system under observation with just the outputs. A system, in this case, is the collection of interrelated objects that are treated as a whole to model behavior. For example, you might want to observe a single host, container, or complete distributed service.

Observability is not monitoring, and monitoring is not observability. Observability is a system property; monitoring is a multistep process of observing a system. Often, individuals think of monitoring as dashboards and production alerts. Framing monitoring in this manner leads people to define monitoring as a subset of observability. The problem with this definition then becomes: what do you call the other activities that you need to monitor? You end up with overlapping terminology to cover all the potential use cases while also increasing the potential for misunderstanding. Monitoring has always been a process with various practices across organizations.

In some ways, it's a lot easier to think about the "unobservability" of a system. For example, imagine that your customers experience a problem that your dashboards and alerts don't identify or explain. If your underlying data doesn't help you explain why and how the problem occurred, that indicates a lack of observability.

You can monitor the observability of your systems by assessing the variety of problems that occur, how often you can answer questions with existing data, and how often the final assessment of why a problem occurred is "I don't know."

It would help if you had observability when you want to find problems you don't know about and better tune the system's response. Observability is in the details.

You don't need observability in every system. So, for example, if you only care about whether a specific system is up and running and aren't trying to tune its resources, you don't need to figure out that system's observability. Implementing extensive tracing, even with sampling, just like configuring every metric on the off chance you need it, is a negative pattern.

Let's examine a real-world scenario. When I'm working on my MacBook Pro and the system starts to lag, how do I figure out the underlying cause? System logging collects events by default. I have installed iStat Menus to collect data from the physical components so I can see CPU, memory, and network exhaustion at a glance. And I haven't invested in any other monitoring, so when something goes wrong, I have to dig into system tools to observe the system.

How observable is my system? It depends. If I collected every single metric on my system, it would become unusable. So, instead, I have application and system tools as needed to trace down problem areas. I don't have deep visibility or automated problem identification and resolution of my system, but I do have the tools necessary to figure out most software issues on my laptop.

 Terms are constantly evolving across teams, organizations, and the industry. As a result, conflict arises in the monitoring community of practice, signaling a lack of shared context over how terms such as *monitoring* and *observability* are used and whether observability is a subset or superset of monitoring. When vendors want to market their solution, they may use the same terminology with subtle differences in meaning, leading to increased misunderstanding.

Take time to build the shared context within the team around your use of monitoring terms. Then as you assess different vendors' monitoring offerings, you will be better prepared to compare implementations and choose solutions that support your team.

Monitoring Building Blocks

Let's start by understanding the building blocks of monitoring: events, monitors, and the data to be collected.

Events

An *event* is a thing that happens, a fact you can track. An event may be system, application, or specific service. Events occur regardless of whether you monitor them. Here are some examples of events:

- CPU utilization at a particular time
- The execution of specific code
- A sysadmin shutting down an application

Monitors

A *monitor* is a tool that defines and captures the events of interest. Monitors are either fixed (predefined things you know about) or flexible (ad hoc things you don't know about yet). Fixed monitors are specific functional checks against known issues you don't customize at runtime. You might use fixed monitors with event logs and CPU or memory gauges. Flexible monitors are checks that you can change ad hoc. Tracing is an example of a flexible monitor that captures and records events. For instance, on a Linux system, you can run strace on a process to capture all the system calls made. You use flexible monitors when diagnosing issues, qualifying performance, or exploring how the system works.

Additionally, monitors can be either narrow or broad. Narrow monitors might define an event as a single instruction, like a triggered log. Broad monitors might define an event as an aggregate of instructions, for example, a single web request that results in many system activities.

Monitors can be event-driven or sampled periodically. Event-driven monitors execute when the event occurs and aggregate over the reporting period. Periodic sampling monitors run at a specific time interval, collecting a statistically significant number of events.

Data: Metrics, Logs, and Tracing

Monitors collect data about configured events into three main types: metrics, logs, and tracing. You automatically collect data from systems, devices, applications, and networks. You may be able to apply filters to limit your data collection or selectively sample to estimate rather than collecting everything accurately. I will dig into the finer details of monitoring data in Chapter 16.

First-Level Monitoring

The monitoring process includes a set of sequential steps: event detection, data collection, data reduction, data analysis, and presentation (see Figure 14-1).

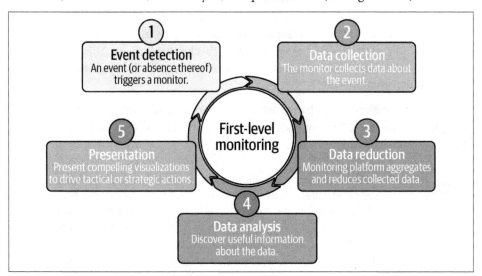

Figure 14-1. The five steps in first-level monitoring

Let's look at these five steps as depicted in Figure 14-1 individually.

Event Detection

The first step in the monitoring process is *event detection*; events trigger monitors. In addition, some monitors track the absence of expected events.

Data Collection

The second step in the monitoring process is *data collection*, when monitors collect data about triggered events. Monitored data can be collected by the monitored system in the following ways:

- Pushing the data to the central monitoring server on a schedule or based on an event
- Signaling the server to push the data
- Pulling data via a health check

Depending on the size of your environment and what you are measuring, a centralized monitoring system pulling data can create a scaling issue to process the number of monitored events on time and not make a backlog that impacts the performance of the service or discarded events.

The method of collection may create an observer effect; imagine the impact of a time-based collection strategy where every monitor checks at midnight. This frequency of monitoring can cause CPU or disk resource exhaustion, which increases latency and leads to unnecessary alerting.

The collection method may change what you monitor and how you monitor it. For example, metrics are generally event-driven and aggregated over time to compress data.

If you have metrics representing people, ensure you protect their privacy and obtain their consent to collect their data. With personal data and PII, you may have additional rules and regulations to follow, so avoid infringing user privacy by not tracking it in the first place.

Additionally, don't assume permanent consent, especially if you change the context or method of data collection. An example where you might need to think about this is telemetry data collected and logged from an individual's use of an application.

Data Reduction

In the third step, your monitoring platform aggregates and reduces the data. While data aggregation and reduction may happen at collection time, you may want to isolate these activities, particularly with distributed data.

Your monitoring agents collect data from many different sources. Your monitoring platform may aggregate, edit, sort, or compress the data into its essential parts.

For metrics, the older data is sometimes aggregated for storage purposes while providing some historical accounting to show differences against baselines. "Older" is contextual and could be weeks, months, or years. For example, monitoring request counts might not need six months of five-minute interval data. Instead, aggregate the count data for a baseline to compare against, accepting that you can't examine the original data with the reduced resolution.

Utilization over time of some metrics may be less useful. But on the other hand, storing metrics costs money, so aggregation is a balance of cost and usefulness.

Data Analysis

In the fourth step, you analyze the data to discover useful information about business and direct action. During this analysis, you identify a set of service-level indicators (SLIs) that help you measure the reliability of your system. Reliability may be measured by different dimensions depending on your service:

- Availability measures the length of the time the system functioned as expected.
- Latency measures the end-to-end time from source to destination to service a request. Latency of successful requests should be measured separately from failed requests. Often failed requests can be very fast.
- Throughput measures the number of requests passing through the system.
- Durability measures long-term data protection; the stored data doesn't degrade or get corrupted.

Once you have SLIs, you can identify the achievable and appropriate levels of reliability through setting service-level objectives (SLOs), which measure the expected system behaviors. Because it is challenging (and costly) to provide better reliability than what you depend on from external service providers, you must factor in those dependencies when setting your targets. Don't forget to factor in network and DNS.

Learn more about SLOs in Chapter 4 (*https://oreil.ly/KCy2H*) of Google's *Site Reliability Engineering* book and how to implement them in Chapter 2 (*https://oreil.ly/acmoK*) of *The Site Reliability Workbook*.

Learn more about the practical implementation of SLIs, SLOs, and error budgets from Alex Hidalgo's *Implementing Service Level Objectives* (O'Reilly).

Data Presentation

The fifth step in the monitoring process is the presentation of information. To transform data into information, you create visualizations. First, you collect charts into dashboards covering known bottlenecks and elevated risk areas. Next, you make other ad hoc visualizations to explore available data.

You may create charts based on real-time offline data. For example, alerts should be as close to real-time data as possible to limit the impact of problems. Quarterly capacity planning for a Hadoop cluster may be aggregating various data sources and processing offline.

Dashboards aggregate a set of visualizations to communicate information and are specific to your needs. For example, you could make a one-time strategic decision, determine day-to-day operational direction, or review the system weekly or monthly to establish a tactical approach. These dashboards are products that drive action. Outcomes and information should feed back into the various team and organizational processes.

Second-Level Monitoring

Your systems exist to do something, to provide a specific service. Monitoring doesn't keep your systems "safe." It helps you provide your organization's particular services by supporting the "when" and "why" of your work. Sidney Dekker introduced the concept of *drifting into failure*, that systems decline gradually and incrementally due to normalized growth of risk:

> Drifting into failure is not so much about breakdowns or malfunctioning of components, as it is about an organization not adapting effectively to cope with the complexity of its structure and environment.[1]

---

1 Sidney Dekker, *Drift into Failure: From Hunting Broken Components to Understanding Complex Systems* (Boca Raton, FL: CRC Press, 2011).

Jens Rasmussen developed a state-based model of a sociotechnical system surrounded by three boundaries (economic failure, unacceptable workload, and acceptable performance) to conceptualize the risks to the system of operating near these boundaries.[2]

Adding more critical analysis—double-loop learning—adds a second level of monitoring as you incorporate the data from your first-level monitoring back into your system to visualize better where the system is heading and the emergence of the system properties in operation. Double-loop learning is predicated on leadership entrusting people to learn incrementally through trial and error, analysis, and reflection and make the appropriate changes.

 Learn more about this state-based model from Dr. Richard Cook's 2013 Velocity NY speech "Resilience in Complex Adaptive Systems" (*https://oreil.ly/l1fw7*).

Wrapping Up

You need a data-driven approach to manage your infrastructure and implement a monitoring framework to answer "when" and "why" questions about your systems. The information provided by monitoring can help you discover problems, improve processes, mitigate risks, validate resource allocation choices, and make informed capacity planning decisions.

Monitoring and observability aren't the same concepts; depending on who you ask, you may get a different answer. Observability is an intrinsic property of a system that exists regardless of whether you are monitoring that system; monitoring is the multistep process of observing the system. Monitoring involves event detection, collecting, filtering, distilling, analyzing data, and presenting. This process drives decisions you make about how to manage your systems.

By adopting double-loop learning and incorporating feedback from your monitored system to introduce change in your system, you better avoid drifting into failure.

---

2 Read more about modeling risk management from Jens Rasmussen's paper "Risk Management in a Dynamic Society" (*https://oreil.ly/ewYMX*).

CHAPTER 15

Compute and Software Monitoring in Practice

Supporting a service for a long time attunes you to operational cues that warn of system problems. You can quickly glean helpful information from event logs. But someone new to the team doesn't have the benefit of time and experience with your systems, so they won't be able to get useful information from trawling through the same event logs and metrics. Moreover, if the job requires distilling all the nuance about the system from logs and metrics alone, there is inadequate monitoring and documentation.

If you manage a wide range of systems, the questions you must answer are: what can you monitor, and what has business value? Your environment and business goals are unique, so your answers to these questions may not look like anyone else's. For this reason, I will not prescribe a specific monitoring strategy in this chapter or tell you to monitor four metrics to complete your monitoring setup.

Instead, in this chapter, I will help you discover what monitors matter to you and offer methods for evaluating different tools and frameworks to help you imagine how to use them. Monitoring outputs must tie directly to your business value and encourage team resilience.

Identify Your Desired Outputs

When planning a monitoring strategy, many start with "What should I monitor?" Instead, I propose that the first question should be "What do I need now?" or "What is causing problems with the way my team works?"

At the top of Figure 15-1, the typical metrics show everything is fine, but the customer has a specific expectation for the cupcakes and is unhappy. Of course, the system administrator could add chocolate. Still, effective administration requires considering what data to collect, how to capture it, and what overall service level indicators should be used to change the system's outcomes.

At the bottom of Figure 15-1, the system administrator identifies a missing quantitative measure of chocolatey-ness. There are still standard metrics to assess the final product. And they've added a monitor that measures the chocolate of the instance so that they can add more chocolate as needed by a customer's specific expectations. Now they can respond directly to the customer's needs and improve the value of the delivered service.

Figure 15-1. A system administrator monitoring the output of their system, adding a new monitor, identifying that they have insufficient chocolate monitoring, and responding accordingly (image by Tomomi Imura)

Recall the steps in the monitoring process from Chapter 14, as shown in Table 15-1.

Table 15-1. Examples of the different monitoring outputs

Monitoring process step	Outputs
Event detection	Monitors
Data collection	Metrics, logs, traces
Data analysis	Service level indicators, logging platform queries, alerts
Data presentation	Service level objectives, charts, dashboards

Each step of the monitoring process has specific artifacts that arise as outputs. So instead of thinking about what to monitor (and focusing on event detection), think about the specific outputs that will improve your processes or overall outcomes (e.g., dashboards, service level indicators, detailed metrics, or monitors).

Of course, outputs that come later in the monitoring process depend on earlier steps, so when planning a project, recognize those limitations in dependencies to limit unexpected slips and missed deadlines.

Now that you've considered the different monitoring steps, consider what you should monitor.

What Should You Monitor?

Start where you are. Use what you have. Do what you can.
—Arthur Ashe

Figuring out precisely what you, in your specific situation, should be monitoring requires a multipronged approach: narrow the scope of what you're trying to accomplish in any project to increase your chances of success (do what you can now), figure out the right questions to ask yourself (monitor what matters), and then make small changes with an iterative approach and a continuous learning mindset.

Do What You Can Now

Monitoring can be overwhelming, especially when you know some of what needs to change and those changes all require funding and executive buy-in that will take months to achieve. The secret to sustainable real-world monitoring is to focus on what you can do now—make incremental changes possible today and continuously work toward your larger goals. Monitoring is never "done." So it's best to get yourself into a continual-process mindset.

I've been part of many "implement monitoring" projects where management wanted a quick win and to be finished with monitoring. If you find yourself in this situation, repair the misunderstanding about your project. Narrow the scope of your monitoring project to something you can track successfully and ensure the opportunity to improve.

Think back to the six areas of monitoring covered in Chapter 14: problem discovery, process improvement, risk management, baseline behaviors, budget setting, and capacity management. The first step in communicating your project's scope is to define your focus areas. The more areas you include in the project, the bigger and more prolonged the project. The longer the project, the harder it will be to come up with an accurate completion date. As with software development, you should prefer small incremental changes to your monitoring strategy because this allows you to roll back or modify changes that are not helpful (or actively harmful). Explicitly communicating your project goals can help convince upper management of the changes you suggest.

Define explicitly what your project entails and don't try to do everything immediately. Narrow your focus and start with what you have now, including the benefits and problems with your current solution. Think about which outputs of your monitoring process will be improved or changed. When communicating to your management and peers, be clear about the objectives rather than overusing terminology (e.g., "Improve problem discovery for identifying issues in long-tail web requests" versus "Fix monitoring"). Don't get into how your methods might change as you progress in your project, but provide the desired outcomes.

Assess what you have in place now. Note how the current implementation helps or hinders the monitoring process, including how to analyze and present information. For example, while you can collect data about all the different applications, operating systems, and compute resources, are you trying to create a single dashboard to encompass all of the collected data? Simplify the dashboard to focus on what matters most to your customers, as you can't pay attention to everything. Even trying may hinder you from seeing key problems that impact customers. Doing this review may help you uncover an area of focus that is highest in priority.

Suppose you are trying to implement exploratory monitoring with the ability to analyze data for unknown trends or performance issues. In that case, you probably want a minimal proof of concept focusing on areas that can show business value.

 Document issues in your work tracking system as this information adds depth and coverage to your monitoring assessment. For example, each page out to an on-call engineer that led to no completed work is a rich area for process improvement. Without supporting documentation, you may not focus on the most necessary improvements.

Monitors That Matter

You may have heard of the four golden signals (latency, errors, traffic, and saturation) from Chapter 6 (*https://oreil.ly/HqYFQ*) of the *Site Reliability Engineering* (O'Reilly) book from Rob Ewaschuk. In addition to the four golden signals, there are a couple of other commonly recommended monitoring methods:

- The RED Method, a microservices-oriented pattern for instrumenting and monitoring introduced by Tom Wilkie that encourages you to monitor the following (for every resource):

    — Rate (the number of requests per second)

— Errors (the number of requests that are not successful)

— Duration (the length of time that a request takes)

- The USE Method (*https://oreil.ly/H4N9E*), a system performance methodology introduced by Brendan Gregg that encourages you to monitor the following (for every resource):

— Utilization (the percentage of time that the resource was busy)

— Saturation (the amount of work the resource has to do, often queue length)

— Errors (the number of error events)

If you look at your environment from the top down, from the user's perspective, focus on the RED method. Otherwise, use the USE method if approaching from the bottom up and focusing on the resources with user impact.

You may have noticed that these signals aren't sufficient to cover your concerns in your environment. That's OK! Golden signals are a starting point and do not apply to every environment. My goal here is to encourage and empower you to decide for yourself what is most important for you to monitor.

Plan for a Monitoring Project

Start with reviewing the architecture for the specific system associated with the problem you want to solve. This may be a single system with different components or a complex service with multiple applications. As you go through the process, you can update your architecture diagrams. Ask yourself these questions:

- What OS is used (including specific distribution, version, patch level, and installed packages)?
- Are there any network access control lists (ACLs): subnet configurations?
- What does my traffic look like (e.g., requests per second, request types, and data written/read)?
- What kind of computing environments are in use (e.g., how much, and what type? What are the specific configurations in use?)?
- How is my compute infrastructure built, configured, and updated?
- Is there an application service layer that is serving requests?
- What are the different services running on the system?
- How is data stored? There might be multiple data stores.
- Is there a backend database? If so, what database software, software version, and database schemas are in use?
- Is data replicated to a secondary location?

- Is data backed up?

- Are there data processing pipelines? Are they stream-based or batch-oriented?

- Is there a load balancer? What kind of load balancer?

- Are there specific user API endpoints? Are there system-level API endpoints that users shouldn't use?

- Where is caching enabled? At the application level, within a database, in memory, externally on a CDN, or within a user's browser?

- Is there a message queue?

 Readily available tools in self-managed infrastructure are not generally available with serverless platforms. So you can see overall health, but digging into specific problems can be confusing, if not completely impossible.

Monitoring serverless services may require additional collaboration with the software engineering team building the functions, apps, or containers. For functions, all the code needed at function invocation time needs to be bundled in with the function deployment. You will need to write and commit the monitoring code directly to the project repository to deploy it with the function's code.

As you examine and assess your environment, think about these questions:

- What data am I missing about events in my environment?
- What data am I collecting?
- What data should I stop collecting?

You may have overlap in monitors, although sometimes this is for different purposes with varying levels of granularity. Intentional overlapping monitors are acceptable if you don't use the monitors for the same purpose. For example, if a single event causes multiple pages to an on-call engineer, that is problematic because it contributes to alert fatigue (desensitization to noisy alerts) and should get deduplicated.

Assess and document which of the various OS, system-level, network, and application monitors are informing which parts of necessary monitoring. You don't want to accidentally remove critical monitors. Sometimes as your monitoring matures, it seems like an easy win to simplify and ease storage costs by removing monitors. However, if you are looking only at a single focus of visibility (i.e., problem discovery), you might miss the reason for those monitors' existence (i.e., budget planning or capacity management).

Remember, there is a difference between what you monitor and what you alert on. Consider eliminating alerting on some events. Continue to refine what you are working on, and don't try to do everything; start with what you have and work on the problems with your current solution. If you have no monitoring, that's the first problem to solve!

Think about the underlying TCP/IP limitations and whether network bandwidth limitations constrain the total number of metrics and logs you can measure in a time period. Note all the tools and scripts in use for monitoring. Document overlapping monitors and their purpose. Note areas where refactoring of monitors may improve storage and network costs. Also, document areas where visualizations are confusing or distracting.

There may be additional areas to assess for missing monitors. Don't get distracted trying to identify all missing monitors, as that is a large-scale project. Instead, be really specific about the focus area of your system.

Recall from the Introduction that reliability measures how well a system consistently performs its specific purpose. To measure reliability, you must understand the system's purpose and underlying expectations. Each infrastructure component will have a different way to assess reliability.

Case Study: Examining a Message Queue

Let's look at an example of assessing reliability for a single component of a system—a message queue. Recall from Chapter 1 that a message queue comprises an event producer, a queue, a broker, and event consumers. Based on the implementation, consider these areas when collecting information to measure reliability:

Message storage
> The size of messages stored.

Message latency
> How quickly does a message of a specific size take to get from producer to consumer? Depending on the architecture of your system, you may need multiple metrics that cover within a single region and across regions.

Message throughput
> The size and rate of messages sent and consumed per time period.

Consumer lag
> The number of messages waiting to be consumed by a consumer.

Connection load
> The number of message producers and consumers and the number of concurrent connections the system supports.

Hot topics
> Topics that have higher rates of requests.

Quotas
> If a quota is implemented to prevent hot topics, be aware of limitations as topics approach that quota.

Errors
> And of course, you want to collect any errors that are reported by your system.

The message queue software will also have specific application metrics based on its architecture. In addition, the underlying compute infrastructure may have other metrics that matter.

This is just a single component of a system, and if you alert on every single part of this component, you could get duplicate alerts when something goes wrong. Depending on your monitoring framework, a standard recommendation or dashboard may present data as long as you are collecting it. (e.g., Datadog, a monitoring and analytics platform, provides a Kafka dashboard (*https://oreil.ly/s8K3R*).)

These recommendations might be a good starting place for you if you have no monitoring, but you are the best expert to analyze which data has direct business value.

What Alerts Should You Set?

In the past, sysadmins based alerts on system metrics like low CPU and memory or latency of requests rather than any direct user impact. Unfortunately, focusing on system metrics can lead to excessive effort and disruption in daily work.

In large-scale environments I've managed in the past, this might look like getting paged for a disk failure, high CPU utilization, or a stopped single virtual machine. And, when there was a real problem with the service, multiple alerts would go out. I would have to acknowledge alerts when I was already figuring out what was wrong. During my regular workday, these excessive alerts were yet another interruption. But, at night, these interruptions could add to significant sleep disruptions. At the time, this was considered acceptable. I was frustrated. During planning cycles, these interruptions were considered nonimpactful, so no one felt any urgency to repair the underlying problems.

So how do you get out of this style of alerting trap? First, what is important about the system(s)? What is urgent to repair? For every alert, it should be evident what the impact of the failure is, even if the underlying cause isn't understood. Present the data that has led to the alert so that the on-call engineer can take the appropriate next steps.

Based on the assessment of your environment, your system should produce data that you can use to measure your system's state with the sustainability measurements that matter. Then, look at the data and identify suitable candidates for SLIs or service quality measurements that align with user impact. A good SLI measures from the user's perspective. For example, for a web service, taking a user perspective might be whether a page loaded successfully and in a timely manner.[1]

Measuring in Percentiles

Tracking every event in your system is prohibitively expensive. Instead, sample. A sample is a part of the total population of measurements.

Percentiles are a common statistical measurement that splits a sample into one hundred equal-sized intervals. Percentiles are more accurate than averages, which assume that the distribution of measurements follows a bell curve. With percentiles, you can better communicate the measurements' distribution.

Learn more about sampling from "Cheap and Accurate Enough: Sampling" (Chapter 17) of *Observability Engineering* from Charity Majors et al. (O'Reilly).

As with other parts of your monitoring strategy, you should continuously improve the alert configuration as you learn from the system.

 Talk about alerts. The earlier, the better. When alert fatigue sets in, people start ignoring alerts or disabling them, and those adjustments can get lost in the mix of all the other work leading to more impactful system failures.

Sometimes, you may avoid alerting by incorporating failure handling within the system's design. For example, your system might automatically serve a degraded service rather than error out. While you still want it measured, the paging service doesn't need to alert you at 2 a.m. because your system is still serving your customers.

From SLIs, you can identify acceptable reliability and define your service-level objectives (SLOs). To start, your SLOs need to match up to your current environment. Then, as you make improvements to the system, you can update those SLOs. SLOs are either a specific target value or a range of values for a system that you are measuring. For example, the web service from the previous example might have an

---

1 If you're working with websites, you need to understand why page load time matters. Pingdom.com offers data analysis on bounce rates based on page load time (*https://oreil.ly/m82hX*).

SLO of "99% of web service requests should complete successfully in less than 1 second."

You may modify these up or down depending on the team's current state. For example, for teams that spend too much time on the toil work to keep the live site up, it might be that adjusting the SLO down to spend engineering cycles to improve the systems in use is critical.

 As mentioned in Chapter 14, Alex Hidalgo's *Implementing Service Level Objectives* is a great resource for learning the practical implementation of SLIs, SLOs, and error budgets.

Examine Monitoring Platforms

Early monitoring shaped many of our current platforms and assumptions about monitoring. One of the first-generation monitoring platforms was Nagios (*https://oreil.ly/oDQsk*), open source software that provides monitoring and alerting along with community-contributed plug-ins (*https://oreil.ly/FdZRS*). Many sysadmins deployed Nagios for host monitoring and alerting. However, there were no ready-made packages and configurations, no infrastructure as code, and no GitHub. While Mark Burgess had introduced CFEngine, it was not widely understood or used.

You had to download the Nagios source code, configure the software, and build it before installing it. The configuration of the running system was complex, and if there was a misconfiguration, it was possible to break your monitoring. If you didn't have monitoring for your monitoring server, it could be difficult to recognize that you didn't have active monitoring of the rest of your site or services.

You configured Nagios per host with associated services and specific checks. That check was the event monitor deployed to the system. Over time, with increasing complexity in systems, the limitations of Nagios frustrated users. Some of these limitations included the following:

- Duplication of alerts leading to excessive notifications
- Static configuration that isn't easily updated in a dynamic environment (e.g., every time an IP address changed, you had to restart Nagios)
- Easy to forget to turn a silenced alert back on
- People forgetting to silence alerts for planned outages
- Challenge to maintain checks
- Lack of complex integrated service checks

Even with all these frustrations, Nagios enabled sysadmins to discover problems before support calls, which helped reduce customer support costs and increased business value.

 Be aware that there are still many environments that use Nagios. However, it is possible to have an improved alerting system through modern integrations with incident resolution service platforms like PagerDuty (*https://oreil.ly/u35Bz*).[2]

Monitoring platforms continue to evolve as the community shares recommended practices, leading to improvements in the platforms, new practices, and specialization to focus on specific parts of the monitoring process. Platforms are getting more complex and changing rapidly, so look directly at the resources for those platforms to get up-to-date information and how-to guides.

There is no single solution for all steps in the monitoring process, so depending on your project scope, make sure that the solutions you are examining target that particular step of the process. You can install and manage the software yourself, or leverage hosted solutions like these:

- Metrics Collection (e.g., Prometheus, Graphite, InfluxDB, Datadog, Azure Monitor, AWS CloudWatch, and Google Cloud Operations)
- Visualization (e.g., Grafana and Kibana)
- Alert Management (e.g., PagerDuty, Opsgenie, VictorOps, and xMatters)
- Log Management (e.g., Splunk and Humio)
- Data Analysis (e.g., Google Data Studio)

Choose a Monitoring Tool or Platform

The challenge of choosing a monitoring tool or platform can be complex and fraught with emotion. Hosted monitoring solutions can be perceived as expensive compared to in-house custom solutions. Individuals can be wary of security compromises because there may be personal data that hasn't been adequately filtered out of logs. So when the CIO or CTO hears that fancy and convincing marketing presentation on observability and decides the organization will implement monitoring based on a specific tool, they may not have the specific context of what is already happening. Given some top-down-driven request, your first job is to find out what is already in use and if it's working or not.

---

2 One integration is the Perl Wrapper Nagios Integration for PagerDuty (*https://oreil.ly/v9fBp*).

Suppose you are managing an in-house custom monitoring system. In that case, this is an opportunity to escalate to your leadership to obtain a budget (resources and time) to assess and eliminate the bottlenecks preventing your team from having a contemporary monitoring strategy that leverages available solutions. The work of maintaining a custom system hinders your ability to focus on the systems that derive business value to your organization. In addition, it requires specialist knowledge about the custom monitoring solution that may not be translatable to other common skills in the industry (making it harder for you to find new opportunities in an industry where you can apply those skills).

To implement monitoring platforms (whether self-managed or hosted), you will likely need a combination of tools rather than one single tool to provide all desired results. There are two absolutes:

- Don't choose a tool because it's the one everyone else is using.
- Determine your outcome and desired behaviors before selecting a tool.

If you're looking to track and display and analyze collected, fixed monitors (i.e., you want to configure specific events against known thresholds), ask yourself these questions when evaluating monitoring platforms:

- How are metrics collected?
- What data model is used for metrics collection, and how is it stored? (Don't make assumptions about how data is stored. Just because a specific monitored event occurred does not mean that data about that specific event is stored in a way that you can describe it accurately based on querying your metrics data later.)
- Can you query the raw data? Do you need to learn a different language, and is it similar to other languages that your team already knows?
- How is data aged out?
- What integrations do you need? Do you have third-party services that the tool needs to work with? Are there ready-made integrations available, for example, Slack or PagerDuty?
- Is the tool extendable with plug-ins or mix-ins?
- For application monitoring, are the languages used within your applications supported with instrumentation? (Even if developers are responsible for instrumenting the code they write, you still need to understand what is happening and how it's getting monitored. You may need to provide guidance on what to instrument and the specific tool usage.)

- How quickly do events get detected, collected, reduced, and presented?

One challenge to be aware of when looking at data collection of a monitoring platform is the data resolution. You need subsecond monitoring when building platforms and services that require customer commitments of seconds. If your monitoring system can get data only at one-minute intervals, the sampling is biased and may not be accurate to the customer experience.

Another challenge is that you may need to connect and contextualize data from different applications, systems, regions, or colocated data centers to identify and debug a problem. Time is relative, especially if NTP isn't running, and timestamps for connected events widely vary.

If looking at hosted services, examine the following:

- Integration with configuration management systems.
- Ephemeral instances can be costly depending on whether the cost of the service is per instance and the period at which instances are counted.
- Whether it's possible to test integrations.
- Isolation of non-prod from production systems.

For visualization, don't limit yourself to what your monitoring platform provides. For example, with R and D3, it's possible to create visualizations as long as you have access to the raw data. Every tool will have strengths and weaknesses depending on what you are monitoring.

You may want to reread Chapter 10 to apply the skill of distilling information to convey meaning and drive your desired goals with your systems.

Wrapping Up

This chapter provided a framework to assess and plan monitoring projects to meet your organization's needs. Consider the problems you might want to address: problem discovery, process improvement, risk management, baseline behaviors, budget setting, and capacity management. Achieving all of these in a single project is unrealistic. Narrow the project's scope, communicate specifics with stakeholders, and include assessments for what is in use.

A reliable system should be a sustainable one in which you are not paged needlessly. Service-level indicators (SLIs) help you define benchmarks for the metrics that matter and the results that align with customer impact. With the right SLIs in place, you can define service-level objectives (SLOs) that set expectations for how well the system performs. SLOs can be a valuable lens for ensuring that the high-level results your customers want to see and the backend technical details your team needs to manage are appropriately aligned.

Several products have emerged to deliver facets of monitoring pipelines. If your organization uses homegrown tools, it may be time to consider a modern approach. Additionally, consider how a collection of these different tools can fit together to give you and your stakeholders a complete picture of your system's reliability and sustainability.

CHAPTER 16

Managing Monitoring Data

Five hundred years ago, sailors learned that casting a line behind their ships could calculate how fast they were moving. They used a line knotted at regular intervals and a log tied to the end. First, they would toss the log overboard and count how many knots on the rope had spooled behind the ship in 28.8 seconds to calculate its speed. Then, they would record the observed speed (number of knots) in a logbook or log journal.

These logbooks became an essential reference source, recording daily information and significant events, including speed, course, astronomical observations, weather events, crew information, ports visited, and maintenance records, which are vital for safely navigating journeys across the open ocean. In addition, navigators used the journals in future trips with the additional context about the present weather conditions to decide what course to steer to reach the desired destination safely. Finally, the logbooks are used as official evidence if an unfortunate event occurs.

Modern computing doesn't use knotted ropes, but it still uses logs metaphorically, in addition to metrics and tracing. So, just as sailors used maritime logs to record observations of speed and position on journeys across the oceans, you keep track of your systems with metrics, logs, and tracing so that you, as the "navigator" of these systems, can keep track of the state of your systems and make predictions. This chapter will help you manage your monitoring data (metrics, logs, and tracing) as a crucial part of your journey to navigate present and future system conditions and provide historical context when debugging an event.

What Is Monitoring Data?

The call comes in. It's late, after midnight. A critical outage is in progress, and the team has been trying to figure out the problem for hours, but they're stuck, and now you've been pulled in. Where do you start?

With your monitoring data. *Monitoring data* is all the events that you've decided are necessary to collect about your systems. This data may be in the form of metrics, logs, and tracing. It may be temporary or saved to disk, continuous or rare. As discussed in Chapter 14, there are many reasons to collect this data.

Effective monitoring data management requires that the data is immutable, that it can't be modified once created, that it has an explicit policy around how long it's stored, and that you have the correct data accessible when needed.

There are trade-offs to consider when implementing metrics, logs, or traces.

Metrics

Metrics are measurements of event properties of interest. Most system metrics are timestamped numeric values represented as a counter or gauge. For example, you might collect requests per second for a web service to measure a site's popularity.

A *gauge* is a value that reflects a point in time, although it doesn't tell you anything about the previously measured values.

A *counter* is a cumulative value that reflects events since a point in the past. It may roll over when a counter reaches its upper or lower limit. For example, you can use counters to measure per time interval and reset at the time interval. You can also reset counters based on certain system events (such as reboots) or on request.

Let's look at the difference between a gauge and a counter. A car's speedometer is a gauge that tells you how slow or fast you are driving. You use that information to guide your immediate actions by knowing whether you are traveling within posted speed limits. On the other hand, the car's odometer is a counter that tells you how far you have gone. You use that information to guide preventive services like tire rotation and oil changes.

For each monitoring platform under evaluation, carefully examine the provided metric types, as the implementation will affect how the data about your events is collected and stored. For example, if the platform reduces or aggregates data too early, it may provide insufficient information for debugging purposes. On the other hand, if data reduction and aggregation are too late, your monitoring traffic may flood your network, impacting network performance and the quality of service.

Logs

Logs are append-only, immutable, timestamped records of events. Logging allows you to preserve a history of activities on a system. Events such as system startup and shutdown, service start and stop, and network activity are examples of recorded activities in logs. When you need to know what has happened on a computer, you depend on logs to provide this information. Here are some examples:

- At boot time, your OS dutifully checks for obsolete and inapplicable hardware—floppy drives, modems, printers, fax machines—and reports a "warning" or "error" if such hardware isn't detected.

- A cron job runs every 10 minutes and logs to the system logs the status of its run.

- A background process faithfully logs an error in a config file thousands of times daily.

Generally, logs are unstructured; the file format does not provide context or meaning to fields. Everyone has different ideas about what activity goes into a log file and how it should be structured. While certain conventions exist per language or application, people don't always choose to follow conventions.

For example, consider timestamps. Applications log in different date formats (e.g., YY/MM/DD, MM/DD/YY, DD/MM). Then there are time zones and daylight saving time adjustments. A typical exercise of collating a sequence of events from different log files becomes a journey of discovery with your favorite scripting language's regular expression syntax. Moreover, event timestamps are only as precise as the date format allows: reconstructing a rapid sequence of events that spans multiple sources is difficult if the dates don't have subsecond precision.

 Learn about different log formats in Graylog's tech series post called "Log Formats—A (Mostly) Complete Guide" (*https://oreil.ly/ Xim6V*).

Structured Logs

Structured logs have a key-value format that makes it easier for computers to process but harder for humans to read. Application configuration changes may affect which fields are displayed but won't impact existing scripts to parse logs.

Structured logs allow applications to use arbitrary text to describe events but enforce consistent use of a defined list of fields with uniform data types. Dates, for example, are encoded in UTC with microsecond precision or better; the log management software handles rendering timestamps in a user-friendly format. This is also more space-efficient: a text timestamp like "Thursday, May 4, 2017 6:09:42 AM GMT-04:00" is 42 characters long but is 1,493,908,962,000 microseconds in Unix epoch time, which can be encoded as a 4-byte decimal integer.

Early sysadmins became fluent with reading through streams of log text, but this doesn't scale for the complex systems you oversee today. First, there's too much inconsistency in the individual log files; maintaining tools for analyzing such text streams is a never-ending task. Worse, there are just too many logs for anyone to read them all.

Modern operating systems provide a logging framework consisting of an indexed database with structured fields: journald on systemd-enabled Linux distributions, Apple System Log (ASL) on macOS, and the Windows Event Log on Windows.

Tracing

Tracing is a specialized form of logging that allows you to see into a running system. A *trace* is a rich set of data that tells the (ordered) story of an event through a system. Examples of tools that provide tracing include strace and tcpdump.

Distributed Tracing

Distributed tracing is a specialized form of tracing that instruments an application to provide rich logs and metrics across different systems to connect contextual data across systems.

Consider the (simplified) sequence of events involved in responding to a user request for a contemporary product website:

1. Browser resolves website URL into an IP address.
2. Browser sends a web request (e.g., HTTP, HTTP/2 or QUIC).
3. Server responds (i.e., 200 for success, 400 errors for client side errors, or 500 errors for backend server errors) with static resources such as images, CSS files, and JavaScript.
4. Browser begins to render the page.
5. Browser issues additional requests.

A tech-savvy user can use browser-based tracing to step through the elements of such a transaction, providing feedback about how long each stage of the request took to fulfill and any reported errors.

For your system, you need instrumented deployed code that tells you what's happening during request processing. There is no guarantee that you will be able to replicate what a user is experiencing from your own browser, and you are not guaranteed a tech-savvy user who can provide you with a detailed browser-based trace.

OpenTelemetry (*https://opentelemetry.io*) is an open source collection of tools, APIs, and SDKs for providing telemetry in software. In OpenTelemetry, a span is a single named and timed operation. Multiple spans make a trace.

Choose Your Data Types

How you collect, store, and explore your monitoring data is the basis for answering questions about what your systems are doing and what you need them to do next. Because most metrics are numeric values, they are optimized for storing, processing, and analyzing large amounts of data. As a result, metrics are great for dashboards, historical trends, and the system's overall health but provide only a limited amount of context, which minimizes the number of overall resources required to store them. In addition, they have a consistent format so you can easily size them over time; if you have a week's worth of a metric, you can estimate the growth of storage you will need over time.

Logs give you more context for the data you collect, but they take up more room in storage and take more time to process. Traces have the highest amount of context per event and require the most storage resources. With both logging and tracing, data can be lost. Logging libraries that leverage the Reliable Event Logging Protocol (RELP) can improve the reliability of message delivery, but this reliability does come with increased costs in infrastructure and may result in duplicate messages.

The cost of reliability with protocols like RELP may be worthwhile only for financial data, billing, or payment or to meet compliance regulations.

Additional thoughts to consider when choosing the type of data you need:

- Measure your daily volume and account for spikes.
- How long do you need the data?
- How are you going to use the data?
- Do you need live monitoring? (This requires low latency.)

Retain Log Data

Unbounded, log data will grow until it fills up the disk it is stored on. Traditional log management approaches to this problem included the following:

- Rotating log files regularly
- Compressing older logs
- Removing logs when they reach certain size or age thresholds

Unfortunately, some services don't play nicely with log rotation and will continue to write to the "old" log if allowed. So, your log rotation tools need to implement logic to force the software to reset itself at log rotation time when needed. Because log rotation typically happens once a day, if an application goes haywire, it can fill up the disk before the daily cleanup gets a chance to run, requiring manual intervention to resolve.

Modern log management frameworks handle log rotation automatically, allowing admins to set simple rules such as "use no more than 10 GB" or "keep at least 5 GB free." Furthermore, these policies are adhered to continuously, so if a service generates a sudden flood of log events, the framework takes action as needed to ensure that the rules are always followed.

Analyze Log Data

With traditional logs, finding a specific word meant opening the log in a text editor or leveraging a command-line tool like grep to search through the events in the file. Of course, this slowed down as log files grew. Filtering events by time spans, host, or other criteria is all possible, but knowing how to use regular expressions to construct complex search filters was a necessary skill.

When the logging framework is a database, you can issue queries in a mode similar to using SQL SELECT statements, using any of the indexed fields as filters. With an indexed database, the data is organized in a way that makes it efficient to randomly access information scattered throughout even large volumes of event data, for example, "Show me all events of severity WARN or higher since yesterday" or "Show me the events prior to the previous reboot." You can even perform retroactive debugging by requesting a detailed view of recorded events.

Monitoring Data at Scale

Now that you've aggregated all of this data, you need a framework for understanding what your systems are doing.

It's critical to record and expose the right information. Recall from Chapter 14 that observability is a property of a system—how much insight into your system's operation you are able to gain from the monitoring you have. Improving your systems' observability is an iterative process. If this is your first monitoring project in this system, you'll have only your team's experience and intuition as a guide. That's OK. As you gain system experience, be sure to incorporate that knowledge into your data pipeline.

Post-incident review is a great place to assess your monitoring data. Consider the following:

- How much of the troubleshooting was done by viewing your monitoring data? Those are your wins; your data saved you time and effort in those cases.

- Based on what you are already collecting, how much more could have been done? Those are data presentation opportunities. When it makes sense, add additional dashboards, alerting, or other visualizations to get more help from the data you already have.

- What troubleshooting steps had to be taken ad hoc because the necessary data didn't exist? Are you able to gain access to that data somehow? Perhaps the events are being collected but not stored, or there are additional configurations to increase the verbosity of logs. If your organization writes the software in question, should additional logging features be added to enable better detection or prevention of this type of incident?

Storing and analyzing monitoring data is costly, especially with logs and traces, so regularly check your data to ensure it is still valuable. You may be able to save money by reducing your collection parameters or incorporating more sampling.

Access control and data governance is another key concern for a maturing log management project. Perhaps you start by aggregating logs for your sysadmin team; everyone has access to everything. In that case, you won't have strict access control needs, but if your system is successful at saving you effort, word will get around. Soon others will want to share those benefits. Logs frequently contain sensitive data, and sharing everything with everyone isn't appropriate. Privacy requirements will dictate who can access logs that contain personal information. Data lifespan policies are also likely to apply depending on the data's nature and your environment. You may only be allowed to retain some logs for only a certain time—or required to keep others for at least some time.

Wrapping Up

Your monitoring data is crucial knowledge about your working systems that provides a historical recording of events and the success and failures that occurred. Effective system monitoring accounts for collecting the right data, storing it in a useful way, auto-expiring data that is no longer relevant, and using systematic methods for analyzing and presenting the information obtained about the running system.

Metrics are data presented in gauges and counters that provide insight into how the system is operating at a point in time and can be rendered in charts that reveal trends, patterns, and anomalies over time. Logs are how software records a history of events, and traces are a specialized form of logs used to provide a more detailed understanding of a particular aspect of how the system is operating. Both logs and metrics are useful for understanding the behavior of your systems, understanding the root causes for incidents, and making forecasts about how the system will need to evolve in the future.

Monitoring data, like any other data, needs to be managed thoughtfully. As your monitoring data archive grows over time, you'll need to pay attention to how much storage it consumes. Use your monitoring data to study incidents occurring on your systems, review how the data helped solve problems, and learn what gaps you need to fill. Making sense of incidents that span fleets of systems can be a real challenge, but a well-tuned approach to monitoring data can make this work easier.

CHAPTER 17

Monitor Your Work

Do not confuse things that are hard with things that are valuable. Many things in life are hard. Just because you are giving a great effort does not mean you are working toward a great result.

—James Clear

Across my career in operations engineering, I've experienced a challenge that stymies many in our industry: inadequate visibility. It is frustrating to have my impact minimized or misunderstood; finding the right narrative takes having the right metrics to tell that story. And, I haven't ever seen lines of code or the number of resolved issues as quality metrics to show my impact.

As an industry, we are starting to recognize the importance of sustainable systems. A system's health affects an individual's health, and their health in turn can impact the managed systems. In this chapter, I show the importance of monitoring your work so you can improve your effectiveness—much like your managed systems. The result is improving your consistency and reliability and achieving sustainable outcomes—for the system and yourself.

Why Should You Monitor Your Work?

Monitoring your work is about explicitly coordinating and collaboratively identifying appropriate and valuable work. In addition, visualizing the data you collect about your work helps you show your work in context versus using a list of completed tasks and projects.

Unfortunately, external pressures may push you to work on the wrong things or the right things at the wrong time. Sometimes you may feel driven by your expectations; your identity and self-worth often get intrinsically tied to specific work that may not serve you as a way to grow or leverage new opportunities.

Monitoring your work provides a mechanism that can signal when you reach a career rut. Doing the same task over and over can lead to stagnation, especially when it's work that you don't enjoy. It happens easily if you are good at that work, especially if no one else takes responsibility for it.

 Stagnation in a job is when you've done a job for 10 years but you don't have 10 years of experience. When you interview for a new job, prospective employers want to see that you have 10 years of different experiences showing your growth, not repetitive task management.

As illustrated in Figure 17-1, when you visualize your work, you can see better how your skills and talents overlap with the work you enjoy doing. It can also help you know where to focus your skill development and hone your abilities. And, it can help you see why you may be unhappy with your current job if you aren't doing any fun work.

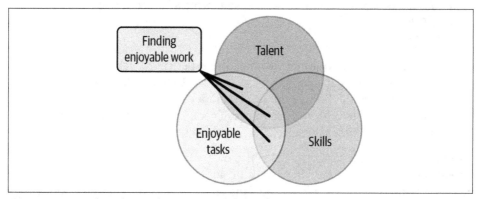

Figure 17-1. Finding the work you enjoy doing

You can do many types of work in your career as a sysadmin. Choose your path intentionally rather than letting arbitrary deadlines and emergencies dictate your direction.

When you track your work, you can better see your successes and use your time effectively.[1] It can also improve your feelings of agency:

- Feeling control and autonomy
- Identifying work that matters

---

1 Learn how to better manage your time from Thomas Limoncelli's *Time Management for System Administrators: Stop Working Late and Start Working Smart* (O'Reilly).

- Responsibility
- Identifying competence and expertise

<hr />

Impacts of Monitoring Your Work

Monitoring your work can have impacts beyond you. Consider the following:

- At the team level, you build stronger relationships and trust by seeing your coworkers' progress on critical tasks and projects by monitoring your work.

  In addition, visibility in the team's work helps to inoculate the team against support heroics by measuring and supporting sustainable practices.

- At the company level, monitoring your work helps to provide team-level evaluations and shift the perception of operations from the lone sysadmins to one of more collaboration and visual feedback.

<hr />

Manage Your Work with Kanban

There are many different ways to monitor and share the progress of your work. One option is Kanban, the Japanese word for visual signal and a visual workflow management system developed initially by Taiichi Ohno, an industrial engineer working for Toyota in the 1940s.

Adopting Kanban for your personal use is different than planning and implementing it for a team; in a team, no person should dictate how the team implements Kanban. Instead, team processes should support and integrate each person's needs, and people should be involved in designing and implementing a board that will manage their work.

Kanban hinges on understanding where you are now and your current state and provides mechanisms for introducing change in manageable ways. For a personal Kanban, the following rules will help you align with this objective:

- Start with what you do now.
- Agree to pursue incremental change.

The core principles of Kanban serve as guidelines for organizing and managing work:

- Visualize your workflow by tracking your work on a board.

- Limit your work in progress (WIP) so you can focus on completing what you start.

- Manage your work's flow to monitor its progress and understand how quickly you get tasks done.

- Continuously improve by evaluating the data about your work to identify areas of improvement and reduce the constraints that reduce the speed of work, also known as your bottlenecks.

Break work into chunks that you can get done in an approximate time. Remember, these are just estimates; no one expects you to predict the future successfully. Rather than nail down a specific time with numbers, use a "T-shirt size" that reflects the estimation. It helps avoid misusing or misunderstanding the time estimate. In Table 17-1, you can see an example of breaking down chunks of work into sizes.

Table 17-1. Approximating sizes for tasks

Size	Timing
XS	< 1 hour
S	< 4 hours (1 day max)
M	< 8 hours (2 days max)
L	< 20 hours (a week)
XL	> L; This is a project, not a task.

For example, adding a user to a system would be an "XS" task. Adding a new user to all the systems and services in an environment might be an "S" task based on the complexity of your environment. Setting up a new service would need to be broken up into several jobs, including setting up system accounts, which could be a large task or something more extensive than a task.

Projects have a more extensive scope and would have a different set of sizes. Table 17-2 shows how I size projects.

Table 17-2. Approximating sizes for projects

Size	Timing
S	> 1 week
M	> 1 month
L	> 1 quarter
XL	> L

Imagine that there is a critical upgrade that must happen by January 1. You estimate that this project is "Large." Based on that estimation, you won't complete the requirements if you wait until December 10 to start the work. Having a way to visualize this requirement provides you with the ability to push back on nonurgent, nonimportant requests that could make this slip.

When used in a team, sizes can support discussions with external stakeholders about prioritizing tasks and projects based on what's currently in progress when additional work is requested.

Once you can size your work, you can approximately compare it, and you're ready to map tasks to cards. Create a card for each task. Label the card with the information about the task (e.g., name, estimated scope, category of work). These cards can be different colors for various types of tasks. You might also add additional information like the value of the job (i.e., business value, customer requests, employee-driven). Furthermore, talk to a business stakeholder who can help you understand the critical measurements that they track. And then identify how to categorize your work to measure that impact.

Business needs and customer needs are often conflated. Something may be necessary to the business that isn't directly of interest to your customer. Additionally, you might identify critical work that isn't perceived as business value to your company. If you ignore all the things you think are important, you will not be happy. Finding the right work to provide the most value for the company and sustain your psychological and physical effort is essential.

You can start with a chart with three columns (ready, doing, and done) that represent a basic workflow:

Ready
　A bucket of your incoming work. This column reflects your to-do list.

Doing
　For all the work you have started (but have not yet completed).

Done
　For the work you have completed.

Over time, you may want to evolve the columns in your board so you can measure your workflow accurately and identify areas of improvement. Start by thinking about how you completed tasks and projects. Phases of the work should be reflected in the columns. You may find that tasks and projects have different phases. For example, maybe you regularly find your work blocked by someone else, and you want to keep track of that bottleneck (e.g., how long you have to wait on someone else to do the next steps in a task or how many blocked tasks you have at one time).

After you have the board and cards, stick the notes in the appropriate columns based on the task's phase. Now, you can view your backlog and active and completed work.

Next, you do work! When someone asks you to do something, you start working on a task, or you complete a task, and the card representing that task progresses through the stages.

Don't forget to track metrics about the work. These metrics may be something you manually have to update in a spreadsheet or provided by your chosen tool. After a couple of weeks, review the work you've completed and assess what you've accomplished. Then, think about a potential change you could make to improve your effectiveness.

Choose a Platform

There are so many tools available to track and visualize your work with varying levels of customization, including Trello, Atlassian Jira, GitHub Projects, Kanbanize, and Microsoft Azure Boards. Each tool varies in cost, metrics collected, dashboards, and API integrations. If a platform doesn't have integrated metrics, measure your work manually at the start so you have information about the impact of changes you make.

When making decisions for a team-based tool, know that no platform or technology will be perfect, especially if multiple teams have to use it. Sometimes sacrifices in the workflow have to be made based on cost and visibility across the organization. Management needs to be aware of that impact, help folks navigate the differences as much as possible, and recognize the criticality of the work that folks do regardless of the tools chosen.

For example, Scrum is generally not a great way for sysadmins to work, but plenty of folks try to force the team into that working model because Scrum is already in use within the organization. Tools implementing a Scrum style of project and task management will be frustrating if the team isn't already scrumming.

No generalized list will dictate what tool you choose personally, as every sysadmin will have different responsibilities and ways of doing their work. Some factors to consider, though, include the following:

Budget

> If you have to pay out of pocket for a tool, you may consider free options (i.e., GitHub Projects or Google Sheets).

Existing tools

> If your team is already implementing work tracking, you may want to use what's already in place. Additionally, you may be using other tools that can easily support you in importing your work into a visualization.

Features

> Every tool will have features; some have better metrics collection and visualization than others.
>
> Another feature might be the available APIs for integration. In the past, I have leveraged integration APIs to pull data from Bugzilla to populate Leankit. While the underlying concepts differed between Leankit (i.e., Board, Cards, and User) and Bugzilla (i.e., Product, Bug, and User), I wrote scripts to map those concepts to Task, Project, and Goal. Without the APIs, there wouldn't have been a way for me to map these one to one, and I would have had to wait for Leankit to provide that functionality.

Here are some additional questions that may help you decide:

- Can you query the raw data? Do you need to learn a different language to access the raw data? It's not helpful to put a bunch of data into a system if you can't get it back out in a usable way.
- Is data aged out?
- What integrations do you need? Do you need to work with third-party services? Are there ready-made integrations available?
- Is the tool extendable with plug-ins or mix-ins?
- What reports or dashboards are available to you?
- Can you categorize a task in multiple ways (i.e., with some tag)?

Even if additional reports or dashboards are not directly available in the platform, if you can pull raw data out to leverage other tools to create the necessary reports or dashboards, this may be sufficient for your purposes.

Find the Interesting Information

Once you track your work with a management system, you can start analyzing your collected data. Again, depending on the tool and what work management tool you use to track your work, you will have different metrics and visualizations available.

Let's look at interesting data from a "Ready, Do, Done" Kanban board (Table 17-3).

Table 17-3. Metric types for "Ready, Do, Done" Kanban

Type	Definition
Speed	The time that it takes for you to move a task from Ready, Doing, and Done, also known as the lead time
Throughput	The total number of jobs you completed for a unit of time
Load	The number of tasks in Do, also known as WIP
Process Efficiency	Work in progress/speed, also known as Little's law

By collecting metrics (i.e., speed, throughput, load, and process efficiency), you might find some interesting information:

Variability
> Keeping track of speed per task type can help you uncover areas of variability. For tasks with lower variability, you can better estimate the time it will take to complete a request.
>
> Keeping track of the types of work you are doing can help you monitor your job stagnancy. In this case, lower variability over time can signal that you should consider alternate work to ensure career growth.

Too much work in progress
> Keeping track of your load can show you how much context-switching you may be doing, impacting how quickly you can get work done or your overall throughput of completing tasks.

The balance of thoroughness and efficiency
> You are always making a trade-off between the resources (time and effort) you spend on researching and preparing to do an activity (thoroughness) and the resources (time, effort, and materials) you spend doing it (efficiency). This trade-off is known as the efficiency-thoroughness trade-offs (ETTO) principle.[2] When you prioritize throughput, efficiency is more important than thoroughness. When you prioritize the outcome's quality, thoroughness is more important than efficiency.

---

2 Erik Hollnagel, *The ETTO Principle: Efficiency-Thoroughness Trade-Off: Why Things That Go Right Sometimes Go Wrong* (Boca Raton, FL: CRC Press, 2009).

If you spend too much time thinking about how to solve the problem, you might not have enough time to do the work, and you might miss incoming requests. On the other hand, if you act too quickly without sufficient thought, you might not have enough information to do the right work, or you'll be poorly prepared.

You can understand and analyze any adjustments for every task to approach the task type more systematically. Additionally, you can examine the specific categorization of tasks and look at the following:

- Specific types of tasks that take longer.
- Tasks that get blocked frequently. Look for bottlenecks.
- Tasks where the work gets scrapped regularly. Lower the priority and urgency when you get these kinds of requests.
- Tasks that were fun (or problematic). If you can categorize things in different ways or mark tasks with this sentiment, you can measure the psychological effort of the workload and the impact of those tasks on your total throughput.
- Time spent learning or practicing specific skills. You can be more intentional about improving your skills in an area.

Wrapping Up

Once you have a method for tracking your work, you may want to support this more broadly across your team. Work with your team on making everyone's work visible.

In Chapter 21, I share a bit more about how to monitor your team's work. You need to integrate many people and diverse perspectives to get the job done. Bringing everyone together to share their vision can help visualize cross-team dependencies to understand better and prevent long wait times or wasted work.

> ## More Resources
>
> Learn how to manage your work and identify areas that may improve your processes with Dominica Degrandis's book *Making Work Visible: Exposing Time Theft to Optimize Work and Flow* (*https://oreil.ly/va8cC*) (IT Revolution Press).

PART V

Scaling the System

In the final part of this book, we'll examine how to prepare your system to scale (whether expanding or shrinking). It's not easy to know what and when to consider system changes. While experience can inform your approach in different environments, relying solely on this experience increases your risk of bias-informed planning. Eventually, you are going to do the wrong thing. Instead of trying to attain perfection and always do the right thing, build the guardrails in your system that support you when you make an incorrect prediction so that your system can adapt sustainably to the humans who are part of the system.

The landscape of user expectations has changed, with visible places of customer (dis)satisfaction. And to maintain the trust of your users (and potential users) so that you have the opportunity to grow your systems, you need the following:

- Capacity planning
- Resilient on-call practices
- Robust incident response to issues when you discover them (or worse, when your users find them)
- Leadership that empowers and fosters learning

CHAPTER 18

Capacity Management

Capacity management is the process of maximizing system output based on customer demand and business value while minimizing the costs to the humans supporting the systems. Historically, sysadmins focused on tuning system utilization to maintain good latency for real-time access systems or to reduce job runtime on batch systems. In contemporary environments, sysadmins may focus on scaling resource pools in self-maintained data centers, applications in cloud services, or both for hybrid environments.

In this chapter, I define capacity and capacity management and provide a framework to help you understand your capacity management planning process. This will help you prioritize the different engineering tasks involved in capacity management.

What Is Capacity?

Before I define capacity management, I need to talk about capacity. Capacity goes beyond just the absolute value of CPU, disk, or memory. Defining capacity also includes the measurable quantity of output producible while maintaining standards of quality and performance.

Capacity is not an exact measurement in systems but rather an approximation based on the information that you have. Over time, accumulated experience with how your customers use your system will allow you to fine-tune the capacity indicators you use to understand your system's capacity.

There are different measurements of capacity, depending on the specific metrics that matter to the system you are supporting. And there are a few ways to define capacity when describing your systems:

Design capacity

> When designing or evaluating the architecture of a system, you estimate the maximum potential output based on whatever tools you may have or previous experience. This estimation is the design capacity of that system. For example, you may benchmark a website and identify as a result that it supports one thousand concurrent user logins.

Production capacity

> When your system is faced with actual normal working conditions, you will be able to measure the real maximum output possible (including all of the operating constraints), and this is your production capacity. When a system is live, you have the data to drive observations based on the site's usage under normal working conditions to better qualify the capacity of the system. For example, users start experiencing impactful latency in your deployed system in production before hitting one thousand concurrent user logins. The site's production capacity is eight hundred concurrent user logins.

Effective capacity

> When your system is under normal working conditions and real-world constraints are added (impacts due to seasonal or economic events), maximum output is your effective capacity. For example, during an after-Christmas sales event, you notice that there are a number of cascading degradations in the system, leading to an effective capacity of three hundred concurrent user logins.

When describing capacity, be specific about which of these—design, production, or effective capacity—you are measuring or analyzing. The capacity constraints are the resources that limit the output of the system and can help you think through likely failure scenarios. These are sometimes called the bottlenecks and are generally where the system will fail first. Capacity constraints in your system might be limitations due to an underlying service dependency, specific hardware resources, or available individuals to do work. Based on the risk of the event, you can plan whether the constraint is acceptable or needs mitigation.

The Capacity Management Model

Capacity management is one area of engineering that sysadmins have the opportunity to focus on when not overwhelmed with toil work. Some parts of capacity work are day to day, and other parts are medium- to long-term design and planning projects.

Operational cost reduction is not the goal of capacity management, though it may be an outcome of applying quality capacity management practices. The goal of capacity management is to balance resource costs and customer demands through the following actions:

- Gathering knowledge over time to guide growth and declines
- Qualifying availability of people and resources to support new projects and changes in current projects
- Identifying periodic cycles from holidays, special events, site-specific tax season in the US, and elections.

With capacity management, it's crucial to understand the business value of the system you are managing. Failing to practice capacity management leads to missed deadlines, lost opportunities, and customer attrition.

Take a look at Figure 18-1 for the four resource components of capacity management.

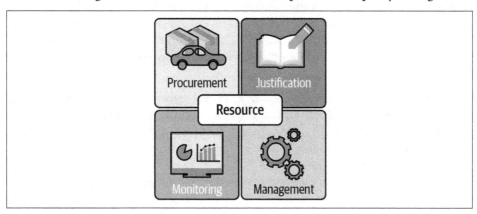

Figure 18-1. Capacity management model

Let's look at these different components in more detail, starting with procurement.

Resource Procurement

Procurement processes vary based on the behaviors and structures of differently sized companies. Small companies may pay more for equipment or resources because of the size of their order but may have fewer gating factors to approval, while larger companies may be oriented to have multiple groups involved and approvals needed before a requisition can begin in earnest.

When planning for the data center, factor in overhead, long-term hardware costs, and supply-chain constraints. In the cloud, you have increased reliability but the possibility of unconstrained complex costs.

The complexity of setup within a data center versus cloud varies widely. For example, compare the long lag times for hardware delivery and setup in the data center versus the near-immediate delivery from a cloud provider.

Regardless of your environment, ask yourself these guiding questions:

- How much performance and availability do you need? Is it variable?
- Will the cost for static instances or servers be more than the cost of auto-scaling options month over month? Year over year?
- Should capacity be built to handle the spikes in activity or regular load?

Justification

Understanding the procurement process that you need to navigate helps inform your justification process. If you have long delivery times, you may need to do the appropriate work to justify resource purchases well before you need them. If resources can be made readily available at a moment's notice, you can delay justification until you are ready to do the necessary associated work around deploying the resources. As with procurement, the processes required within an organization to justify resource procurement vary in implementation, from something ad hoc to very formal, with a review board assessing the strength of the proposal.

Even if the environment doesn't require a formal review process, it's important to have this information on hand to better understand the decisions made, including what was considered and ultimately discarded. Circumstances change, and maybe a formerly inappropriate solution becomes a better fit for a future project or a new direction for the current project. And it can also be worth having a record of why a particular solution was discarded—maybe there's a fundamental flaw that others should steer clear of as well.

Document the following items:

- Describe your problem assuming no prior understanding of the circumstances.
- Describe the potential solutions.
- Explain your choice of solution, for example, "With this resource, I expect this amount of improvement in a specific measured value with an estimated increase in revenue or business value."
- Provide supporting data for answering why and how much.
- Address any other potential constraints and risks to success.

Management

Resource management covers the entire lifecycle of resources from deploying to deprovisioning and varies based on the type of resources and how much automation is in use. A resource's lifecycle helps you to plot a set of actions in alignment with business objectives.

As shown in Figure 18-2, with managed physical infrastructure hardware, you plan provisioning, configuration, deployment, and eventual retirement; you have to think about these concerns before you even purchase the hardware.

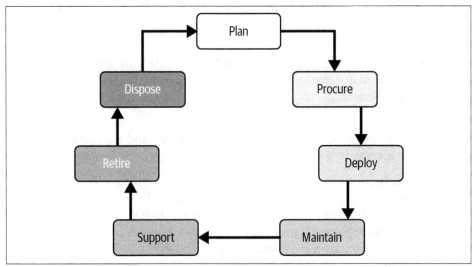

Figure 18-2. Physical infrastructure hardware asset lifecycle

These are the phases of the hardware asset lifecycle:

Plan
> You plan hardware purchases, taking into account space, cooling, and power needs in addition to your currently owned hardware.

Procure
> After identifying the hardware, you determine whether you are buying or leasing it based on the availability of the hardware and vendor pricing aligned to your plan. Building solid relationships with vendors in servers, storage, and networking helps you get the best prices and necessary support for your hardware.

Deploy
> Once the equipment arrives, you need to verify that the systems come as specified. A different team may be responsible for the physical deployment into the racks, or it may be part of your job responsibilities.

You install the required OS and necessary updates. Generally, hardware follows a "bathtub curve," where defective components show failures early in their lifecycle. You may perform some amount of burn-in testing to verify that the system isn't going to fail prematurely, the system behaves as expected, and there are no component performance differences.

Finally, you install and deploy the necessary software and services to make the system live.

Maintain

You update the OS and upgrade any hardware as necessary to support the required services.

Support

You monitor the hardware for issues and repair based on any expectations of services. This may mean coordinating support or physically swapping in new hardware as necessary.

Retire

You identify when the hardware is no longer needed and deprovision running systems. This may be a long process to identify any access to the system.

Sometimes, new hardware is brought into service to replace older hardware. If the system architecture can be scaled up gracefully by adding new hardware and then scaled down by removing the older hardware, this allows for easier retirement and deployment processes with minimal impact on the end customer. If you have to shut down a system to remove hardware altogether, this will cause some amount of end-user impact.

Dispose

Once you have retired software from the system and removed it from service (and if it is no longer useful within your organization in any other capacity), you have to dispose of the hardware. In addition to ensuring that no sensitive data remains on the system, you may need to be aware of specific laws and regulations around the disposal.

When planning hardware requirements, it's common to think about a three- to five-year life span for nonspecialized hardware. In part, this is due to advancements in physical technology that improves the cost of running servers. It is also due to advancements in the system software, where older hardware might not support current operating systems.

With specialized hardware like storage appliances, the lifecycle changes slightly in that the costs can range from the tens of thousands to close to a million dollars. On top of that, maintenance and support are separate costs and longer-term investments.

It's not uncommon for IT departments to be structured organizationally within finance, leading to accounting depreciation schedules that trickle down into IT policy.

Organizations may use a different strategy for depreciation, and there may also be specific legal/tax guidelines to follow, but three- to five-year schedules dovetail with how the expense of expensive equipment is amortized over multiple years.

Planning for Failure as Part of Capacity Management

Consider the "bathtub curve," the curve of a bathtub with steep sides and a flat bottom, as depicted in Figure 18-3.

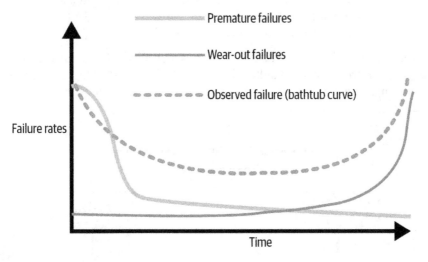

Figure 18-3. Charting hardware failures over time with premature, constant, and wear-out failures

This model depicts observed hardware failures over time. Physical resources typically follow one of three phases: premature failure due to defective products, random failure during regular use, or end-of-life failure due to wear. Observed rate of failures will follow this bathtub curb with a high number of issues early (so make sure to exercise the hardware with a burn-in to cause this fast failure outside of production environments) and toward end of life (make sure to monitor the age of hardware, and preemptively plan to cycle it out).

Even if a system is still doing useful work, like an older car, it's necessary to evaluate whether the ongoing cost of repairs exceeds the cost of replacing it and avoiding failure completely.

When implementing quality hardware management in your infrastructure strategy, challenges with staffing, tool availability, and the complexity of hybrid environments will arise. Operation engineering teams are often understaffed, which can lead to not having enough time to spend on developing quality practices for managing hardware effectively. This could mean hardware arrival and delayed deployment or a lack of retiring aging systems in a timely manner.

Another challenge is the lack of investment or availability of quality tools. Often spreadsheets are used to design data centers (including cooling and power) and manage vendor relationships and inventory (from the physical hardware itself to the cabling organization). This can hinder collaboration, communication, and knowledge transfer throughout the organization.

A hybrid environment where part of the infrastructure is on-prem and part is managed by a cloud provider adds additional complexity. This might be acceptable if there is no in-house knowledge for managing necessary services.

Take a look at Figure 18-4. With cloud services, consider this modified lifecycle of assets. The service provider handles the physical racking, stacking, security of the hardware, maintenance, and disposal of systems. You are left with the following phases.

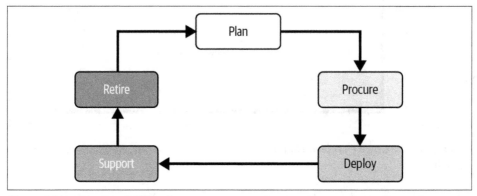

Figure 18-4. Cloud asset lifecycle

Plan
> You focus on identifying specific cloud services to use (e.g., specific machine types or reserving capacity versus on-demand) and budget forecasting.

Procure
> Instead of having to plan for expenditures all at once, you set budgets per individual or team to align spending and leverage purchasing power across the organization. You build relationships with different cloud providers and identify compatible services that align with business requirements.

Deploy

Instead of physically deploying servers, you write infrastructure code to provision, verify, and deploy necessary cloud resources programmatically.

Support

Through careful monitoring of systems in use, you identify areas for cost savings. You assess, monitor, and repair security vulnerabilities in the software and underlying layers depending on the service in use. You may also be the central contact with the service provider to coordinate support.

Retire

Rather than worry about maximizing the value of physical hosts for three to five years, configure instances to live only as long as needed, eliminating cloud resources that are running and providing no value-add. You can configure policies to shut down and deprovision resources that are no longer in use.

Migrating to the cloud may ease some of the stress on operation engineering teams, allowing them to focus on the practices involved in managing infrastructure. However, with the ease of quickly provisioning resources, visualizing resources in use is critical to preventing costly mistakes.

Finally, take a look at Figure 18-5. Serverless is a special type of cloud compute, storage, and networking. With serverless, the lifecycle of assets is simplified because the provider handles many of the step.

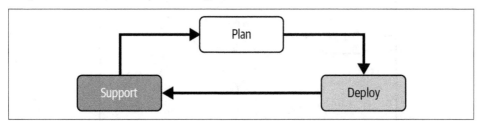

Figure 18-5. Serverless asset lifecycle

Plan

You need to research and design the architecture and services necessary to provide the expected experience.

Deploy

You need to deploy any configurations, applications, connected services, and instrumentation for monitoring.

Support

You are responsible for your users getting the benefit of your systems. When something goes wrong, you need to use logging and traces to handle and debug problems.

Monitoring

Resource monitoring is monitoring the specific resources in use with the goal of balancing resource costs, customer demand, and business value. This area of capacity management is covered in detail in Part IV.

The Framework for Capacity Planning

You should consider documenting capacity management components per environment, as underlying processes to follow will vary from team to team and across organizations. While I can't define what they will look like for you, I can provide a framework to guide you on what you can do next once you understand the processes and policies in place within your environment (Figure 18-6).

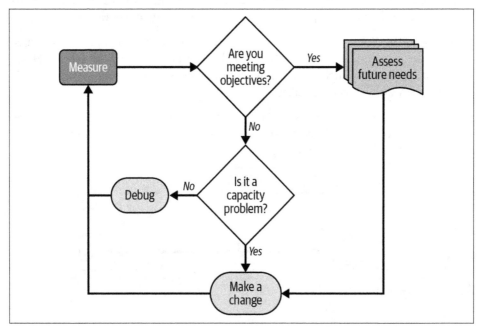

Figure 18-6. Capacity planning process framework

Let's look at the steps in Figure 18-6:

1. Measure the current workload for all the components of the object in your system under evaluation.

2. Evaluate whether you are meeting the SLOs based on demand.

3. If you are meeting objectives, spend time assessing your future needs (e.g., is there new compute technology that may replace current requirements?).

4. If you are not meeting the objectives, assess whether this is a capacity problem. Sometimes you need to resolve other issues before making changes to capacity. There may be optimizations possible in configuration tuning that will lead to performance improvements.

5. If it is a capacity problem, identify changes that can be made and apply one of the changes to see the impact of making that change. Make sure that information gleaned about the change is understood by the relevant team or teams to help guide future decisions. If you don't have enough information because you don't have the right measurements, make changes to your measurements.

How Organizational Strategies Influence Planning

Organizations use three main strategies to assess future needs: lead, lag, and match. Any of these strategies can help inform and prioritize action and reduce friction.

With the lead strategy, you add capacity as you receive indicators that system demands will increase. Often employed with on-premises resource management, this strategy compensates for not being able to make fast changes in the event that demand is higher than capacity since ordering and delivery of hardware can be highly variable. Overhead costs increase if user demand doesn't materialize after capacity is increased.

With the lag strategy, you meet demand after it occurs. If you cannot fulfill demand in a timely manner, the lag strategy can increase the chance of losing customers and impact trust or confidence in the company. The lag strategy isn't realistic for on-prem resource management for small companies due to the length of time it takes to order and receive hardware. In large companies, resource allocation to individual teams can be made from other teams within the organization. Resource-driven conflict occurs when popular projects that didn't do adequate capacity management "steal" resources, leading some teams to greatly exaggerate the estimations on resources that they need to accommodate for losing some portion of expected resources, which can reduce financial investment for other projects.

The match strategy attempts to compromise between the lead and lag strategy by incrementally increasing capacity with demand. For example, capacity may be preemptively expanded by a fraction of the forecasted future need, with the remainder waiting until the need actually appears.

Another term for the lag strategy is *just in time* (JIT) approach to resource allocation.. With JIT manufacturing, rather than maintaining inventories of components, parts are acquired as they are needed based on production demand. This reduces costs and minimizes unwanted surpluses, both of which increase profitability. But this efficiency relies on accurate predictions of future demand; incorrect predictions will disrupt the pipeline.

Consider the economic effects of the COVID-19 pandemic on global supply chains. Shortages of products like toilet paper arose not because people started using more toilet paper; offices and schools didn't need commercial single-ply toilet paper, but consumers needed more household toilet paper. It took time for paper manufacturers to shift production from commercial to domestic distribution, and in the meantime, retail shelves were empty even as warehouses of commercial toilet paper piled up.

As you evaluate your capacity planning needs, think about the variables that inform your predictions, and consider contingency plans for how you can respond to unexpected shifts in demand.

Do You Need Capacity Planning with Cloud Computing?

Even when using cloud services, you need to develop an explicit capacity management strategy. Even for services that provide dynamic scaling, at minimum, you need to focus on resource management and monitoring. Consider the following limitations:

- Time to spin up new resources.
- Resource ceilings set by the provider based on instance types chosen. CPU, network, and storage throughput are limited to what you chose in the initial configuration. While in some cases these can be changed, downtime may be required, depending on the cloud provider. Some limits require contacting the cloud provider to adjust, which can have varying times to resolve. Contrary to the idea that everything is API based and instantaneous in the cloud, service providers institute certain limits to better serve the average use case.
- Managed datastore configuration limitations. Cloud providers create tiered offerings that simplify some of the management challenges of sizing databases, but you may need flexibility you hadn't anticipated. The more expensive the offering, the more of the fine-tuning with resource management they generally cover. You still have to select the specific functionality, whether sharding, replicating, or load balancing, and these choices can be very expensive. Right-sizing your resources follows the flow of the capacity planning process.
- Capacity limitations of the cloud provider itself. At certain levels of scale, the assumption that more resources can be added on demand breaks down due to the real limits of how much hardware the provider has available.
- External dependencies may have additional limits or lack dynamic scaling functionality. Examples include gateways and proxies.

Cloud computing makes it easier to adjust dynamically to real demand. Engineering requirements can be more finely tuned to better approximate the variable nature of demand and inform staff of the impact of making changes to core infrastructure.

Service providers set varying limits for services. While the service provider handles scaling, individuals still have to be aware of the impact of dependent services and the limits across all of these services as well. Without oversight, it could be quite easy to run afoul of these limits (e.g., 75 GB max limit on function and layer storage in AWS (*https://oreil.ly/jmOPe*)).

Wrapping Up

The future is unpredictable; deploying new resources can take time, but over-provisioning costs money. Capacity planning is the art and science of matching your resources to anticipated future needs aligned with the demands of your organization without constraining your system's potential or spending too much.

Take these steps when considering the capacity of your systems:

1. Identify the need and justify how a particular resource will meet that need.
2. Procure the resource, along with any overhead expenditure to maintain the resource.
3. Monitor the resource.
4. Manage the resource throughout its lifecycle.

Capacity planning is important for all resources you oversee, including both physical and cloud-hosted systems, but the procurement characteristics are distinct. With hardware systems, it takes time to acquire and deploy new equipment, and it's generally harder to scale up or down as demand evolves. With systems built with cloud services, scaling can be automated, but it's also easy to overspend if you aren't keeping an eye on things. Effective capacity planning requires ongoing assessment and adjustments to your processes.

More Resources

Check out these additional resources on capacity management:

- Learn more about capacity planning for websites from *The Art of Capacity Planning: Scaling Web Resources in the Cloud* by Arun Kejariwal and John Allspaw (Pragmatic Bookshelf).
- See the case study of capacity management from Capital One from Kevin McLaughlin at Velocity 2016 New York "Is Capacity Management Still Needed in the Public Cloud?" (*https://oreil.ly/MHR8v*)

CHAPTER 19

Developing On-Call Resilience

The most visible responsibility of supporting a service or system is on-call and managing impactful events. When your alerting system constantly pages you, you may not have the time or energy to improve the system's infrastructure effectively. In extreme situations, you may avoid thinking about the on-call experience when you are not on-call because it feels better to accomplish project work. In this chapter, I propose a framework for building resilience, investing early and regularly to prepare for on-call so that you can cope with the challenges and stress that come from being available to handle any issues that arise.

What Is On-Call?

On-call is a temporary rotating role assignment that may include being reachable outside of normal business hours (e.g., evenings, weekends, and holidays) to answer requests for support and handle discovered alerts. When you are on-call, you are one of the people responsible for this work for a specific length of time. Depending on the size and distribution of the team, on-call rotations may consist of 8- to 24-hour shifts for one to two weeks.

On-call duties vary widely within different organizations, from failed application services to power outages. You may be the person to respond to services going offline or provide escalation support. You may have to investigate why a website went offline in the middle of the night or scramble to restore backups when a file server crashes. Some on-call is for the sporadic issues "just in case"; in others, paging is so frequent that it feels like a full-time job. Often on-call and interrupt-driven work tend to merge into a single work queue.

Many contributing factors lead to unsustainable on-call practices that transform the sysadmin job into task-based reactive work that lacks growth opportunities. Two prime factors are misalignment in severity and priority assessment.

When individuals assess the severity of a problem as too severe, they may demand a fix for an issue even if a viable workaround exists; setting the severity too low can lead to under-prioritizing a problem that affects many people. The operations team may have difficulty assigning priority. Problematic practices include the following:

- Automatically setting all interrupts at a high priority
- Failing to rank incoming issues
- Not combining duplicate reports that are the same issue
- Failing to clean up known problems to eliminate the possibility of duplicate reports

Ideally, the urgency of a request and the impact of the problem are known and shared, including the following issues:

- How many people are affected?
- Is there a satisfactory workaround?
- Is data at risk?
- What's the business impact on your organization?
- What's the business impact on your customer(s)?

Let's discuss what tools and techniques can help you improve your resilience by refining the on-call process.

Humane On-Call Processes

I've been there. Late-night pages and interrupted sleep. Years of waking up in a panic, wondering if I missed an alert. Skipping vacations and missing meals or eating whatever cold pizza was left from the team huddle as we resolved a significant revenue-impacting incident. Missing out on family and friends' events, and relatives expecting that I would bail again. I have painful memories of on-call that have had long-term impacts on my relationships and mental and physical health. I eliminated the very activities that could have helped because I didn't see the path to a more sustainable experience.

It doesn't have to be this way. While you have an obligation to your company, you also have a responsibility to yourself and your health. You can be a responsible and attentive worker who is on-call while simultaneously advocating for yourself and maintaining relationships with your friends and family.

In the following few sections, I will share my recommendations for a sustainable on-call shift, from the preparation steps you can take before on-call even begins through your on-call shift and the handoff meeting. Then, compare your processes to what I describe here and adopt practices that help you.

Check Your On-Call Policies

Ideally, the on-call policy is documented clearly. If there isn't a documented policy, when I'm looking to understand expectations, I ask these questions:

- Am I compensated for my time on-call or when I'm actively working outside of normal business hours? This includes compensation for on-call and call-out, whether additional time off or additional pay for the impact of needing to be available for out-of-hours work.

- How does the team prioritize incoming requests? How do I know which problems *must* be resolved outside of business hours? Prioritize requests to clearly define examples of what constitutes high impact and high urgency to guide effective and consistent collaboration.

    Use Figure 19-1 to categorize request types. The items that have high urgency and impact have higher prioritization than items that are low urgency and low impact.

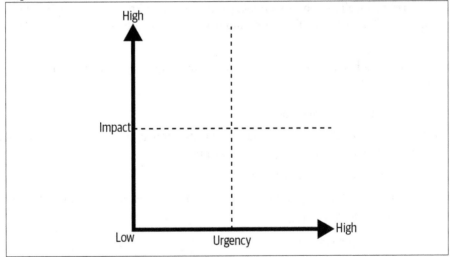

Figure 19-1. Impact and urgency matrix

- How long do I have before I'm expected to respond? Do different types of requests have different levels of response?

- Who else can I page if I need help in networking or security? What are the on-call support expectations for subject matter experts, especially for areas where there is only a single person with expertise?

- Who do I need to notify about incidents, and when should I notify them? Does the escalation process vary during working hours and after hours?

- How long am I on-call for?

- How long do I need to sustain active call-outs? Is there a route to rotate to the next on-duty if I have a significant issue?

Preparing for On-Call

During the weeks leading up to your first on-call shift, ensure you know about all the systems you're responsible for and the escalation path, in other words, who you ask for help and when you should pull them in. Part of understanding your systems is knowing the availability expectations for the systems you are responsible for: in some cases, an outage of minutes or even seconds is a critical problem, while in others, an outage might not have a customer-visible impact, and it's enough to leave a note for someone to deal with it the next day.

Regardless of whether there is a formal process of participating with other on-call engineers (also known as *shadowing on-call*), ask if you can shadow others on the team. Shadowing allows you to see tools and processes in use, see examples of how to respond and interact with the team, and assess the cost of the on-call experience to you.

Shadowing also helps you get a sense of paging frequency and the typical response norms:

- How are new incidents reported?

- Is there an email or SMS message, a notification in a messaging service like a Slack channel, or a status report in a dashboard?

- Does a service ticket get generated?

- If so, does this happen automatically, or does someone need to file one manually?

- How promptly do requests need acknowledgment?

- How quickly is a resolution required?

- If a solution requires specific expertise, what is the escalation procedure?

- When is it considered appropriate to escalate?

- After resolving an issue, what additional steps do you take to ensure the problem doesn't happen again?

Make sure your laptop and phone are charged and up to date with software requirements and that you can access the services you need from home and wherever you may be during your on-call shift: your favorite coffee shop, the soccer field, or bike path. Depending on the nature of your on-call rotation, you should have the latitude to do these sorts of things as long as you receive and acknowledge requests promptly and are prepared to help resolve problems.

Bookmark the different services you need, and make sure you can log in and access them. Then, when you get paged, you don't want to be fumbling around trying to find where you need to go to learn more about the pages.

Configure your phone and other devices in your alerting service. Services have different escalation policy customizations, so make sure to enable more than just email. For example, I focus on alerts when I'm on-call, so I prefer to minimize the distraction of future alerts on the same issue while still enabling redundancy. For an expected response time of 15 minutes, I like email and SMS, with a 10-minute follow-up phone call if I haven't responded. This configuration gives me 10 minutes to respond to the SMS before I get another alert, which reduces potential duplicate alerts and gives me time to respond within 15 minutes.

While teams have a specific expected response time, you can also configure your preferences. It's essential to consider the requirements of the on-call rotation and response time and your way of working. Find the balance of being responsive while not getting frustrated by noisy notifications.

Check your company's expense policy and talk to your management about expensing additional charging cables for all your devices to help eliminate the dreaded "did I leave that cable" panic. For example, I like to have extra power cords for my laptop and phone in my on-call bag, ensuring that I don't have to break down any part of my day-to-day setup or worry that I've forgotten a cable.

 Battery packs or power banks can give you extra time to resolve issues on your phone and laptop.

While you may not make and receive phone calls regularly, be prepared to have voice or video conferences during your on-call rotation with a hands-free headset so you can continue to type without sacrificing sound quality with the speakerphone.

A mobile hotspot or WiFi tethering device can support sustainable on-call rotations by enabling you to work from anywhere. Instead of being limited to the distance between your working station and the expected response time to resolve an issue, you can find an available spot and connect when you get paged. Having a mobile hotspot allowed me to enjoy family picnics and log in from the park to resolve issues that often took only a few minutes.

A separate device allows you to use the phone to further alert on other issues or dial into conferences as needed. In addition, it increases the diversity of connection options—if your phone has service from one provider and the device gets service from another, you're more likely to have access to a viable signal.

One Week Out

The week before your on-call shift, you can notify any stakeholder teams depending on your work and update associated project tickets to share status information. Updating the project tracking system with information about your upcoming on-call will minimize the unplanned stress folks might have about specific work. Ideally, proactive updates also reduce the project work interrupting on-call. If there are critical time-bound tasks, let your manager know, and support the delegation of those tasks. An up-to-date documented state of the project means others can chip in to keep the project moving forward if you get pulled into supporting a long-running incident.

If possible, send test alerts to confirm that you're enabled to receive alerts. Even if you have checked for past rotations, ensure configuration changes haven't eliminated your notifications. I have uncovered problems with alerting services blocking my phone provider, which saved me from dealing with failed system alerts and debugging why the phone provider was blocked.

Plan your snacks and meals ahead of time. Self-care is especially critical during an on-call shift. When and how often you'll get paged is unknown. While you can estimate what will happen based on past performance, it's not a guarantee. For the things that you can plan, this will help eliminate additional stressors when cascading failures occur. Energy bars can fill the gap, for example, when you have to start your day earlier than expected and need something quick to get your brain going.

Relationship building: do you have family or friends you can depend on to support you through on-call? Ask for help. Bring people into your experience. You don't have to be isolated, and giving people the opportunity to help you can help build connections, especially if you reciprocate when you're no longer on-call.

Plan for any additional coverage. Do you have a long commute or a regularly scheduled doctor's appointment? Do you need to drop your kids off at day care or attend a soccer game? Do you need to take your pet to the vet? Talk to the secondary or, ideally, another engineer that can provide coverage. Remember to reciprocate support when others need it.

Configure these overrides in advance. On-call rotations need to factor in the actual demands of personal life responsibilities and be flexible. A team that already practices this will be more able to handle additional short-term demands from outages.

> While you don't have a responsibility to reach out to everyone on-call, doing so helps build and sustain meaningful connections for successful, minimum-drama rotations. By reaching out, I've identified gaps in coverage where folks hadn't identified replacement coverage for their planned vacation. Instead of experiencing the support gap during my rotation, I helped get support coverage.
>
> It's also helpful when the on-call team is a virtual team composed of folks from different roles who may not be aware of the other skills that the individuals bring to the on-call rotation.

Connect with the rest of the on-call team. Ideally, the on-call team is made up of a primary and secondary on-call engineer, individuals who are designated escalation points of contact, and an on-call incident manager. Meeting with the rest of the on-call team helps make sure that everyone is ready to be on-call. As the primary, you get additional peace of mind about the support available to you.

Connect to specialized engineers. While they might not be officially on-call, you need the contact details for your security, network, or database engineer if there are single points of responsibility within the organization. Since a single person can't support an on-call rotation sustainably, document under what escalation conditions you should notify them.

Talk to your family or roommates about upcoming on-call. Set the expectations around what an event looks like and the expectations they may have of you. Set boundaries around acceptable behaviors (e.g., no hosting parties on your on-call weekends).

Preparatory work is necessary for going on-call. Make sure that time allocated for the week doesn't focus on a project's progress to the detriment of on-call preparation.

The Night Before

Verify that your notification device is charged and not silenced or in do-not-disturb mode. Get enough sleep; feeling rested is a crucial component to being able to sustain alertness in a changing environment. If you're fatigued going into an on-call rotation, it will hinder your effectiveness at sustained attention.

Often overlooked is preparing comfort for future you. Here are a couple of suggestions from other experienced sysadmins:

> Keep a warm hoodie/dressing gown near the bed for less cognitive load on those 2 a.m. wakeups.
>
> —Sera (@tsdubz), September 19, 2021

> Tea/coffee beverage of choice set up and ready to make should you get paged in the night.
>
> —Yvonne Lam (@yvonnezlam), September 19, 2021

Think about the specific accommodations (beverages, food, and/or clothing) that will provide comfort of convenience when your time is constrained to respond to an outage that may last for a while.

Your On-Call Rotation

Throughout your on-call rotation, the overall process may vary based on your team's expectations, but a general approach includes the following:

- Receive alert(s)
  — Acknowledge the alert(s)
  — Triage
  — Fix
- Improve on-call experience
  — Documentation
  — Monitoring
  — Assessing normal

When you receive an alert, the first action is to acknowledge the page. An acknowledgment lets folks know that you have received the alert and will help minimize further interruptions for the same issue. Next, triage or assess the severity and urgency of the problem and, based on these factors, route the alert to the appropriate action. Finally, fix the problem that is being alerted. Fixing includes adjusting a noisy alert that pages with no expected action.

Assess your on-call readiness. High-impact lengthy incidents and numerous frequent alerts are both concerning. It may be better for you and the team to hand off primary on-call to someone while you take a break.

> ## Formalizing On-Call Processes
>
> Assessing on-call readiness needs to be formalized within the team's processes. This helps set expectations and supports modifications to working norms that otherwise might affect an individual's health or the perception of that individual's work ethic. Here are a few examples of what that would look like:
>
> - If a team member gets paged after standard working hours and the issue takes more than an hour to resolve, they may modify their core working hours the following day.
>
> - If a page takes more than eight hours to resolve during the workday or four hours to resolve after hours, then the team member automatically gets the next work day off.
>
> With these kinds of explicit policies, individuals have more certainty about expectations and are more willing to be a member of the on-call rotation and provide coverage when someone needs a break.

During the typical on-call workday, when not receiving an alert, the focus is on improving the on-call experience (versus working on project work). Workday tasks could be improving documentation or monitoring or learning more about what "normal" behavior looks like in your systems. Sometimes in the process of examining the live system, you'll discover something that needs to be fixed. Make sure that these discoveries are documented (in the work queue as well as the on-call handbook) and alerts are configured.

On-Call Handoff

OK, so the clock hits the magic hour, and you are no longer the designated on-call. You want to be done. But you're not done yet. You still need to hand off to the next on-call engineer. Making this an official sync meeting will do two things. First, it will support the incoming engineers by informing them of the past week's issues and any remaining open issues so they're set up for success. Second, it will give you a much-needed psychological release to have an explicit stopping point to the hyperalertness required of being on-call for production. It's a ritual of finality that tells your body it's OK, you can stop now, and it is glorious.

But it's also a ritual of beginning because it sets the starting point for when the next person needs to take on the mantle of hyperalertness. When it's time for you to start on-call, your colleagues should be handing off to you in the same way; otherwise, you may stress more about expectations and whether something is already a problem depending on the state of the systems you are managing.

You may think, "My environment doesn't have these concerns, my environment isn't that complex, we don't get paged a lot, etc." But we're not trying to optimize for environments that are calm without regular issues; we're trying to create team processes that are sustainable regardless of the inevitable issues and incidents that may arise: data corruption, loss of data centers or cloud provider outages, or security incidents. A clean handoff sets yourself and your team up for success when problems do arise because the team is already well practiced in how to hand off responsibility with ongoing issues so that individuals are well rested and at their best when tackling thorny or complex ongoing problems.

Part of the handoff includes a weekly review document. Here's an example of information that could be included:

- Time period
- Individuals who made up the on-call team for the time period
- Incidents and relevant links to more information about those incidents
- Open incidents
- Resolved incidents
- Incidents that were not captured by alerts
- Manual work
- Opportunities for automation and improvement
- Open questions; while there may no longer be an impact on consumers, there might still be unanswered questions
- Call-outs for specific items that went well and what needs improvement

The weekly review document is crucial. I can trust that the person before me has handled things and is supporting me through documentation, and the next person can trust that I will handle things and will support them through my documentation.

Handoff procedures are vital for effective collaboration across regions. A good practice is to have quick standup video conferences for shift transitions, where the people who are ending their day can bring the next group up to speed on what they've been working on. On an ongoing basis, sharing case notes in a ticketing system like Zendesk or a chat system like Slack can make it much easier for regional teams to be able to pick up where their colleagues left off. Additionally, searchable case notes lay the groundwork for internal and customer-facing documentation, as well as bug reports for the software team.

The Day After On-Call

When you're finished being on-call, it doesn't mean that you're finished working to improve on-call. While the events are fresh (either the same day as the handoff or the very next day), revisit the issues you filed. This is the best time to have those creative epiphanies to improve what you just experienced. Update necessary documentation, clean up any noisy alerts (which includes reducing the severity of alerts as appropriate), and record any project-related work required for long-term improvements. For any incidents, add relevant information to the incident report.

 One way to help continuously improve on-call alerts is to have a regular alert review with your team to talk through the impacts and values of the alerts.

Variability in the On-Call Experience

By Chris Devers

Reading this chapter, I was struck by how the on-call experience where I work differs from what this chapter describes. Most of the on-call work I've had in my career deals with humans as much as it deals with the systems, e.g., "The news system just crashed, and we're on the air in 17 minutes, help!" Yes, there's a technical aspect to the response, but there's a great deal of human interaction, talking to frustrated people and improvising solutions to get them to acceptable states of resolution.

My employer builds solutions for the media and entertainment industry, where on-site server deployments continue to play important roles. People working in this field need to deal with things like cameras, tape decks, satellite links, broadcast systems, and vast archives of media, and the servers we build help tie it all together so that the show, as they say, can go on.

Many of the systems we sell are physical servers, which our customers install and manage themselves at their studios, offices, and data centers, wherever in the world they may be. Routine administration of these systems is the customer's responsibility, but if they run into problems, they can turn to us. Our tech support staff are, in effect, a team of consulting sysadmins, providing escalation assistance for the on-site admins at individual customer locations.

We're not a huge company. But we do have offices around the world, and this has been key to maintaining a sustainable approach to on-call work. If a broadcaster in India reports an overnight problem, the on-duty team in Europe is ready to assist; if the problem extends past the end of the workday in Europe, the case is handed off to the Americas team as their workday begins. Similarly, global staffing allows holiday coverage. Regions adjust shifts to provide coverage so that we minimize impact to customers when our regional offices close for holidays, whether it's Lunar New Year in East Asia or Thanksgiving in North America. And when the COVID-19-driven shift to widespread remote work came along, we took this in stride, because we were already used to collaborating with remote colleagues and customers.

We do a shift rotation for weekend coverage that resembles the rotation described elsewhere in this chapter: people need to watch email and Slack notifications on their phones and be ready to get on a laptop at a moment's notice. Or perhaps a customer has scheduled a weekend maintenance window, and the engineer on duty knows in advance how their Saturday is going to unfold. But late-night investigations are rare, because cases are handed off regionally, just as they are during the workweek.

We also encourage a close working relationship between our support and dev teams, which brings a variety of benefits. The support team, of course, is keenly aware of the customer pain points, but they also get excellent feedback about how to improve and extend the product. At the same time, it can be rewarding for developers when they see that the work that they're doing is meaningfully improving things, not only for customers but also for support staff. This collaboration also helps distribute knowledge: if a particular individual is a recognized subject matter expert on a particular aspect of the product, it makes everyone's jobs easier when that person shares their bag of tricks. Obviously, having a lot of interruptions can make it difficult to focus and get things done, and everyone tries to be mindful of this. But when the benefits of such collaboration are recognized, it seems to be easier to get more people on board, and this can lead to a positive feedback loop: the support team levels up, the escalations get less frequent, and the devs aren't consulted as often.

Each organization needs to craft an approach to on-call that is adapted to the problems you need to solve and the resources you have to work with. In my case, working with a global team has led to a low-impact approach to on-call duty. Think about how your own organization may apply creative solutions to sustainable on-call coverage.

Monitor the On-Call Experience

Once again, monitoring is not just for production systems; it's also important to monitor the human systems. The on-call process itself requires monitoring in order to be aware of what is not working and proactively iterate on improvements. This is tied into advocating for yourself. To know whether on-call sucks and to provide that supporting information to management who can make change, you have to have monitoring that measures and presents that information in compelling ways. See Chapter 11 and apply these improvements to how you share the measurements you make about on-call.

The first measurement includes monitoring work in progress, even if you're the solo on-call engineer and you don't need to explain your work to anyone. Ideally, work associated with alerts should come into a shared work queue. You want to be able to share visualizations over time of the work, and when you make a change, you want to be able to see the impact. By measuring first, you can establish the baseline and can then observe the impact that changes (like more people on-call, specific improvements to code or infrastructure) can have on the work being measured.

Here are a few questions to think about and consider monitoring:

- How many on-call hours are there per time period?
- How many active on-call hours are there per time period?
- How often does an alert page?
- How often is it actionable? Does the alert self-resolve?
- When was the alert last updated?
- When was documentation last updated?
- What is the impact of the failed system? Does it need to alert outside of hours?
- How much coverage is available? If an individual is paged out and resolving an issue, who takes the next page?
- How often does the person on-call get diverted from normal life activities, including sleep, meals, and showers?
- How often are family gatherings and obligations interrupted? There are many activities that can't be rescheduled and are critical to maintaining healthy relationships.

Rather than just focusing on system time to recovery and time to discovery, these metrics help to classify and direct improvement in the on-call experience. During production meetings, it's helpful to talk about these metrics so that the team notes the necessary action items to improve the observed trends.

If your team has periodic retrospectives, think about the on-call progress. Potential remediations you can suggest may include updating the paging schedule and escalation policies. (If your team doesn't have retrospectives, I encourage you to suggest them.)

Let's look at some other mitigation strategies once you've identified specific issues with your on-call:

You're having a difficult time unwinding after an on-call rotation
Look at the underlying cause. Is this about the total amount of time required for the job, and is your availability to do the rest of your work leading to incomplete recovery?

The mitigation here is to make sure you are tracking how much free time you actually have and how restricted you are with that free time and the type of activities you can do. The problem is with the system if you have insufficient unrestricted free time. Work with your management and your team to identify ways to repair this; long term, this isn't healthy. Left unchecked it will lead to fatigue and emotional exhaustion and eventually burnout. Set healthy boundaries for yourself.

If it's not because of work, it may be that you have other areas you need to invest in. It's OK to ask for accommodations to support you resetting.

People who are on-call don't know enough about the system

The mitigation here is to help folks grow their skills to understand more about the system. Take this as an opportunity to grow the knowledge base about the system and find areas of improvement. If you are the person who doesn't know enough about the system, if you are in an environment that encourages psychological safety and sharing your concerns, speak up about what you need. You can ask to have a shadow or to shadow someone else's on-call shift to get better acquainted with the system.

There are not enough people to cover the hours expected for on-call

Unless you are a manager, this is a really hard problem. Document the cost to you and your team. Based on this data, ask for either additional head count whether that means hiring additional people, proposing that others in the company also take on-call responsibilities, or consider lowering the priority of responding to on-call, i.e., availability is only during normal working hours. If you can't change the system's expectation, you need to change your job. It becomes harder to navigate the interview process for other companies when you are burned out, and your health will continue to suffer.

There is an inconsistent approach to on-call

First, inconsistency in itself isn't a problem. While you may want to have a nice, neat, perfect system, people are going to be messy and inconsistent; no one can predict how any human will respond on a given day. This is one reason that solving problems gets so ambiguous at larger scales.

If the inconsistent approach is caused by lack of understanding or education, fix the documentation. If the inconsistent approach is intentional and harming the team, there are two possibilities of action: a team with high psychological safety can hold its members accountable for the work and the expectations of the work, otherwise, management needs to take on this role and set the expectations clearly and follow through when expectations aren't met to repair the harm.

On-call shifts are unpredictable

On-call by its nature will be unpredictable. The better you and your team get at handling and prepping the live environment, the more unpredictable the work can get, especially as the usage of your system grows. Monitoring for patterns early and distributing work fairly can help individuals on the team feel mutually supported to weather any unpredictableness.

Lack of compensation for perceived work

This is outside your scope as an individual contributor. Take a look at Chapter 21 for ideas on how to mitigate this, and share with your manager if you need help in this area. I included this in this list of challenges because when individuals start feeling this way, it can impact how they approach on-call and the work as a whole, even if they don't feel the same way about their compensation. Rather than take it out on each other, recognize that this is a valid concern that individuals may have.

Wrapping Up

Supporting your system through participating in an on-call rotation is part of managing systems, but on-call can be handled in a humane way that is compatible with a healthy lifestyle that includes spending time with friends and family and engaging in activities outside of work that you are passionate about. You can take time to step back from your usual routine and focus on how the systems you oversee can be managed in a more maintainable and sustainable way.

More Resources

Check out these resources about on-call:

- "Crafting Sustainable On-Call Rotations" (*https://oreil.ly/eaCvN*) by Ryn Daniels
- "The On-Call Handbook" (*https://oreil.ly/zJKwv*) by Alice Goldfuss and contributors (GitHub)
- Chapter 10, "Notifications," in *The Art of Monitoring* (*https://oreil.ly/p6bMj*) by James Turnbull (Turnbull Press)

CHAPTER 20

Managing Incidents

As we explored in Chapter 19, the purpose of on-call is to be aware of your systems so you can keep them healthy. But as much as you strive to reduce risk, failure will happen—there will be incidents. Incident management begins when you detect a problem during an on-call rotation, but management often extends beyond on-call when other subject matter experts and teams are required for issue resolution. The aim of incident management is to minimize the impact of an incident.

You, as an individual, need the kinds of tools, techniques, and practices that will not only get you through an incident with minimal suffering but will also help you feel prepared ahead of time and able to react effectively when an incident occurs. You need good, clear communication across teams so that the appropriate subject matter experts can share their knowledge and minimize time to resolution. And you need a way to capture and apply what you learned from the incident to improve overall production, reduce future impacts to customers, and reduce the team's toil.

In this chapter, I share the framework for collaborative and sustainable incident management from identifying incidents to conducting post-incident reviews and identifying the actions required to improve the live environment.

 I am assuming your team has incident management and that you'll have some framework to which you can apply what I'm sharing to improve your experience. If your team doesn't currently do incident management, then share this book or Chapter 21 with your leadership team.

What Is an Incident?

The definition of "incident" varies across organizations; an incident may be anything that pages the on-call engineer, or it can specifically mean security breaches. In this book, I define an incident as an *exception* to a *live* site, service, or software application that has an *impact*.

Let's break this definition down into the components, starting with exceptions. Exceptions occur when the system doesn't behave in an expected way. Exceptions can be bugs in the code, failures in underlying systems (like DNS or the network), or misunderstanding in the project planning that led to a different implementation.

A *live* site, service, or application is something that is in use by clients or customers. In many cases, this is the production environment for a site or service but also includes applications installed on devices.

Impact is the qualitative effect that the exception has on the clients or customers. Sometimes, this impact may be visible externally. Other times, the impact isn't visible and a decision needs to be made about whether to disclose the incident or not.

Here are some examples of incidents:

- In October 2021, the loss of IP routes to Facebook DNS servers led to a global outage of more than six hours to Facebook and its subsidiaries' sites. When the system went down, it also took down the system that controlled keycard access to the buildings and server rooms, so nobody could access the servers remotely and the sysadmins on-site couldn't get into the buildings and server rooms to do hands-on mitigations.

- In July 2020, an expired server certificate and a data outage prevented the California Reportable Disease Information Exchange from accepting COVID-19 lab results from external partners, leading to discrepancies and under-reporting of case information.

- In October 2019, Docker experienced an incident where the Docker Hub registry was down. Any organization that relied on directly pulling images from the registry would have experienced issues. Organizations that cached Docker images or hosted their own registry would have minimized their impact.

- In May 2019, Slack (*https://oreil.ly/Z18FC*) started a deploy of a feature that prevented some customers from connecting to and using Slack. For organizations that were impacted, this was a complete outage.

As you can see from these examples, incidents can vary in degrees of external impacts. Additionally, incidents may be near misses that your customers have not (yet) observed.

What Is Incident Management?

Managing an incident is more than responding to the impactful event and restoring your system to its operational state. Incident management is the process of planning, preparing, responding, investigating, and learning from the incident.

Take a look at Figure 20-1, which shows this continuous learning cycle.

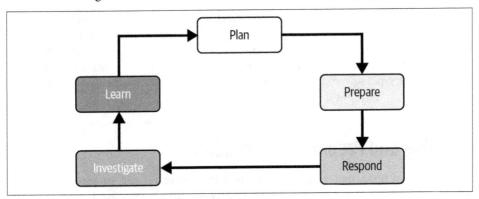

Figure 20-1. Incident management cycle

Outcomes of these different parts of incident management lead to the following:

- Reducing damage, costs, and recovery time
- Identifying code or process issues
- Repairing issues to prevent repeat incidents
- Documenting incidents
- Learning from the investigation

Each step in the incident management cycle shares basic principles that include clearly defined roles and responsibilities, as well as opportunities for continuous collaborative learning. Effective incident management may lead to data to support head-count requests, improved training, and promotion artifacts.

Recognizing When It's Really the System, Not You

In Chapter 19, I talked about building your individual resiliency to support your production services during on-call. Yet, sometimes there are components of the work that are outside of your control, and no amount of individual resilience is going to support sustainable work.

When it comes to managing incidents, there are some warning signs that your role has limited growth opportunities, including:

- Lack of transparency around failure
- Blame and fear culture where folks are afraid to talk about mistakes
- Repetitive incidents without improvement or long-term correction

There are other problematic issues, but these are especially harmful because they hinder learning, disrupt trust and relationship building, and promote burnout, which can compound the impact of incidents. If you see these signals and can't change your work to make it more sustainable, find a new opportunity before you burn out because it is especially challenging to interview for a new job when you're already depleted.

Planning and Preparing for Incidents

While you can hope that nothing happens during your on-call rotation, inevitably something will happen, so have a plan and regularly prepare for incidents. With contemporary systems, this requires collaboration and coordination within and across teams to communicate to the various stakeholders with a consistent and reliable response. In some organizations, an ad hoc temporary team such an incident response team (IRT) or incident management team (IMT) is created to coordinate and collaborate to resolve an incident.

The following subsections cover the planning and preparation steps you need.

Set Up and Document Communication Channels

During an incident, a team shouldn't be trying to figure out the process for how everyone will communicate, especially when individuals might not be in the same place or even time zone.

There is no one right way to handle incident discussions. One approach is to create a single #oncall channel where on-call discussion occurs. When a significant incident is identified in the discussion channel, a new #incident_NUMBER channel is created, keeping the primary #oncall channel uncluttered by the highly focused incident needs so that other potential problems aren't hidden. A problem with this approach is managing and tracking a lot of short-lived channels.

Another approach is to create a single #oncall channel and discuss incidents in threads. This helps with organization and visibility of incidents, but it can also make the channel overwhelming, especially when incident-related threads stretch to hundreds of messages.

A third approach is a compromise: start with threads in the main #oncall channel and be mindful of the scope of the investigation. Break out into separate channels when it becomes necessary.

Choose a standard, and change the approach based on how it works for your team.

Train for Effective Communication

Being explicit about the expectations around communication during an incident reduces mistakes and time to resolution. Recall "Case #2: Telling the Same Story with a Different Audience" on page 104, and consider also the level of detail that is appropriate for your different audiences: internal teams working a case need to share unfiltered real-time information, but managers overseeing things might want only periodic status reports, and customers and other external stakeholders may need only a brief summary.

People practicing communication protocols helps encourage speaking up and sharing their knowledge during an event.

The Launch of Crew Resource Management in Airline Training

On December 28, 1978, as the landing gear of United Airlines Flight 173 was lowered on approach to Portland International Airport, the crew felt problems with the aircraft and didn't have a solid signal that the landing gear had lowered successfully. The crew asked for a holding pattern so they could prepare passengers for a potential emergency landing. The captain was focused on resolving the landing gear issue and wasn't monitoring the fuel gauges. Flight engineers expressed concerns over the fuel but didn't manage to successfully communicate the concern to the captain. When some of the engines flamed out due to the lack of fuel, they had to try to land immediately and crashed.

After investigation by the National Transportation Safety Board (NTSB), other flight accidents were discovered to have been caused by similar problems with lack of communication and ability to work together; some crew members had critical information and didn't share it or question the decisions that were made. The NTSB identified a need for new training that would improve how the crew would make decisions, solve problems, and work together effectively. NASA's Ames Research Center developed the original crew resource management (CRM) training through a workshop in 1979.[1]

---

1 Jerry Mulenburg, "Crew Resource Management Improves Decision Making" (*https://oreil.ly/Z5cbE*), APPEL Knowledge Services, last modified May 11, 2011.

Collaboration is difficult. You have to understand how to do it and regularly practice it, and it's going to vary across situations and the people that make up the team. You don't want to try to learn how to do this when the incident occurs.

Additionally, you need to build the confidence that enables you to question leaders or subject matter experts. Everyone makes mistakes. If you hesitate to speak up when you observe mistakes, it could lead to more negative outcomes.

Create Templates

Templates help guide consistency across incident management and improve efficiency because individuals have a structure and layout to start from. Templates set expectations and standards.

People may chafe at templates with too many rows or fields. Make sure that templates focus on the minimal required information.

Maintain Documentation

On-call and incident handling documentation should be reviewed and updated regularly. Stale documentation that doesn't reflect the processes in use hinders organizational learning as well as frustrates engineers. Make sure to review the processes to handle alerts, disaster recovery, and other artifacts that might not seem to be documentation at first glance.

Document the Risks

What are the risks that you are exposed to, what's the probability of those risks occurring, and what are the associated impacts? The goal of incident management isn't to eliminate incidents but to reduce risks in a way that lets your organization continue to make changes.

Imagine potential failures and explain what would cause them. This also helps you prepare backup plans and highlight factors that could influence successful resolution.

Read more about risk in Chapter 3 (*https://oreil.ly/es3Qs*) (written by Marc Alvidrez) of *Site Reliability Engineering* from Google.

Practice Failure

Exercise and review your incident handling procedures so that the steps are automatic. Much like testing in development and the live running of your system, practicing your response to simulated failure is a very different experience from handling a live incident. But even with a practice run, you can still identify gaps in documentation and processes that will provide a much better experience for you when responding to an event at 2 a.m..

Understand Your Tools

Your team will have a collection of tools, practices, and processes for incident management. Table 20-1 shows examples of tools to be aware of.

Table 20-1. Tool categorizations

Category	Purpose
Monitoring	Measure, collect, store, explore, and visualize data from infrastructure.
Alerting	Manage on-call rotations and escalations and notify designated on-call responders.
Chat service	Provide real-time communication to share observations, links, and screenshots.
Video chat	Provide real-time communication to discuss and agree on approaches for incident response.
Incident tracking	Process, troubleshoot, and track the overall progress of the incident.
Documentation	Categorize and aggregate artifacts (incident management reports, incident research).
Issue tracking	Process, troubleshoot, and track the overall progress of issues with your systems and software. This may or may not be the same tool used for tracking incidents.

Make sure that you have an account on each of these tools as necessary and the method for accessing each tool, whether it's a special application that you install on your phone or a URL.

Clearly Define Roles and Responsibilities

Incident response teams vary across organizations. If your organization has an IRT, there may be different names for specific roles and more or less differentiation. A few significant functions (whether they have these names or not within your organization) are the incident commander, subject matter expert, liaison, and note taker:

Incident commander (IC)
> Responsible for driving an incident to resolution. During an incident, there is always a single acting lead to coordinate the various activities. The responsibility may be passed from one individual to another throughout the resolution of the incident.

Subject matter expert (SME)
> The on-call engineer or the designated owner of a particular part of the service. A number of SMEs may be required to resolve a specific incident.

Liaison
> Responsible for communicating internally and externally about the status of a current incident. There may be multiple liaisons for handling the different messaging internally and externally for a specific incident depending on the scope of the incident.

Note taker
> Takes notes, filling in details about the important actions and follow-ups that occur during the incident. The note taker can use software that responds to special commands or a chatbot. Handling incidents via a chat tool like Slack or a recorded video conference can fulfill this role too, because both of these provide timestamped transcripts of what was discussed. These notes are critical for providing the context for the narrative that will drive learning for the incident later.

If your organization doesn't have an official defined process for incident response, this may be an area to refine to help support sustainable on-call and incident management. This will require leadership buy-in.

Understand Severity Levels and Escalation Protocols

When you are paged while on-call, you need a reliable way to prioritize pages and identify an issue as an incident; understanding how your team assesses severity levels helps you decide what to do and who to tell.

Lower-number severity levels generally indicate more highly impactful incidents. This might look like the following:

Severity 1
> A critical incident with high impact; for example, this could be a completely compromised system that is impacting all customers, a privacy breach due to a hacked system, or the loss of customer data.

Severity 2
> A major incident with significant impact; for example, this could be a degraded system that is impacting some customers.

Severity 3
> A minor incident; for example, the system may be slower to respond but not completely down.

When a team has a common understanding of what severity levels mean, they can communicate the severity level and quickly initiate appropriate escalation protocols that bring the right level of response. The more severe the incident, the more important it is to have different people handling the different roles of incident management.

Responding to Incidents

Every team has some sort of process (whether documented or not) for handling incidents. Reflecting and explicitly documenting what each part of the process looks like can help in improving coordination when you are actually handling an incident. Figure 20-2 is an example of the process of managing your incident response with clear roles and responsibilities for the different parts of the incident management team.

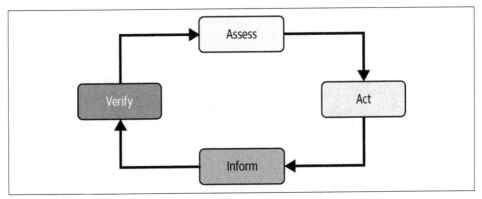

Figure 20-2. Incident response cycle

The IC *assesses* the incident through the observed symptoms, scope of the problem, and potential risks based on the symptoms.

When it's time to *act*, the following steps occur:

1. The IC identifies possible actions and associated risks.

2. The IC makes a decision, saying their decision out loud if on a call and in a channel if on a chat platform.

3. The IC obtains consensus on the decision by asking whether there are strong objections. The IC adjusts actions based on feedback, but ultimately the IC makes the final determination.

4. The IC delegates stabilization actions. The assignments must be clear and specific with explicit timing information about when the individual will update the team with progress.

Sometimes, an individual might not have the skills to do the identified action. It could be a good time for the individual to learn from someone with the experience. If there isn't sufficient time or there are too many tasks, the stabilization step should be handed off to someone more experienced.

Assignments should be adjusted based on feedback and required timelines. Depending on the severity of the incident, this may require pulling people on to the incident response team to complete the required tasks in a timely fashion.

The next phase of the cycle is to *inform*. Depending on the size of the team handling an incident, the IC may name an explicit liaison to handle updates. Liaisons shouldn't be actively investigating and repairing the system. Shifting contexts from debugging to communications to executing critical commands can exacerbate stress and increase mistakes.

When the live site is in a degraded state, clear, timely communication to customers requires skill. Poorly worded explanations can cause more problems than the actual outage.

The liaison sends regular updates to the team, customers, and executives. The frequency and content of the communications will vary by audience. Updates should include what is happening and the steps taken. As an individual's expertise is no longer needed, the IC reduces the scope of the incident. The IC informs the incident response team, who is still required to resolve the incident and encourages folks who are no longer needed to take a break.

The final step in the incident response cycle is to *verify*. This includes checking that stabilization actions are complete and verifying the outcomes of those actions. If there is continued impact, the incident commander repeats the steps starting from the assessment of the incident.

Learning from the Incident

After the incident has been resolved, collate information from all the participants of the incident response. The goal of this is not to place blame but to uncover what happened and drive conversations. One way to help prevent blame is to make sure that the focus is on what happened and what people decided to do based on that information rather than on what should have happened or could have been done.

How Deep Should You Dig?

Organizations vary in size and complexity. There may be regular incidents of varying degrees. Have you ever been in a post-incident review meeting where it felt like the goal was just to go down a checklist rather than focus on the impact of the incident and how it was handled? I've definitely sat in my share of meetings thinking about strategies to avoid those meetings ever again. To learn from an incident, you need to be open to discovery and exploration rather than follow a strict checklist.

Every incident is a special snowflake; even when it looks familiar. The combination of computing, storage, or network choices in the system implementation might be different. It could be a different software (or version or or configuration of software). It could be different people. Depending on the maturity of your organization, the set of tools you have, and the people in the mix, there may be limited time to analyze all incidents. So, how do you figure out what to investigate and to what degree? Really, it depends on what your team wants or needs to learn. Interesting incidents might include those that involve multiple teams or large impacts, incidents due to new systems or features, or events where an incident was actually avoided.

The Danger of Cognitive Biases

A number of cognitive biases can hinder your identification of the systemic causes of incidents:

Anchoring bias
> Relying on one piece of information or single source when making a decision rather than considering things holistically. Checklists reduce anchoring bias by helping you make sure that important details haven't been overlooked.[2] Following a checklist isn't a sign of incompetence; it's an admission that even professionals make mistakes and seek to minimize them.

Availability bias
> Occurs when you are influenced by memorable or easily accessible events. One way to minimize this bias is to maintain a searchable library of previous incidents so that you can compare the current incident to ones that your team has handled in the past.

Confirmation bias
> Relying on data that agrees with your preexisting opinions and beliefs while filtering out evidence that doesn't. To counter this bias, look for and include countering evidence and include diverse perspectives and points of view.

Hindsight bias
> Assuming that it was possible to predict that a particular event would occur.

Status quo bias
> A preference for things staying the same, leading to a resistance to change.

---

2 As an example, even highly trained surgeons benefit from checklists; surgical safety checklists (*https://oreil.ly/DSJIq*) have proven to be an effective way to improve medical outcomes for surgery patients.

To counter biases:

1. Obtain the facts first without assuming an immediate cause.
2. Flag potential causes.
3. Look for and evaluate contradictory evidence.
4. Revisit the data.

Aiding Discovery

The "should've" and "could've" can derail learning about what happened. This doesn't mean you shouldn't acknowledge mistakes. Mistakes need to be talked about and understood. Without psychological safety on a team, it can be really hard to admit to being wrong or having made a mistake. If people don't speak up because they are afraid they did something wrong, you miss an opportunity to repair systemic problems or mistaken assumptions about recommended actions.

Depending on your role in the discovery and investigation process, especially if you weren't part of the incident response team, you can ask the following questions:

- How were you notified of the event?
- Has this type of incident occurred before?
- If the incident has occurred before, what was the past impact?
- What surprised you about the incident?
- Could this incident occur again?

You may discover varying perspectives on the system and what went wrong as well as hidden differences in how people make decisions about managing the systems.

Documenting Incidents Effectively

Incident reports are artifacts for the team to help spread knowledge and prevent stagnation. Team artifacts should be stored in a central place. Depending on the organization, these artifacts may be useful to other teams.

Each artifact may have slightly different content based on the nature of the incident. The intended audience of the team incident report is the individuals on the team, so these reports can be longer and more detailed than external or executive briefings. Here is an example template for a team incident report:

- Title.
- Date.
- Author(s).

- Summary of the incident.
- Incident participants and their role(s).
- Impact.
- Timeline.
- Graphs and logs that help support the facts described in the timeline.
- Lessons learned about what went well and what needs improvement.
- Action items—these should include who, what, type of action, and when. Others outside of the incident response team might think of additional action items after reviewing the narrative.

Everyone involved in the incident response should review the record of the incident and add information that might be missing, including areas where they might have been confused or uncertain about next steps.

Team incident reports aren't the only artifacts of interest. In my experience, when the focus is on creating a single artifact, it can feel like a way to direct blame and can lead to ingrained fear that hinders collaboration on learning what happened. A lot of data is generated, many graphs are examined, and many people may have been involved in getting the service back into a healthy state. Sift through all this information and compose the necessary artifacts; this may be an executive report for a CEO or customer communication, in addition to the team incident report.

Distributing the Information

After documenting the incident, share what you learned from the incident with the organization. You might do this by sending an email, updating a website, or presenting the information in a meeting. The post-incident meeting is a critical part of continuous learning in an organization.

Everyone heading to this meeting should have shared objectives to help align efforts. A post-incident meeting without shared objectives is often worse than no meeting at all. If there are misaligned incentives or individuals are not getting recognized for the value they bring to the process, this can lead to heroics or dismissal of the whole process.

Objectives shouldn't reflect an idealistic "perfect" world. For example, there is no way to prevent incidents from ever occurring, so having an objective to eliminate incidents isn't reasonable or attainable.

Instead, aim not to repeat the same incident in the same way. Other helpful objectives might include identifying specific areas where information about why something occurred isn't understood clearly and where single individuals knew specific information that wasn't known by the entire team. In other words, the outcome of this meeting should increase knowledge and identify areas of focus. Some documentation may need to get updated after information has been distributed to the larger group.

Next Steps

Often, incident management success metrics are focused on improvements to mean time between failures (MTBF), mean time to failure (MTTF), mean time to detection (MTTD), and mean time to recovery (MTTR). These metrics were useful when reading hardware specifications to schedule optimum proactive replacements to avoid outages. These metrics are much less valuable when it comes to modern cloud-centric systems, because their focus on predicting hardware failure trends no longer applies, now that the focus has shifted from physical servers to virtualized compute. Additionally, averaging response times for different times of failures isn't providing useful and actionable information. Better success metrics can be uncovered through continuous collaborative learning from incident reports.

A successful incident management process could result in the following outcomes:

- Less people in incident response (folks feeling more confident in the process)
- More people attending incident reviews (folks feeling like the use of their time is valuable)
- More time allocated for event investigation

Wrapping Up

Incidents are exceptions to a production system that have an impact on the users of that system. It's unrealistic to think you can eliminate all incidents. Instead, focus on improving your incident response with deliberate and measured change. Consider how well your team responds to and learns from incidents.

You and your team can prepare for incidents by establishing processes for communication, training, and documentation. When an incident happens, communicate clearly to internal and external stakeholders, customers, and the team; pull in the necessary subject matter experts; and learn from the outages to improve the systems.

Incident resolution needs to include sharing learning from the incident, identifying where things went wrong, and considering changes to reduce future risks where patterns can be detected around events that affect your systems or across incidents that occur.

More Resources

Learn more about incident management from the following:

- Vanessa Huerta Granda's blog post "Making Sense Out of Incident Metrics" (*https://oreil.ly/mLpOt*)
- John Allspaw's blog post "Moving Past Shallow Incident Data" (*https://oreil.ly/SLnMR*)
- Richard Cook's treatise on the nature of failure, "How Complex Systems Fail" (*https://oreil.ly/uxHqA*)
- Community-curated collection of resilience engineering papers (*https://oreil.ly/xjkf1*)

CHAPTER 21

Leading Sustainable Teams

Let's revisit some concepts from the previous chapters and apply a leadership lens. Throughout my career, I've seen how the overall systems impact the flexibility and capabilities of a team. As a leader, there are additional opportunities to foster and support the team by changing how the overall system works.

OK, this chapter is explicitly for individuals in leadership positions. While I believe strongly that everyone can be a leader, I know that different organizations block functional leadership. If you aren't leading now, I encourage you to read this chapter and share it with your management if you like what you read here.

In this chapter, I will share how to lead teams with a whole-team approach that centers on continuous learning throughout every phase of a system's lifecycle without siloing or centering any specific role (i.e., development, quality assurance, or operations).

Collective Leadership

> *A leader is not one who wishes to do people's thinking for them, but one who trains them to think for themselves.*
> —Mary Parker Follett

Leading is required when the problem is bigger than one person can solve or influence. It's not specifically about management, and it's not telling someone to do something. It's a lot of work to convince others that a problem exists and that you can fix it together.

Additionally, I recognize that there is formal power in an organization. The individuals with authority over money decisions (e.g., hiring, firing, retention, reorganizations) have more capabilities in creating and maintaining sustainability.

Leading comes with great responsibility and privilege. What happens on your team and at your work impacts people's lives, health, personal relationships, personal goals, and dreams. You affect how they spend their time, the most precious resource any of us have. You have a responsibility to the company but an equal commitment to the people.

Instead of a lifecycle that silos development and operations, in Figure 21-1, I present a devops lifecycle model of continuous learning that eliminates the silo and focuses on continuous learning throughout every phase with monitoring to enable observation and experimentation regardless of role or stage.

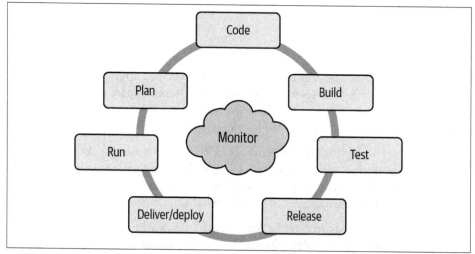

Figure 21-1. A modern devops lifecycle requires continuous learning

 Organizations often base funding decisions (head count, projects, tools, and technology) on early requirements and ignore the rest of a system's lifecycle. For example, when building software, resource allocation is centered on the developer's experience and coding rather than on making a system supportable after it has graduated into production. In addition, people take for granted that "somebody" will know when something has gone wrong and will be there to respond immediately.

Watch out for this pattern in your organization, as it signals that the human(s) responsible for the system's operation will bear the brunt of running the system.

Adopt a Whole-Team Approach

A whole-team approach is one in which the team includes everyone (e.g., system administrators, developers, security admins, network admins, product managers) involved with the system, and everyone is held responsible and accountable for the success of the system.

This approach requires that every person values the strengths and skills of the others on the team. There is no way to know everything, and operating in isolation limits the perspectives anyone can take in solving the problems.

Consider a whole-team approach to maximize the comprehension of complex environments where a shared understanding of the system's components helps mitigate the risks that can negatively impact the experience of using or running the system. You are not striving for a "perfect" system with zero downtime where you eliminate all risks. Chasing zero downtime is costly to the business and potentially harmful to the humans supporting the systems.

Combining a whole-team approach with a question culture encourages individuals to ask for clarification, which supports an increased shared understanding, as people don't make assumptions in isolation.

 An important note, particularly for managers, is that while retrospectives and reviews of incident response protocols have their place, you want to avoid second-guessing the details of the resolution while you're trying to provide social support. In research founded in the Jobs Demands-Resources model, both autonomy and social support may reduce exhaustion and other consequences from heavy workloads,[1] and even a well-meaning and insightful critique can appear to yank away both when someone is sleep-deprived and frazzled.

Let's look at adopting a whole-team approach to on-call and building a resilient on-call team.

Build Resilient On-Call Teams

A resilient on-call team is one that can manage the stress of handling the unknown problems that occur in a system. It's the virtual team of folks who care about the service or system and treat the live system with a co-ownership model to distribute responsibility.

---

1 A. B. Bakker et al., "Job Resources Buffer the Impact of Job Demands on Burnout," *J. Journal of Occupational Health Psychology* 10 (2005): 170–80.

On-call provides direct insight into the value of the software in use and customer commitments. The people who build the product have the most understanding and context about how the product should work. Still, the system administrators have often learned how the product works in the production environment. Having developers respond to first-level alerts ensures that the people building the product have insight into the most painful parts of the system.

Additionally, when developers handle on-call, they can better prioritize feature work, whether refactoring existing systems, implementing new features, or removing functionality crucial to the system's operation. Finally, when developers ask for infrastructure support, they will better assess the severity of the problem based on their knowledge of the system's operation.

Some organizations embraced adding developers to on-call rotations and started to advocate for the elimination of operations teams. A "no-ops" team can be problematic because many developers don't have operability skills. Lacking these skills isn't a reflection on the individuals; there is always a trade-off in skill specialization. Developers often focus on the software to solve a specific business problem, whereas sysadmins specialize in reasoning about the systems in operation. The problem arises when you don't have the perspective of people who understand the systems in operation that need continuous care and feeding. One way of identifying whether this is causing a problem in your organization is to examine whether there is friction in describing the team's work.

While devs may be on-call for a specific component, sysadmins are usually the ones with knowledge about the interoperation of all of the different systems. Operations teams play a part in on-call, whether through primary rotations or second- or third-tier support. Beyond first-tier support, system administrators assist product integration with other dependencies or standard operability (i.e., backups and recovery).

Sysadmins often have administrator visibility across system resources with cloud providers and third-party services. As a result, they have insight into how production systems can vary from other engineers' experimental and testing instances.

It can be hard to change a team dynamic where folks assume on-call work is the responsibility of a single individual who must be held accountable. Incentives and rewards need to align with the importance of the customer-impacting environment. Support the co-ownership model and keep the reliability and robustness of the live system in as high esteem as feature work.

 Check out this case study on changing the on-call practice at LinkedIn (*https://oreil.ly/DYZjR*).

You don't have to set on-call rotations in stone. They can be the plan of record that allows and responds to changing situations. Form a supportive team with sustainable practices that encourage folks to sub in and swap mid-rotation, thus giving the on-call engineer respite as necessary.

Update On-Call Processes

High-stress on-call without relief harms mental health and can lead to anxiety, depression, burnout, and other issues. Also, individuals may ruminate about production in unproductive ways, shifting focus away from the creativity required to work on complex projects and develop plans that can efficiently solve the underlying problems.

Teams that apply continuous learning to on-call can help lower the risks of this harm to the individual and improve the team's resilience to respond to outages. Suppose on-call is sustainable to the engineers responding. In that case, everyone benefits from having the mental space to incubate ideas because people no longer have to worry or fear more significant impacts or interrupts.

Update the on-call process by doing the following:

Monitoring the on-call experience
Lots of pages and long-running events tire out on-call engineers. When folks are tired, they are more likely to make mistakes. Monitoring the on-call experience improves the general health of individuals and the team by ensuring tired folks don't stay on-call and encourages a culture of support and care.

To do this successfully, you must have earned the team's trust so that individuals don't feel like someone is virtually looking over their shoulder, holding them accountable to optimize key performance indicators. Instead, the whole team is approaching the goal of this initiative to measure, learn from, and alleviate the innate pressures of the work to enact sustainable and lasting change.

Embracing the whole-team approach
Encourage folks to reach out for help to increase the overall resilience of the team. Planned escalations reduce the stress of the unknown.

Monitoring and maintaining alerts
Noisy alerts are frustrating and reduce vigilance (alert fatigue), increasing the risk of mistakes. If you use an SLO handbook, make sure that documentation is updated to reflect changes to the SLIs, including why you made the change.

Establishing incident protocols
Not every event needs to be measured. Not every measured event should be an alarm that pages individuals. Not every page is an incident. Establishing explicit,

clear protocols helps reduce fatigue and promotes alert maintenance. It also provides people with a process to follow for those business-critical pages at 2 a.m.

Monitoring the impact of the schedule

Humans make schedules that others may perceive are unfair or unbalanced. Proactively planning and adding individual needs can promote better, more flexible schedules that work with humans.

Ultimately, companies that build sustainable on-call will have a competitive advantage over those that don't, as systems take on more complexity.

Incident teams should have a plan for obtaining inclusive snacks and meals. For distributed teams, it's critical to have contact information for the on-call engineers and delivery options or have a policy that grants a stipend for folks to expense a meal.

People forget to eat when focused on repair and recovery. This exacerbates the fatigue that comes from sustained attention to a specific problem. Team leadership should make part of the assessment process a check-in with the humans that are part of the system.

Monitor the Team's Work

As I discussed in Chapter 14, you monitor to increase the visibility into your systems and the potential risks to those systems, which includes gaining more visibility about the people and processes. When thinking about a team's work, what are you trying to assess, and what are the desirable outcomes? What are the signals that will help you identify and reach your goals? How do you determine the complex issues that need to be solved to improve the team's efficiency?

Why Monitor the Team?

Monitoring at the team level helps build stronger relationships and trust as the individuals on the team have more visibility and context of the work each contributes to the team effort. Visibility into all the work also helps to inoculate the team from support heroics by measuring and supporting the right actions.

Providing team-level evaluations of work can help shift the perception of operations from the lone sysadmin to one of more collaboration and visual feedback. It also allows for in of how individuals do the job. allowing the most important and urgent work to get done while also providing the flexibility to incorporate other work as needed in the absence of that urgency.

The monitoring process is iterative. Monitoring provides information to help you analyze what is happening and gives you the supporting evidence to educate the team and drive changes. Sometimes these changes are to the compute infrastructure; other times they are to the human processes. People are part of the systems you manage, from development to support in production.

For example, I have been in environments where the average workload for the ops team meant that we each worked at our full capacity. If anyone took time off, whether planned or unplanned, this led to extra stress on the system, which led to increased mistakes in resolving incidents and frustration among team members. Monitoring helped us establish that we needed additional people on the team based on our expected workload. This gave us extra capacity when everyone was available but reduced friction when people needed time off.

Increasing Staffing

If you recognize that your team is chronically understaffed, how do you go about getting more people? There are different ways to approach this problem, especially if you are on a "team" of one, but here's my advice.

First, do not start any request with "We're understaffed." Also, when growing the team, recognize there are limits to how many new people can start at any one time. Research, plan, get buy-in, and execute as with any project:

Research
Identify who has decision-making authority. Don't undercut your manager or skip levels. Find the critical, impactful projects your team has been involved with that have value to the authority. Brevity is key here; don't document everything you've done.

Plan
Put together your proposal with the specific work that the additional people will do and what impact they will directly have. Speak in the language of the business and the decision-making authority. Provide possibilities that might not be top of mind: internships, temporary team rotations, etc.

Get buy-in
Empower your manager and skip levels to support your efforts by inviting them to review, give feedback, and approve your plan.

Execute
If you get the head count, write up that job requisition based on your plan. Then, follow through on the commitment so that what you promised happens such that people want more.

If you don't get the head count, hear the feedback and act on it. Maybe the team is working outside its remit and should stop doing some of that work. Sometimes this means part of the system starts failing. Recall from earlier in the chapter that you're not trying to have a perfect system and that the failure may be acceptable to the business.

What Should You Monitor?

Talk about the meta-work, how you do the work, to identify the events to monitor. Also, this discussion isn't a one-and-done. Over time, the team's processes will evolve, and regular retrospectives to document emerging practices need to occur.

A *retrospective* is a meeting held at the end of a specific period to reflect on how the team works and identify ways to improve.[2] When work is visible, folks can reflect on the data and make decisions based on that data rather than on what they imagine has happened based on memory.

Recall "Case #1: Charts Are Worth a Thousand Words" on page 103, the story I shared about tracking work. In addition to prioritizing work as a team and visibility improvements to our stakeholders, we had better visibility about what was happening. With regular retrospectives, we identified and corrected the underlying problem of having too much work in progress.

When we implemented a shared board for tracking our work, regular retrospectives helped narrow our goals to what we could accomplish in a quarter (decreasing our work in progress). As a result, we incrementally made a few changes in our processes: we postponed big projects to ensure that everyone had one large project at a time, and we increased our frequency of retrospectives from once per quarter to biweekly.

Even though we had more meetings, these changes helped us accomplish more per quarter because each of us as individuals could focus our efforts.

During the retrospective, when you reflect on what has gone right, include information about who and what supported successful outcomes. Recognizing contributions is a way to fuel trust within the team, even if the assumption is that folks are "just doing their job." When you reflect on what went wrong, include the details about what hindered the goals.

Over time, quality retrospectives can turn teams into great teams through continuous improvement. Without retrospectives, work can feel chaotic and unproductive, and vital tasks and projects get delayed while the wrong ones get completed. Initial topics

---

2 Learn more about retrospectives in *Agile Retrospectives: Making Good Teams Great* from Esther Derby and Diana Larsen (Pragmatic Bookshelf).

to discuss within a team include the team's objectives, task and project definitions, and descriptions of the work and the phases it goes through.

Keep in mind that, in general (regardless of the type of job), people need five things:[3]

Freedom
Having control and autonomy over their work

Challenge
Feeling that their mind is stimulated; they think and fully use their skills to research, design, or implement new approaches.

Personally meaningful contribution
Feeling that their work matters

Positive atmosphere
Feeling connected with their coworkers in a positive way

Education
Increasing competence and growing expertise

Incorporate this understanding into conversations about the team's work. For example, instead of telling someone, "Do this, that way," ask, "What do you think we need to do to solve this problem?"

What are the team's objectives?

The objectives will be the overarching goals of the team that help align the incoming work and performance of the team. For example, suppose the team completes incoming work that is not supporting a team objective. In that case, it's essential that management either help the team to update the objectives so that the individuals doing this work get credit for contributing to company objectives or help the team to say no. For embedded teams, if the leader does not include the sysadmin work in the overall objectives of the team, this work may not be valued and rewarded!

Individuals don't define team objectives. When this happens, the individual who forms the objectives often has to push for those objectives to be met. Ideally, individuals pull work because they are motivated and interested in accomplishing the tasks and not having the work pushed at them to complete.

3 Sheila Henderson, "Follow Your Bliss: A Process for Career Happiness," *Journal of Counseling and Development* 78 (2000): 305–3, *https://doi.org/10.1002/j.1556-6676.2000.tb01912.x.*

What is the team's definition of a task?

A task should be something discrete that can be tracked through the stages of work and accomplished within a specific time frame; for example, use real tasks to illuminate where differences in definitions may be occurring. The specific time frame could be an hour, day, or week. For example, setting up a new service on some teams might be considered a task; for others, it might be a project.

Future discussions can also include characterizations of tasks; is something rote that you can document with a playbook or checklist, or is it novel and requires additional planning time?

What is the team's definition of a project?

I've found it's pretty hard to nail down more than a week to apply myself to a single workstream consistently, so breaking it down gives me a way to progress toward achieving the larger objective. So, I generally consider anything that requires more than a week of my time a project, meaning that there are additional steps that I need to take to ensure its completion.

A project is composed of a number of tasks. To make the work visible, individuals should divide a project into the required tasks and split larger tasks into smaller ones.

There may be additional terminology that you need to define collaboratively with your team to come to a common understanding. For example, I use the word *program* to describe work that is a project with additional collaborators from external teams who may desire different outcomes but have a common purpose in the collective efforts.

What is the service catalog that your team offers?

The service catalog is your team's organized and curated collection of services. Discuss all the different types of work and skill levels so that you can organize (and curate) this offering. The first step is just figuring out the complete list of work and then deduplicating descriptions of the work. Once the team has reached a place of team psychological safety, it can be helpful to ask, "Why do we do this work?" The team may discover that there is work that needs to be deprioritized to focus on the real differentiators in what the team can accomplish.

Examine the work

Once you have the list of work, examine the work more closely and the phases or stages that work goes through. Are they the same or vastly different? Here's an example of what this categorization might look like based on the type of work:

- Bug fixing
- Incident response
- Administrative tasks
- Interrupt-driven requests
- Recurring meetings, including one-on-ones
- Watercooler talk
- Specific project work

Some of this work (such as one-on-ones and watercooler opportunities) can't be automatically monitored or visualized qualitatively. Work following a similar path can be grouped and use the same visualization when monitoring. If work doesn't follow a single path, you shouldn't try to shoehorn it together into a single workstream. Each stage needs to clear boundaries with defined exit and entrance conditions.

On reflection, you may uncover differences in opinions on what stages mean. For example, what does an "Accepted" stage mean? Has the team committed to doing the work? Does it mean someone is responsible for doing this work this week? Giving further definitions helps clarify intent and establish a common understanding.

 Make it a habit to update the team's onboarding documentation with updated taxonomy, processes, and policies with each retrospective.

Measure Impact on the Team

Recall from Chapter 20 that metrics like MTBF, MTTF, MTTD, and MTTR aren't valuable for modern system administration; they incentivize the wrong improvements (e.g., not the right work or work done at the wrong time) or devalue the individual's work and demotivate them by pressuring them to provide metrics that don't make sense (recall the importance of control and autonomy and work that matters to individuals).

Instead of these metrics, based on the business goals, identify how those goals are being met (or missed), and implement dashboards that can support achieving those goals with continuous collaborative learning. If there is no current monitoring, leverage the narratives from what is available. The key point here, though, and it bears repeating, is measure to learn.

When you are assessing the system, sometimes you'll see patterns where the system is the problem. For example, in a past job, testing could trigger a flaw with the network devices. There was an expectation that I would be ready at a moment's notice to come in on the weekend to power cycle a network device that had crashed to ensure that automated testing could continue. The cost at the time to invest in better network gear (tens of thousands of dollars) or a switched power distribution unit (approximately $1,000 per device) never occurred to management as a viable option because my time was not valued, even though I was not being paid for on-call work or weekend work in any capacity.

Falsely pushing capacity limitations to humans creates unsustainable work. Examples of this include the following:

- Not investing in appropriate tools
- Not investing in or supporting enough people for the work required to support the infrastructure needed for a service

Capacity limitations create an additional human workload that is erroneously often seen as "free" but has high costs, like travel time, work time, and the research on the maximum capacity of effective work.

Sometimes you (or your management) may make an intentional decision not to invest in automation or tools because the underlying complexity of a system causes a high risk of failure during implementation. When complexity hinders automation implementation, it may be an area to improve to ease the cost of manual support.

To be proactive at capacity management, you need to understand the labor required to support the current systems. I don't mean predicting the specific labor costs (skills vary across teams, and emergencies and vacations do happen) but knowing how much of a team's time is consumed by each system.

What could be a way to measure this kind of impact? You can better assess time and labor if team members regularly check in about their work (which requires a foundation of psychological safety) and share how much time is needed to support specific projects. Of course, everyone will have a different mix of time spent on types of work, but having everyone on the team share the data allows you to create a shared visualization of the work to surface some of its specificity. Analyzing this data can uncover areas for improvement.

You can use regular surveys to take a pulse on other metrics like these:

- Satisfaction with compensation
- How demanding a particular task or project was
- How work impacted activities outside of business hours
- How individuals were able to relax outside of business hours

 Encourage "swarming" to tackle larger problems that can be broken down into discrete pieces. Swarming engages multiple people from the team to help tackle the task or problem. The individual feels supported, and the team gains a broader understanding of the work.

Support Team Infrastructure with Documentation

Very rarely is it a person choosing just not to do work and shift it onto others. Instead, there's something about the system that we've created in the team/company that is making that the only option for them. So the fix isn't telling them to do better but to change the system.
　—Carolyn Van Slyck (@carolynvs), October 15, 2021

The team is constantly evolving; when someone new joins or an existing member leaves, documentation provides the scaffolding for how the team works and continues to work through change. In addition to documenting the definitions discovered through the meta-work discussions, other areas to support the team include the following:

Include project documentation in the definition of done
　This can consist of all the related tickets, associated communication over ChatOps, and releases or deployments.

Treat documentation like your software
　Version, test, and release.

Document explicit norms and demonstrate those norms
　Sometimes, it can be hard to know what to document and how much time to spend writing, especially when it's unclear who the audience is and you're faced with a blank screen. Managers can help to set the priority of this work, ensure the appropriate tools are available, and clear any potential roadblocks. Leaders can show the way by sharing their documentation, creating templates, and making it easy for others to follow.

Just because norms are documented doesn't mean that someone will follow those norms. When someone isn't following standards, rather than assuming the problem is with the individual, it's essential to take time to understand why.

Document policies explicitly; don't assume that everyone has the same expectations or understanding. For example, as mentioned in Chapter 19, your on-call policy should be clearly documented.

Budget a Learning Culture

As mentioned in the Introduction and throughout the book, the tools, technologies, and third-party services are multiplying. However, if you focus on how things are now and do not incorporate new information, data, tools, and processes, you can get stuck in "how things were."

Funding a learning culture requires process change, time to learn and adapt to change, and money. To estimate and plan for a learning culture, consider the following four items and re-evaluate your assessments on a regular basis:

Establish a training budget
> In addition to establishing a training budget, include time to allow individuals to use the funding.

Encourage sharing of knowledge
> Share knowledge actively with learning sessions (e.g., brown bags, reading groups) or passively through write-ups (e.g., "What I learned from this conference, talk, research").

Practice failure
> Incidents will happen. Teams should practice the process for handling incidents and testing various scenarios that might occur. Much like testing in development, practicing failure is very different from handling a live incident, but it does have value. It can help expose gaps in documentation and help you better understand processes before you have to respond to an event at 2 a.m. or deal with differences in skill gaps.

Provide time for analysis of the work
> Give individuals the time to improve the system. For on-call work, this could be identifying weaknesses in the system and addressing or documenting missed expectations. For toil work, this could be identifying repetitious work and making time to automate tasks.

Adapt to Challenges

Old-school management focused on people as resources and managed those resources as replaceable cogs. Modern management recognizes the nonhierarchical, more matrix-like form of contemporary organizations;[4] people have relationships and emotions and aren't interchangeable.

The old-system administration model separates humans from work; this doesn't work because it creates two parallel systems—the humans and the managed system.

The current system administration model recognizes that humans and work are inseparable. Humans are part of the system. Each human has a distinct set of skills, talents, interests, motivations, work styles, triggers, perspectives of the world, and preferences on how they work. Think of systems more humanely, on the whole, to make them sustainable for the humans in them. People have limited capacity and are prone to "failures." I'm not being callous and advocating treating people like machines because they are part of the system. When the system expects people to do harmful things like 24/7 on-call and then doesn't recognize the impact on the individual, that's inhumane.

You can't control outputs and outcomes, and people are part of the chaos in systems that make them messy. So, you have to be authentic and appreciate people where they are now and all of their emotions and work with them.

At Yahoo, I never thought about myself as part of the system until I took my first vacation and everything caught on fire, even though I'd left several checklists and playbooks. As an industry, we talk about single points of failure in the design of the systems. But, we don't look at the people with the knowledge, understanding, context, or support when evaluating the system. These are all fragilities in the system. You can't automate these fragilities away. Building a self-healing system just makes the system that much more complex to understand for the human that will eventually have to debug or support it.

These systems are built in our image, modeling our relationships. Look to human relationships to inform how we treat the system to better build sustainable systems that support the humans in the systems. Examples are encouraging mutual support, knowing that it's safe to say you don't know something, and understanding that others will support you.

> *A person's on-call shift should not be solely their responsibility. The team, the environment, the situation, and the system all have to support the person.*
> —Ryan Kitchens (@this_hits_home), October 15, 2021

---

4 "DevOps Culture: Westrum Organizational Culture" (*https://oreil.ly/Ar8OL*), Google Cloud, accessed June 13, 2022.

What sustains people—connecting with people, opportunities to learn, and feeling valued (recall these three needs of the five common needs everyone has from "What Should You Monitor?" on page 258)—must be part of a systems assessment. Without this assessment, you may be putting people at risk of burnout. And this can create additional tension between teams.

Our work is becoming more complex, and the pressures on the systems are becoming more complex. You have to plan for unexpected events that are out of your control because they happen all the time (e.g., floods and power outages). Look at COVID-19 in 2020 and what it did to the system: lower team capacity (the formulas for calculating an individual's capacity remained the same) with accelerated demands on the team, which increased the rate of burnout.

Human capacity changes over time and is unpredictable. To be successful, your team needs to adapt to a complex set of messy and chaotic challenges to the system. People need to feel trusted and empowered and build trust in each other so that they will be supported when needed. Managers need to recognize and bring people in to help the team or cut scope and ease the load based on the actual capacity.

Wrapping Up

Lead with a whole-team approach that centers on continuous learning throughout every phase of a system's lifecycle by adopting these behaviors:

- Hold extensive one-on-ones.
- Manage scope and cross-organizational relationships.
- Create space for the team to engage with each other as people.
- Encourage collaborative work and accountability to each other.
- Minimize process overhead that is not helping to ship or pay down technical debt.
- Encourage a whole-team approach to solving common challenges.
- Provide clear and regular feedback about the team's priorities and limitations.
- Empower people to speak in the way they want to share.
- Encourage open and transparent environments.

Conclusion

You've reached the end of the book, and I hope you feel better prepared to face the multiple paths before you, to navigate the chaos in your systems reliably and sustainably, and to adopt modern system administration technologies, tools, and practices.

Throughout this book, I've set a path—to help you understand your existing systems and practices, assemble systems with those practices and infrastructure code, and monitor and scale those systems. You may have followed that path one chapter after another, or you may have skipped around to the most pressing issues you're facing right now. Regardless of where you are in your journey—whether you're an experienced system administrator or an engineer early in your career learning about operability—this resource has given you a path to reason about your systems and understand how to tackle the next challenge, one step at a time.

Recall Figure I-2 from the Introduction and the comparison of system administration to hiking (reproduced here as Figure C-1).

Figure C-1. The future is bright, and your path may be unclear. Still, with your knowledge, experiences, growth mindset, and collaborators, you can confidently move forward, knowing that you'll be able to handle whatever lies ahead (image by Tomomi Imura).

In hiking, once you reach the summit, you must descend again in order to ascend the next mountain. Likewise, with system administration, you must leave a system before you can tackle your next challenge. Leaving might mean migrating your existing customers to a new system, deprecating a system gracefully, handing off the system to be maintained by new engineers, or leaving a company to start a new role entirely. And, as with every journey, you have the opportunity to grow, learn, and adapt your approach as you tackle the new path before you.

Just as I've shared some of my stories and challenges, I encourage you to share your stories and experiences through conference participation (e.g., hallway tracks, birds of a feather, or presenting), blogging (e.g., dev.to, the seasonal sysadvent, or your own platform), or shorter snippets (e.g., LinkedIn posts).

Feel free to share with me by tagging me on LinkedIn (*https://www.linkedin.com/in/ sigje*) or dev.to (*https://dev.to/sigje*).

—Jennifer

Protocols in Practice

Building on Chapter 1, let's look at an example of web protocols in practice: HTTP, QUIC, and DNS. Understanding protocols will help explain the reality of systems communicating. And these protocols are evolving as the needs of the web evolve.

Hypertext Transfer Protocol

HTTP covers a set of web standards describing how systems communicate on the web. A number of different HTTP server types are optimized for different use cases, from application servers that run web app code like Apache Tomcat (*https://tomcat.apache.org*) to cache servers like Squid (*http://www.squid-cache.org*) to web servers like the Apache HTTP Server Project (*https://httpd.apache.org*). A modern web stack may incorporate multiple HTTP servers to provide service.

Originally, HTTP was designed as a client/server, one-request/one-response protocol. You could use Wireshark and tcpdump to look at sniffed traffic and reconstruct web conversations because communication was done in plain text.

Over time, HTTP has evolved. One of the adaptations includes using HTTP headers (*https://oreil.ly/z87B9*) to pass additional information with an HTTP request or response. Historically, custom proprietary headers used the X- prefix, but that's been deprecated (*https://oreil.ly/baSAc*). HTTPS over HTTP/1 and HTTP/2 uses TLS, TCP, and IP (see Figure A-1).

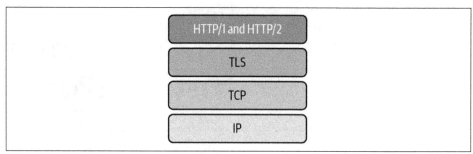

Figure A-1. An HTTPS stack using the TCP/IP model

Before two systems can communicate over HTTP/1, they must establish a TCP connection. HTTP/1.0 opens a separate TCP connection for each HTTP request/response. Establishing a series of individual TCP sessions for each HTTP request adds significant overhead.

HTTP/1.1 introduced the Connection header to allow for subsequent requests to the same server to reuse the TCP connection. Reusing an established TCP connection reduces the overall latency of a request especially when the client is not local to the server because of the overhead of setting up the three-way handshake of a TCP connection.

With the new binary framing layer, HTTP/2 optimizes transport for HTTP requests and reduces the latency of loading web pages with the following:

- Request and response multiplexing over a single TCP connection
- Data compression of HTTP headers
- Request prioritization
- Server push

HTTP/2 maintains the core concepts of HTTP/1.0 and HTTP/1.1, including the methods, status codes, headers fields, and URIs. So you don't have to change existing web applications to benefit from the performance improvements. Instead, HTTP/2 changes how the data is formatted and transported between the client and server.

Multiplexing connections allows multiple streams of data to be processed independently, and packet loss with one stream will not interfere with other streams. But running HTTP/2 over TCP is still vulnerable to head-of-line-blocking problems that can disrupt data flow if any of the packets are delayed or dropped.

The HTTP/3 standard (*https://oreil.ly/raR0k*) switches from single TCP sessions to QUIC connections, as discussed in the next section.

While HTTP has driven web adoption for many years, its architecture was based on trust between peers. People didn't design for integrity or confidentiality because the goal was open access to research and communication, not protection from malicious users modifying or reading traffic. These days, by default, most browsers at minimum require HTTP/2 over TLS and will raise a warning when trying to access an older, unsecured web server.

You can set up a 301 redirect from http:// to https://, but that doesn't eliminate the window of opportunity when a malicious attacker could capture cookies or session IDs or force a redirect to a phishing site. An HTTP Strict Transport Security (HSTS) header tells the browser that it should never use HTTP and should automatically convert to HTTPS requests instead (see Example A-1).

Example A-1. Basic syntax for the HSTS header

```
Strict-Transport-Security: max-age=<EXPIRY TIME>
```

The process looks like this:

1. The browser accesses your site using HTTPS for the first time.
2. Your site returns the HSTS header.
3. The browser stores this information, and all future connections will use HTTPS (within the *max-age* seconds of the expiry time).

As long as a user visits the site within the *max-age* seconds specified in the header, the browser will automatically connect to the secure connection without even trying HTTP. Adding a flag to the header to set includeSubDomains will apply this policy to all subdomains as well.

Be careful with using the includeSubDomains flag. If your organization operates legacy services that cannot be updated to support SSL/TLS, this can cause issues that may become difficult to troubleshoot.

If an HSTS-compliant browser can't confirm the security of the certificate, it aborts the connection to an HSTS-compliant server.

Learn more about HSTS at the following:

- OWASP HTTP Strict Transport Security Cheat Sheet (*https://oreil.ly/09Wim*)
- "HTTP Strict Transport Security (HSTS)," RFC 6797 (*https://oreil.ly/eLrbS*)

The client verifies the authenticity of the server using the server certificate. During the initial TLS handshake, the client and server exchange a secret, which is used to encrypt the session. This secret is required to decrypt and analyze HTTP/2 capture packets. Without it, you can capture the encrypted packets, but you won't have a way to decrypt and make sense of them. Set the environment variable SSLKEYLOGFILE before starting up a capture in order to capture session keys. Browsers will append keys to the file that you define.

If you want to debug a session, on your client, set the environment variable SSLKEYLOGFILE (*https://oreil.ly/9YiIi*) before starting up a capture in order to capture session keys. Your browser will append keys to the file that you define.

To learn more about TLS protocol, see "The Transport Layer Security (TLS) Protocol Version 1.3, RFC 8446 (*https://oreil.ly/IRdTS*).

QUIC

Originally introduced by Google in 2012, the QUIC ("quick") protocol addresses shortcomings in the user experience of the HTTP application layer and the TCP transport layer and became a proposed standard (*https://oreil.ly/6Mg5J*) in May 2021.

The emerging HTTP/3 standard, officially an a proposed standard (*https://oreil.ly/uSfvB*) as of June 2022, includes traditional HTTP semantics (request methods, status codes, and message fields) that leverage the QUIC protocol. As of November 2022, three-quarters of web browsers (*https://oreil.ly/n3qVI*) and one-quarter of websites (*https://oreil.ly/bViGD*) already support HTTP/3, and these ratios are likely to grow rapidly as the HTTP/3 protocol moves through the IETF approval process to become an official standard, as QUIC itself has already done.

As you can see from Figure A-2, HTTP/2 appears to have clean, discrete layers, but the HTTP/3 slice has overlap as the QUIC protocol is one part application layer and one part transport layer.

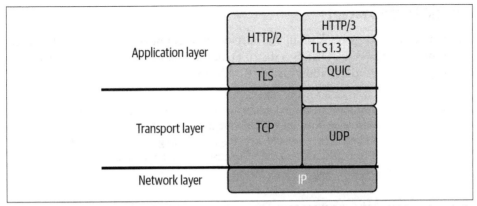

Figure A-2. Comparison of HTTP/2 to HTTP/3—it may help to picture it like a layered cake; you can slice right through each layer

QUIC overcomes the limitations of HTTP/2 by switching from TCP to UDP for transporting HTTP/3 and later traffic. Using UDP eliminates the overhead required for TCP session management, and while this heightens the risk of uncaught errors, in practice, on a relatively stable network, the packet loss rate is low. The occasional need to retransmit data takes less time it took to manage TCP sessions.

Other advantages conveyed by leveraging the QUIC protocol include the following:

- Forward error correction is implemented at the application layer to address the lack of error handling due to running without TCP's session management capabilities.

- TLS encryption is mandatory and has an efficient approach to establishing secure session keys as part of the initial handshake. Session keys are then used for individual request/response cycles, and each packet is individually encrypted with the key, unlike TCP, which typically must wait to encrypt the overall bytestream. This makes QUIC more secure regardless of the service.

- It has better support for network-switch events with connection migration, such as when a mobile device toggles between WiFi and cellular data connections, which would change the IP address of the device. With TCP, this would cause all active connections to time out and fail and then be restarted from the new link. QUIC avoids this problem by seeding each connection with a unique identifier for the client to respond with, so when a network switch occurs, the server recognizes that the same device is now using a different IP address, and the existing multiplexed session can continue as before.

Software attempting to use HTTP/3 must fall back to more traditional protocols when necessary. For example, some network administrators may have chosen to restrict UDP traffic outside their perimeter.

Domain Name System

An organization keeps track of all the hosts within its domains and shares this data with other sites via DNS. DNS is a distributed, hierarchical, and replicated database that maps human-readable addresses to IP addresses.

 DNS is separate from domain name registration. Registries manage the top-level domains (TLDs), the last segment of a domain name including *.com*, *.net*, and *.org*. Registries delegate domain registration to registrars, and then these registrars handle the reservation of domain names.

Some system administrators manage DNS servers. With the advent of cloud services, system administrators more typically use managed DNS services because it's one less service to misconfigure that can bring down a whole site. With global service providers, DNS issues do still occur, but they are much less likely to happen. At approximately $.50 per record, this allows sysadmins to focus time on other operational concerns.

The DNS protocol consists of two parts: the query/response for resolving DNS queries and the exchange of database records between DNS servers.

A DNS query consists of a fully qualified domain name (FQDN), the name that refers to the specific resource within the DNS hierarchy. Clients and DNS servers may provide cached responses up to the time in seconds specified by the time to live on the record. Otherwise, authoritative servers provide DNS responses.

DNS is also used to provide the following features in addition to name resolution:

Load distribution
> Round-robin DNS can be used to provide load distribution without any extra hardware or software. To implement a Round-robin DNS for a stateless service, include IP addresses for all the replicas of the service in the DNS entry. With each query for the IP address, the DNS server will reorder the IP address response so that host requests will be distributed. If one replica fails, DNS does not do any verification, so some percentage of requests will fail until the cache for its IP address is cleared based on the TTL and any client-side caching.

Feature management
> Often, customers use a fully qualified domain name to access a service. By setting up CNAMES that point to specific versions of deployed software, you can update where the CNAME points to when you want to release a new version of the software.

Service discovery

Domain owners define service endpoints by adding an SRV record with the host, accessible port number, priority, and weight for specified services.

Email authorization and authentication

With the increase in phishing and spoofing, mechanisms have been added to leverage DNS to authenticate email, including DKIM and SPF.

As with HTTP, the original DNS protocol did not have any security features and so is vulnerable to problems started by misconfigured or malicious actors. For example, forged or manipulated data can be used for DNS cache poisoning attacks to redirect traffic to impostor sites. The DNS Security Extensions (DNSSEC) specifications provide a backward-compatible way to protect DNS traffic by using cryptographic authentication, data integrity promises, and other improvements. However, DNSSEC does not provide privacy by encrypting DNS traffic itself, so protocols such as DNSCrypt, DNS over TLS (DoT), and DNS over HTTPS (DoH) have emerged to protect DNS traffic.

More Resources

To learn more about DNS, check out these resources:

- *DNS and BIND Cookbook* (*https://oreil.ly/OhGCx*) by Cricket Liu (O'Reilly)
- "Domain Names: Implementation and Specification RFC 1035" (*https://oreil.ly/26quq*)

If you are responsible for managing email or sending email campaigns within your organization, make sure to look into DKIM, SPF, and Domain-based Message Authentication, Reporting, and Conformance (DMARC):

- DKIM (*http://www.dkim.org*)
- DMARC Overview (*https://dmarc.org/overview*)
- Email Authentication for Internationalized Mail RFC 8616 (*https://www.rfc-editor.org/info/rfc8616*)

Resolving Test Failures

Building on Chapter 7, let's learn more about the different types of test failures (environmental problems, flawed test logic, changing assumptions, flaky tests, and code defects).

Test Failure Type #1: Environment Problems

Environmental problems can be super frustrating because so much can go wrong, especially in the larger end-to-end tests that test between different services. Make sure to have sufficient unit test coverage because unit tests are not vulnerable to environmental problems. There are many issues with environments that can arise, including these:

- The testing environment doesn't match the production environment in scale or function.
- Elements of functionality can be costly, for example, monitoring agents that shouldn't have an impact but do.
- There is no local testing environment setup due to lack of understanding that it's possible to have a local testing environment.
- Dependencies aren't locked down and vary in environments.
- Third-party continuous integration and deployment services are having failures.

These are just a few examples of environmental problems that can cause tests to fail.

Problems with shared test environments can lead to folks insisting that no testing environment is needed, and they instead test directly in production with feature flags and canary testing. Feature flags make features available to a subset of users in a controlled manner or turn off a feature if necessary. Canary testing allows you to provide a subset of users access to a feature or product to determine if the quality of the release is OK and, if so, to continue to deploy. If the users report issues, you can migrate them back to the standard experience.

There is no way to replicate a test environment that matches production exactly. So feature flags and canary testing in production are crucial ways to improve feedback and reduce the risk of mass changes to production.

They don't replace the need for ongoing fast and early feedback to developers from the test environment. When you have extended lead times for feedback (i.e., waiting for deployment into production), you lose the context of your work. In this situation, it's the difference between minutes to potentially days, which adds up over time.

Additionally, shared test environments create a safe place for experimentation and exploratory testing. However, leadership can view shared test environments as an expense without adequately evaluating the return on investment.

One way to minimize what folks might consider a waste of resources is to monitor and manage the creation and decommissioning of test environments through infrastructure automation. Test environments are available when needed and are consistent and repeatable so that engineers needing to test can get access when they need them. You can eliminate idle systems and time wasted queueing up to use a single test environment.

Sometimes environmental conditions are entirely outside of your control, such as when third-party CI/CD services have failures like GitHub, Travis, or CircleCI being down. Outsourcing these services has short- to medium-term value in terms of not having individuals specialize in ensuring these work as needed locally. Third-party services will have failures. It's guaranteed. Consider these questions to plan for mitigations:

- How will you work on code while third-party services are down?
- How will you test?
- How will you deliver value to your customers?
- What if there is data loss?

If, for example, the tests aren't warning of failures, this isn't a guarantee that everything is OK. It could be that the third-party system has failed and no longer thinks it is managing the project.

Test Failure Type #2: Flawed Test Logic

Sometimes the problem you discover is due to how you have interpreted the requirements or how a customer expressed their needs. The code does the right thing, but the tests are failing. These failing tests expose some issues with collaboration or communication. For example, there could be missing, unclear, or inconsistent information. Worse, you may not discover the problem if you aren't testing the right thing. When you detect failures due to flawed test logic, modify the test, review the processes that led to the missing context, and address them.

Products evolve. Sometimes specifications change from the initial design meetings to developer implementation, and tests that at one point were valid can now cause failures.

So if a test failure is due to flawed test logic, fix the test and also assess where the problem occurred:

- Did the initial discussions not include the required people?
- Did the process of requirements gathering align the testing acceptance criteria with the customer requirements?
- Did feedback not make it back to discussions and design when the implementation changed?

Depending on your development pipeline and the different gates that you have for software to progress, there are various areas where communication and collaboration can fail.

Test Failure Type #3: Changing Assumptions

Sometimes you can make assumptions about how something happens, and you can be right; other times, not so much. Those assumptions aren't visible until the underlying circumstances change. For example, maybe you change when a test runs, and now different tests are failing that don't align with any revised code. Assumptions can also become visible when the order of operations of a particular task changes and when the database changes.

Failures due to changed assumptions expose previously unknown fragilities in the code or tests.

Automated tests need to be deterministic, so uncovering hidden assumptions and making them explicit will help eliminate flapping tests. It also might be an area where instead of doing an end-to-end test, there could be room for tests closer to the components themselves so that interface changes don't cause failures.

Test Failure Type #4: Flaky Tests

A flaky test is a nondeterministic test, passing or failing with the same configuration, and is generally found in more complex tests like integration and end-to-end tests. When we identify nondeterministic tests, it's crucial to refactor or eliminate them so that they stop being noisy.

Some common reasons that a test may be flaky include the following:

Caches
> Does the application rely on cached data? There are many types of caches and ways a cache can cause problems with testing. For example, with a web cache, files that are critical for rendering a web page may be cached on the web servers, on edge services, or locally within the browser. If the data is stale in the cache at any of these levels, tests can become nondeterministic.

Test instance lifecycle
> What are the policies regarding the setup and teardown of the testing instance? Tests may be invalid or return inconsistent results if the environment is reused or multitenanted. Practicing regular hygiene in test environments and simplifying the setup and cleanup of all test instances reduces the risk of flaky tests.

Configuration inconsistencies
> When environments are not consistent or the testing situations don't match up with real-world production experiences, this can cause problems. For example, suppose something is time-dependent and one environment is syncing to an NTP server and the other is not. In that case, there may be conflicts in how the test responds, especially in special conditions (i.e., during the daylight saving time change). Therefore, use infrastructure code for test environments to maintain configuration consistency.

Computing environment failures
> Sometimes the test itself isn't flaky, but it exposes underlying problems with your computing environment. There should be some monitoring to expose these problems as they occur rather than wasting time debugging issues that don't exist.

Third-party services
> Your organization will rely on more and more third-party services to ensure it focuses on the areas of business value. When problems occur with those services, it can cause issues with your integration and end-to-end tests. Therefore, it's important to isolate those challenges and make sure you can pinpoint where problems are occurring, much like with your infrastructure failures.

Test Failure Type #5: Code Defects

Code defects are last on my list because you have created your tests to look for code defects. So when you are assessing the test failure, it can be easy to focus first on code defects rather than looking at anything else. Instead, look at your environmental conditions, consider flawed test logic, and see if any assumptions have changed before you dive into addressing code defects.

When you discover a problem with code and have been able to verify whether it's repeatable and how often it happens, follow these steps:

1. Describe the problem clearly, including information about what happened and how, the steps to replicate it, and the version of any infrastructure (software, application, computing environments). If you discovered the problem manually, add a test that will find it automatically next time.

2. Once you write the defect report, you need to track it and ensure that someone is responsible for resolving the problem.

3. Work with the team to prioritize the report based on what is in the work queue. Once the team fixes the problem, verify it's fixed, revisit any boundary conditions that might need to be changed, and close the defect report.

4. If the priority of the bug is not high enough to get worked on or assigned a responsible owner, examine whether the report should stay open. Long-term bug reports remaining open puts a cognitive load on the team.

I'm not advising that you assign or close all reports immediately. I am saying, assess the problems and actively advocate for significant problems that you want to make sure get resolved.

Index

M

MAC (media access control) addresses, 8
MAC spoofing, 9
machine images, 122
  code for building, 123
machines, 123
maintainability, 25
  comparison for layered, microservices, and event-driven architectures, 4
  of documentation, 94
managing infrastructure, 129-140
  getting started, 135-140
    identifying necessary skills to be successful, 137
    linting, 138
    managing testing infrastructure, 139
    well-scoped infrastructure management projects, 135
    writing end-to-end tests, 139
    writing integration tests, 139
    writing unit tests, 138
  GitOps, 135
  goal, breaking down to smaller objectives, 136
  infrastructure as code, 129-134
  treating infrastructure as data, 134
manifests, including with applications, 153
match strategy, 215
mean time between failures (MTBF), 248
mean time to detection (MTTD), 248
mean time to failure (MTTF), 248
memory-bound applications, example workloads, 12
message queue, examining (case study), 177
messaging (in event-driven systems), 4
metadata (object), 28
metrics, 165, 192
  about, 186
  benefits and use cases, 189
  collection platforms, 181
  data reduction and, 167
  helping to classify and improve on-call experience, 231
  incident management success, 248
  measuring system impact on a team, 261
  metric types for Ready, Do, Done Kanban, 200
  provided metric types from monitoring platforms, 186

representing people, ensuring privacy of, 166
  tracking for your work, 198
MFA (multifactor authentication), 146
microservices architecture, 3
Microsoft Azure (see Azure)
MirageOS, 15
mistakes, acknowledging and learning from, 246
mitigation strategies for your on-call issues, 231
mkcert utility, 59
mobile HotSpot or WiFi tethering device for sustainable on-call, 223
monitoring
  of alerts, 255
  compute and software, in practice, 171-184
    choosing monitoring tool or platform, 181-183
    deciding what should alert, 178-180
    deciding what to monitor, 173-175
    examining monitoring platforms, 180
    identifying desired outputs, 171
    planning for a monitoring project, 175-178
  in incident management, 241
  managing data from, 185-192
    types of monitoring data, 186-189
  of the on-call experience, 230-233, 255
    questions to think about, 231
  of resources, 214
  of teams and their work, 256-263
    benefits of, 256
    factors to monitor, 258-261
  theory, 161-169
    being your own authority instead, 162
    building blocks of monitoring, 164
    first-level monitoring, 165-168
    observability versus monitoring, 163
    reasons for monitoring, 161-162
    second-level monitoring, 168
    terminology, 164
  of your work, 193-201
    benefits of, 193
    choosing a platform, 198-199
    finding the interesting information, 200
    impacts beyond you, 195
    managing your work with Kanban, 195-198
monitors, 164

About the Author

Jennifer Davis is an experienced engineering manager, operations engineer, international speaker, and author. Her other books include *Effective DevOps* and *Collaborating in DevOps Culture*. She is passionate about community, has organized and contributed to a number of conferences, and founded CoffeeOps, a worldwide community to facilitate conversations and collaboration across companies. Jennifer has worked for a variety of companies, from startups to large enterprises, improving operability practices and encouraging sustainable work.

Colophon

The bird on the cover of *Modern System Administration* is a common paradise kingfisher (*Tanysiptera galatea*). There are nine species of kingfisher, only two of which have a presence outside of Papua New Guinea (in Australia and Indonesia). The common paradise kingfisher lives in the island's rainforests.

Paradise kingfishers have striking bold blue feathers from the crown of the head to the tail feathers and a white breast. The beak is bright reddish-orange, long, and pointed. Two tail streamers extend beyond the tail feathers, stretching the birds' length to 13–17 inches. Common kingfishers weigh about two ounces. They eat insects such as worms and grasshoppers, which they find in the forests they inhabit.

The paradise kingfisher has a conservation status of Least Concern. Many of the animals on O'Reilly's covers are endangered; all of them are important to the world.

The color illustration is by Karen Montgomery, based on a black and white engraving from *English Cyclopedia Natural History*. The cover fonts are Gilroy Semibold and Guardian Sans. The text font is Adobe Minion Pro; the heading font is Adobe Myriad Condensed; and the code font is Dalton Maag's Ubuntu Mono.

O'REILLY®

Learn from experts.
Become one yourself.

Books | Live online courses
Instant Answers | Virtual events
Videos | Interactive learning

Get started at oreilly.com.

©2022 O'Reilly Media, Inc. O'Reilly is a registered trademark of O'Reilly Media, Inc. | 175

CPSIA information can be obtained
at www.ICGtesting.com
Printed in the USA
JSHW022343121222
34811JS00004B/52